Exports to Improve Labor Markets in the Middle East and North Africa

MIDDLE EAST AND NORTH AFRICA
DEVELOPMENT REPORT

Exports to Improve Labor Markets in the Middle East and North Africa

Gladys Lopez-Acevedo and
Raymond Robertson, Editors

WORLD BANK GROUP

Middle East and North Africa Development Report Series

This series features major development reports from the Middle East and North Africa region of the World Bank, based on new research and thoroughly peer-reviewed analysis. Each report aims to enrich the debate on the main development challenges and opportunities the region faces as it strives to meet the evolving needs of its people.

Titles in the Middle East and North Africa Development Report Series

Informality and Inclusive Growth in the Middle East and North Africa (2023) by Gladys Lopez-Acevedo, Marco Ranzani, Nistha Sinha, and Adam Elsheikhi

Exports to Improve Labor Markets in the Middle East and North Africa (2023) by Gladys Lopez-Acevedo and Raymond Robertson

Blue Skies, Blue Seas: Air Pollution, Marine Plastics, and Coastal Erosion in the Middle East and North Africa (2022) by Martin Philipp Heger, Lukas Vashold, Anabella Palacios, Mala Alahmadi, Marjory-Anne Bromhead, and Marcelo Acerbi

Distributional Impacts of COVID-19 in the Middle East and North Africa Region (2021) edited by Johannes G. Hoogeveen and Gladys Lopez-Acevedo

The Reconstruction of Iraq after 2003: Learning from Its Successes and Failures (2019) by Hideki Matsunaga

Beyond Scarcity: Water Security in the Middle East and North Africa (2018) by World Bank

Eruptions of Popular Anger: The Economics of the Arab Spring and Its Aftermath (2018) by Elena Ianchovichina

Privilege-Resistant Policies in the Middle East and North Africa: Measurement and Operational Implications (2018) by Syed Akhtar Mahmood and Meriem Ait Ali Slimane

Jobs or Privileges: Unleashing the Employment Potential of the Middle East and North Africa (2015) by Marc Schiffbauer, Abdoulaye Sy, Sahar Hussain, Hania Sahnoun, and Philip Keefer

The Road Traveled: Dubai's Journey towards Improving Private Education: A World Bank Review (2014) by Simon Thacker and Ernesto Cuadra

Inclusion and Resilience: The Way Forward for Social Safety Nets in the Middle East and North Africa (2013) by Joana Silva, Victoria Levin, and Matteo Morgandi

Opening Doors: Gender Equality and Development in the Middle East and North Africa (2013) by World Bank

From Political to Economic Awakening in the Arab World: The Path of Economic Integration (2013) by Jean-Pierre Chauffour

Adaptation to a Changing Climate in the Arab Countries: A Case for Adaptation Governance and Leadership in Building Climate Resilience (2012) by Dorte Verner

Renewable Energy Desalination: An Emerging Solution to Close the Water Gap in the Middle East and North Africa (2012) by World Bank

Poor Places, Thriving People: How the Middle East and North Africa Can Rise Above Spatial Disparities (2011) by World Bank

Financial Access and Stability: A Road Map for the Middle East and North Africa (2011) by Roberto R. Rocha, Zsofia Arvai, and Subika Farazi

From Privilege to Competition: Unlocking Private-Led Growth in the Middle East and North Africa (2009) by World Bank

The Road Not Traveled: Education Reform in the Middle East and North Africa (2008) by World Bank

Making the Most of Scarcity: Accountability for Better Water Management Results in the Middle East and North Africa (2007) by World Bank

Gender and Development in the Middle East and North Africa: Women in the Public Sphere (2004) by World Bank

Unlocking the Employment Potential in the Middle East and North Africa: Toward a New Social Contract (2004) by World Bank

Better Governance for Development in the Middle East and North Africa: Enhancing Inclusiveness and Accountability (2003) by World Bank

Trade, Investment, and Development in the Middle East and North Africa: Engaging with the World (2003) by World Bank

All books in the Middle East and North Africa Development Report series are available for free at https://openknowledge.worldbank.org/handle/10986/2168.

Contents

Chapter 5. Egypt Case Study: Exploring the Link between Trade and Labor

Boxes

Figures

Maps

Foreword

Standard economics usually points to large benefits of trade openness for a country's economic growth and prosperity. It is rare to find exceptions. But we have a puzzle to solve when it comes to some countries in the Middle East and North Africa: despite significant trade liberalization and strong growth in trade in many of the region's economies, labor market outcomes—average wages, informality levels, unemployment, and female labor force participation, among others—have remained less favorable than in most countries. Why did increasing trade fail to produce better labor market outcomes in the region's low- and middle-income economies (LMIEs)?

From 2000 to 2009, many LMIEs globally experienced a trade-related economic boom, with rising exports of both raw materials and manufactured goods coinciding with falling poverty and inequality. In the Middle East and North Africa, trade liberalization measures accelerated as countries integrated into global value chains to promote economic growth. In response, total trade in the region's LMIEs rose sharply in parallel with GDP.

These are the kinds of economic improvements from trade that we would predict. But we would also expect this kind of trade and GDP growth to improve labor market outcomes throughout the region. Why do the Middle East and North Africa's LMIEs underperform in terms of employment growth from trade, for instance? This is an important political as well as economic issue because job creation has failed to keep pace with the region's growing working-age population, causing particularly high, and dangerous, youth unemployment. Government can absorb only so many graduate employees.

This book, *Exports to Improve Labor Markets in the Middle East and North Africa*, tries to solve the puzzle of why labor market outcomes lag in the region by exploring two theoretical avenues: Do trade agreements not produce the same trade increases for these economies as for those in other regions? And why do increasing exports fail to generate the same kinds of labor market outcomes in these economies as experienced elsewhere?

Of course, not all of the region's economies are the same; most notably, some are highly dependent on oil exports while others focus on manufacturing exports, especially apparel. We looked more closely at three cases of countries that are not highly oil dependent—the Arab Republic of Egypt, Morocco, and Tunisia—and developed approaches to examine how trade policy affects imports and exports and, in turn, local labor markets. We employed economic modeling to evaluate how trade agreements have affected trade flows and labor outcomes in our three case countries, compared those outcomes with those in other regions, and explored firm-level decisions to determine whether differences among firms influence the relationship between exports and labor market outcomes.

We find that trade liberalization has boosted trade flows in the Middle East and North Africa and significantly increased the region's economic growth, but the benefits of this trade have not been equally shared among areas and population groups. Broadly, these results are attributable to the region's unique labor market challenges, including significant gender segmentation in the labor market, high informality, an imbalance between population growth and job creation, and the state's dominant role in the economy. Specifically, Egypt stands out for its apparent absence of a link between trade flows and improved labor markets, while policies and export growth have favored male-labor-intensive sectors regionwide. Clearly, the results mandate a need to support female labor force participation as well as greater private sector participation in job generation.

The book provides some new assessment tools and models to provide insights into analyzing the distributional impacts of trade in the Middle East and North Africa, particularly on the labor market. Our hope is that these findings will help policy makers and other stakeholders design policies to enhance the chances that increasing trade will deliver more and better jobs for a broader group of the region's people.

Nadir A. Mohammed
Regional Director, Equitable Growth, Finance & Institutions
Middle East and North Africa Region
The World Bank

Acknowledgments

The preparation of this report was led by Gladys Lopez-Acevedo (lead economist, Poverty and Equity Global Practice, World Bank) and Raymond Robertson (director of the Mosbacher Institute for Trade, Economics, and Public Policy; professor and Helen and Roy Ryu Chair in Economics and Government, Texas A&M University). The team members included the following consultants in the Poverty and Equity Global Practice: Mexico A. Vergara Bahena, Claudia Berg, Carlos Bezerra de Góes, Eddys Gonzalez, Jaime Roche Rodríguez, and Daniela Ruiz Zárate. The team is thankful to Laura Wallace for her skillful editing of the report and to Aletz Sonidas for formatting and additional editing.

The work greatly benefited from the comments and encouragement of Johannes G. Hoogeveen (practice manager, Poverty and Equity Global Practice). The analysis was improved through consultations with colleagues, in particular Ragui Assaad, Kevin Carey, Nelly Elmallakh, Asif Islam, Daniel Lederman, Bob Rijkers, and Josh Wimpey. The team would like to express its gratitude to Lantoniaina Ramanankasina (program assistant, EFI-MNA-POV) for the assistance provided during the preparation of the report. The team duly acknowledges funding received from the Office of the Chief Economist for the Middle East and North Africa and the World Bank's Trade Umbrella Fund.

About the Editors and Contributors

Editors

Gladys Lopez-Acevedo is a lead economist and global lead for the World Bank's Poverty and Equity Global Practice. Her professional career spans work in five World Bank regions, including as acting South Asia Chief Economist and in various lead and senior economist roles. Currently in the World Bank's Middle East and North Africa Region, she has been leading analytical and operational work on distributional effects of the COVID-19 (coronavirus) pandemic, conflict, informality, trade, digital markets, fiscal incidence, green growth, labor markets, social protection, data and statistical capacity, poverty and equity, and gender. She holds research fellowships at several research organizations, including the Institute of Labor Economics (IZA), the Mexican National Research System (SNI), the Economic Research Forum, Duke University's Global Value Chain Institute, and the 3ie Impact Evaluation Initiative. Before joining the World Bank, she held high-level positions in Mexico's Ministry of Finance and Ministry of Trade and taught as a professor at the Instituto Tecnológico Autónomo de México (ITAM). She has written extensively on economics in peer-reviewed journals. She holds a bachelor's degree in economics from ITAM and a doctorate in economics from the University of Virginia.

Raymond Robertson is professor and holder of the Helen and Roy Ryu Chair in Economics and Government in the Department of International Affairs at the Bush School of Government and Public Service, Texas A&M University, where he also serves as director of the Mosbacher Institute for Trade, Economics, and Public Policy. In 2018, Texas A&M named him as a Presidential Impact Fellow. He is a research fellow at the Institute of Labor Economics (IZA) in Bonn, Germany, and a senior research fellow at the Southern Methodist University's Mission Foods Texas-Mexico Center. He has taught at the Maxwell School of Citizenship and Public

Affairs at Syracuse University and was a visiting professor in the Department of Economics, Graduate School of Administration, at the Monterrey Institute of Technology's Mexico City campus. Widely published in the field of labor economics and international economics, Robertson previously chaired the US Department of Labor's National Advisory Committee for Labor Provisions of the US Free Trade Agreements and has served on the State Department's Advisory Committee on International Economic Policy as well as on the Center for Global Development's advisory board. He earned a bachelor's degree in political science and economics from Trinity University in San Antonio and a master's degree and doctorate in economics from the University of Texas at Austin.

Contributors

Mexico A. Vergara Bahena is a consultant in the World Bank's Poverty and Equity Global Practice. He has been working on female labor participation and distributional impacts of trade in the South Asia and Middle East and North Africa regions. Previously, he worked as an economist in the international economy division of the Mexican Central Bank. He holds a master's degree in applied economics from Instituto Tecnológico Autónomo de México (ITAM) and a master's degree in public policy from the University of Chicago.

Claudia Berg is an extended-term consultant in the Sustainability and Infrastructure Unit of the World Bank's Development Research Group. Previously, she worked in the Bank's Poverty and Equity Global Practice and the Sustainable Development Practice Group, among others. Her primary research interests include assessment of the economic and welfare impacts of policy and investment measures, such as microfinance, road infrastructure, poverty interventions, trade, and currently climate change. Outside the World Bank, she applied her skills at the International Monetary Fund and Inter-American Development Bank. Before joining the World Bank, she taught microeconomics at George Washington University, where she earned a doctorate in economics.

Carlos Góes is a consultant in the World Bank's Poverty and Equity Global Practice. He is a spatial economist whose research agenda lies at the intersection of macroeconomics and international trade. He previously worked as a senior economic adviser in the Office of the President of Brazil and as a researcher at the International Monetary Fund, the World Trade Organization, and some US think tanks. A doctoral candidate in economics from the University of California San Diego, he holds a master's degree in international economics from Johns Hopkins University's School of Advanced International Studies.

Eddys Gonzalez is a consultant in the World Bank's Poverty and Equity Global Practice. He has previously worked in the private sector and other development organizations including the Inter-American Development Bank. His experience includes financial and economic analysis in a wide range of economic sectors, investment advising, and portfolio evaluation. Through the Fulbright US Student Program, he is working toward his master's degree in international affairs at Texas A&M University, specializing in international development and economic policy. His research interests include trade policy, poverty eradication, macro trends, and sustainable development. He also undertook graduate work in economics at Central American University in Managua, Nicaragua, focusing on microeconomic analysis for enterprises, project investment, and project evaluation.

Jaime Alfonso Roche Rodríguez is a consultant in the World Bank's Poverty and Equity Global Practice. His research has focused on the distributional impacts of trade on labor market outcomes, as well as poverty and inequality in the Middle East and North Africa region. He is also an international economist at the Mexican Central Bank, where he conducts labor market research and macroeconomic analysis to support the monetary policy committees. He holds a bachelor's degree in economics from Tecnológico de Monterrey and a master's degree in international finance from Rennes School of Business.

Daniela Ruiz Zárate was a consultant in the World Bank's Poverty and Equity Global Practice. Her research interests include economic growth and development, structural transformation, labor economics, and globalization. She has also participated in projects with other international organizations, such as the International Labour Organization (ILO) and the Economic Commission for Latin America and the Caribbean (ECLAC) of the United Nations. She currently works as an international economist in the Research Department of the Mexican Central Bank. She holds a master's degree in specialized economic analysis on international trade, finance, and development from Pompeu Fabra University in Spain and a master's degree in labor economics for development from the University of Turin and Sciences Po.

Abbreviations

BaTiS	Balanced Trade in Services (dataset)
EFTA	European Free Trade Association
ENPE	National Survey on Population and Employment (Tunisia)
EU	European Union
FDI	foreign direct investment
FLFP	female labor force participation
GAFTA	Greater Arab Free Trade Area
GATT	General Agreement on Tariffs and Trade
GDP	gross domestic product
GVC	global value chain
iid	individually and identically distributed
LE	Egyptian pound
LFS	Labor Force Survey(s)
LMIEs	low- and middle-income economies
MFA	Multifiber Arrangement
OECD	Organisation for Economic Co-operation and Development
RTA	regional trade agreement
TFP	total factor productivity
UN	United Nations
WDI	World Development Indicators
WTO	World Trade Organization

Overview

Introduction

From 2000 to 2009, many low- and middle-income countries experienced a trade-related economic boom. Rising exports of both raw materials and manufactured goods coincided with falling poverty and inequality. In the Middle East and North Africa, trade liberalization measures accelerated as countries tried to catch the globalization wave and integrate into global value chains to promote economic growth. In response, total trade in the region (excluding high-income countries) rose sharply from 61 percent of gross domestic product (GDP) in 2000 to 73 percent in 2008.[1]

However, despite continued liberalization with falling tariffs, the trend of trade expansion was reversed starting in 2008 in the wake of the Global Financial Crisis, with a partial recovery in 2015–17, but still below the 2009 levels since 2017 (figure O.1).

In the early 2000s, trade agreements and other reforms coincided with stable economic growth, with GDP per capita of the region's low- and middle-income economies (LMIEs) growing at an annual average rate of 2.5 percent in 2000–04, rising slightly to 2.7 percent in 2005–09. These results surpassed the performance of other low- to middle-income regions like Latin America and the Caribbean and Sub-Saharan Africa. However, labor market outcomes in the Middle East and North Africa's LMIEs—such as average wages, informality levels, and female labor force participation (FLFP)—remained less favorable than in most others, and these issues persist.

Why did the rising trade fail to produce better labor market outcomes in the Middle East and North Africa's LMIEs? This report tries to solve the puzzle by exploring two possibilities: First, trade agreements might not produce the same trade increases for these economies as for countries in other regions. Second, exports might not generate the same kinds of labor market outcomes in these economies as experienced elsewhere.

1

FIGURE O.1

Trends in Tariff Liberalization and Trade Flows, Middle East and North Africa, 2000–19

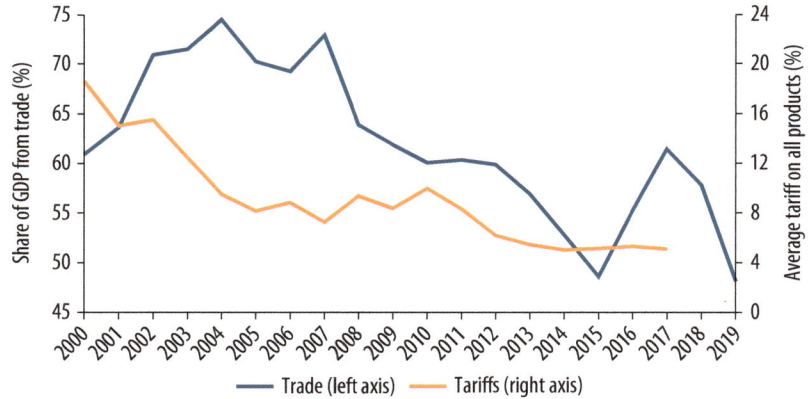

Source: World Bank based on the World Development Indicators Database.
Note: "Trade" is the sum of exports and imports expressed as a percentage of GDP. Average tariffs are a simple mean applied to all products. The available tariff rate data end in 2017. All data exclude high-income countries.

The wide range of experiences across the Middle East and North Africa's LMIEs suggests that these economies must be studied individually to determine the specific link between trade and labor markets. For example, while some countries export oil (such as Iraq, Qatar, Saudi Arabia, and the United Arab Emirates), others have expanded manufacturing exports, especially apparel (as in the Arab Republic of Egypt, Jordan, Morocco, and Tunisia). To examine the effects of trade on labor markets in the Arab Republic of Egypt, Morocco, and Tunisia, the report implements three approaches (further described in box O.1):

- Estimate the impact of trade policy on trade exposure (that is, exports per worker in region)

- Estimate the relationship between trade exposure and local labor market outcomes

- Estimate the relationship between exports and labor market outcomes at the firm level.

To highlight the differences within the region, the report focuses on three lower-middle-income countries—Egypt, Morocco, and Tunisia—which, given their idiosyncrasies in labor markets, export diversification, and trade policy history, offer important lessons for economic development in the Middle East and North Africa's LMIEs.[2]

BOX O.1

Methodological Approach

To trace the relationship between trade policy and labor market outcomes, this report follows a three-pronged approach (figure BO.1.1):

1. As shown on the left side of the schematic, we employ the gravity model to estimate the relationship between trade policy (in the form of trade agreements) and trade flows for our case countries relative to global averages.[a]

2. As shown on the top right side of the schematic, we estimate the relationship between trade flows and labor market outcomes at the subnational or regional level. We use a "shift-share" analysis (following Bartik 1991) to identify distributional impacts of trade and spot which districts win or lose in response to higher export flows.

3. As shown on the bottom right side of the schematic, we focus on firm-level data (a "heterogeneous firm model") to explore whether differences among firms influence the relationship between exports and labor market outcomes, as economic theory predicts. By examining the micro level, we can detect positive relationships that are not perceivable at the macro level.

One of the main ideas behind our approach is that labor markets are localized, so the effects of trade are proportional to trade-related industry employment across different cities or regions. Both imports and exports can have important labor market effects, and we apply the shift-share approach to both.

FIGURE BO.1.1

Approach to Examining the Link between Trade Policy and Labor Market Outcomes

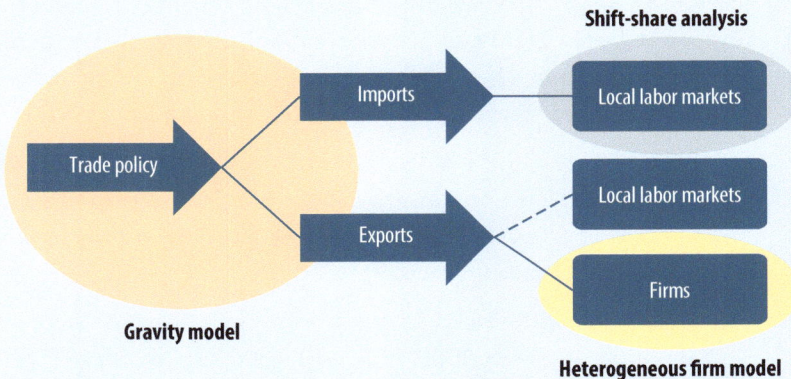

a. The gravity model is the most common empirical tool used by economists to estimate the contributions of various factors—such as trade agreements—to bilateral international trade flows. Our application of the gravity model follows Baier, Bergstrand, and Clance (2018).

This report focuses on four key messages:

- *Message 1:* Liberalized trade policy has successfully boosted trade flows, which are associated with a significant increase in economic growth.

- *Message 2:* Trade benefits have not yielded the hoped-for labor market outcomes.

- *Message 3:* Trade benefits have also not been equally shared among regions and population groups.

- *Message 4:* One obstacle to better labor market outcomes may be widespread exogenous (externally determined) market segmentation by gender, which shapes the effects of trade shocks such as higher exports.

The report provides new assessments of and insights into the trade and labor market picture in various countries of the Middle East and North Africa. Policy makers and other stakeholders can use these insights to design policies that enhance the chances that higher trade flows will not only deliver better labor market outcomes but also ensure that the benefits are more equally shared.

Message 1: Liberalized Trade Policy Boosts Trade Flows, with Big Benefits

Between 1990 and 2019, Egypt, Morocco, and Tunisia signed 19 regional trade agreements (RTAs) (figure O.2) and reduced tariffs (figure O.3). Over the same period, trade in the Middle East and North Africa's LMIEs grew from 49 percent to 59 percent of aggregate GDP,[3] and the aggregate GDP per capita (in constant 2015 US$) increased by 54 percent.[4]

- *In Egypt*, 10 RTAs are in force, 6 of which were signed since 2004. Between 2000 and 2020, export values shot up 196 percent in real terms from a low base, while imports soared 231 percent—and GDP per capita increased 52 percent (in constant 2015 US$).

- *In Morocco*, nine RTAs are in force. Between 2000 and 2018, its living conditions improved significantly—with the poverty rate falling from 15.3 percent to 4.8 percent and per capita income almost doubling.

- *In Tunisia*, eight RTAs are in force, half of which were signed since 2000. Between 2000 and 2010, total exports and GDP per capita (in constant 2015 US$) grew by 79 percent and 37 percent, respectively. However, following the Arab Spring in 2010, this trend plateaued in response to both domestic and global shocks—and both total exports and GDP per capita have been stagnant ever since.

FIGURE O.2

Cumulative Regional Trade Agreements, Arab Republic of Egypt, Morocco, and Tunisia, 1970–2020

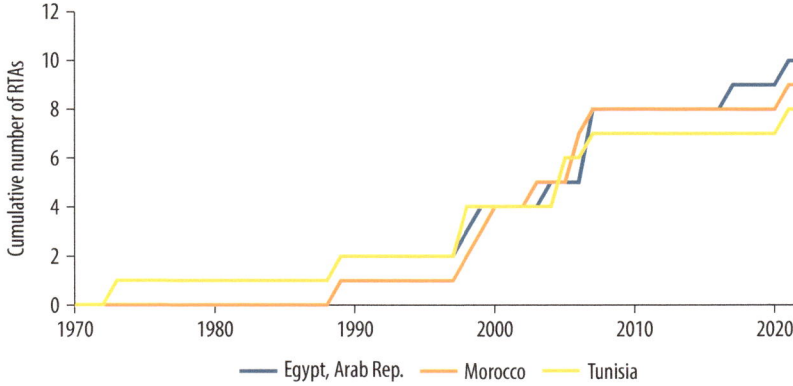

Source: World Trade Organization's Regional Trade Agreements Information System (RTA-IS), https://rtais
.wto.org.
Note: "RTAs" refers to regional trade agreements currently in force.

FIGURE O.3

Tariff Rates on All Products, Egypt, Morocco, and Tunisia, 2000–19

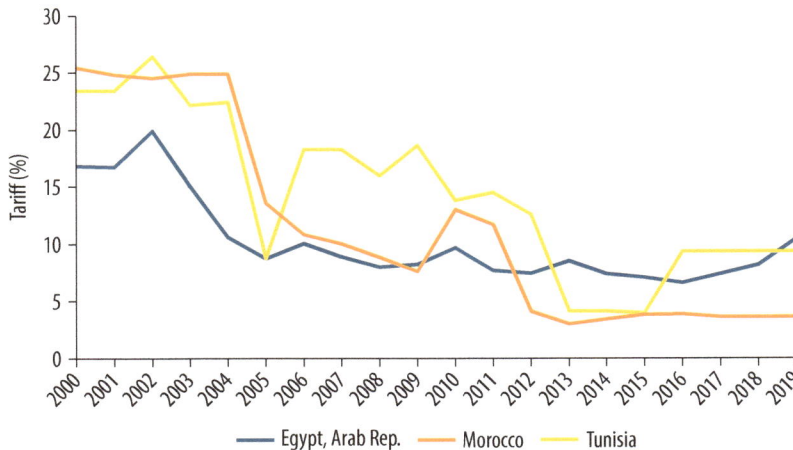

Source: World Bank based on data from the Our World in Data database (https://ourworldindata.org/) of
the Global Change Data Lab and University of Oxford.
Notes: Tariffs shown are weighted mean applied tariffs—the average of effectively applied rates weighted
by the product import shares corresponding to each country partner.

Our study starts by asking whether the recent trade agreements signed by Egypt, Morocco, and Tunisia have been more, less, or equally effective in promoting bilateral trade flows compared with the average trade agreement globally. The results, using a gravity analysis, show that for all three countries, RTAs did a good job of boosting trade flows. In fact, each trade agreement had a larger impact on trade flows than the average trade agreement—and trade flows increased more in each country than in the average country. For each pair of source and destination countries, the average treatment effects are positive and fall close to the middle of the distribution (0.53)—with some agreements more effective than others (figure O.4): 0.57 in Tunisia, 0.50 in Egypt, and 0.48 in Morocco.

FIGURE O.4

Treatment Effects of Trade Agreements in Morocco, Tunisia, and Egypt

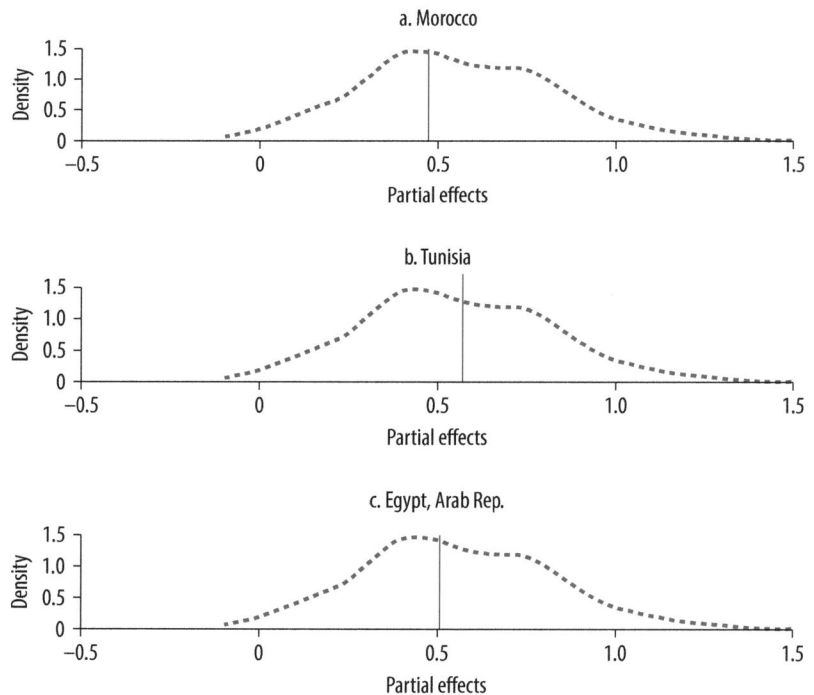

Source: World Bank estimates using data from the United Nations Comtrade database.
Note: Averages for Egypt, Morocco, and Tunisia (shown as solid vertical lines) are juxtaposed against the distribution of treatment effects for every source–destination country pair, as of 2010. Values above zero for a given trade agreement imply that such an agreement has boosted trade between those country pairs, relative to a counterfactual of absence of an agreement. Dashed lines show the distribution of estimated effects.

Thus, it is plausible that signing additional free trade agreements in the Middle East and North Africa would further increase trade flows. And in 2012–14 Arab Barometer public opinion surveys, more than 70 percent of the respondents viewed international trade as having a "very positive" (35.0 percent) or "somewhat positive" (36.7 percent) impact on the economy.[5] However, this is not a universal sentiment. Despite the net benefits of rising trade flows, as exhibited in East Asia's rapid growth, a global pessimism has taken hold as increasing inequality among workers and lagging economic growth in certain regions are frequently blamed on globalization (Artuc, Taglioni, and Zarate 2022).

> *Policy recommendation: Continued trade expansion is called for in all three case countries, given strong evidence that the signing of trade agreements and concurrent tariff reduction by the region's economies have helped boost higher exports and economic growth.*

Message 2: Trade Benefits Have Not Improved Labor Outcomes

In the Middle East and North Africa, as elsewhere, higher trade has gone hand in hand with lower unemployment, signaling better job creation. Yet, the region's unemployment remains high relative to peer economies in other regions (figure O.5). Between 2010 and 2019, the average annual unemployment rate was 12 percent in the Middle East and North Africa's LMIEs. Moreover, certain groups have been hit harder than others. While male unemployment held at about 9 percent, the rate for women rose from 18 percent to 20 percent, and the rate for youth (ages 15–24), who continued to face a scarcity of jobs (as did women), rose from 25 percent to 27 percent.[6]

Key Factors That Increase Unemployment

Why does the Middle East and North Africa underperform in terms of unemployment? The answer lies, in part, in the three key factors that characterize the region's labor market:

- Labor supply rising faster than labor demand

- The state's dominant role in the economy

- Gender biases.

Job creation fails to keep pace with the region's growing working-age population. Although the population of the region's

FIGURE O.5

Average Unemployment Rates in Relation to Trade in the Middle East and North Africa, Regionwide and Selected Countries and Economic Peers Elsewhere, 2015–19

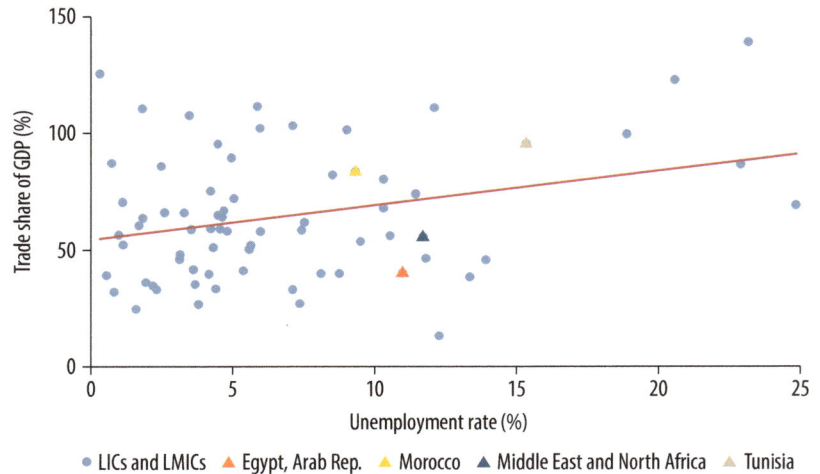

Source: World Bank based on World Development Indicators Database 2015–19.
Note: Values correspond to five-year averages of 2015–19 data. The red line represents the fitted trend of the data. Middle East and North Africa excludes high-income countries. "LICs" are low-income countries and "LMICs" are lower-middle-income countries in other regions. Country income groups are according to World Bank classifications.

LMIEs almost doubled—from 279 million in 2000 to 389 million in 2019[7]—these economies' rapidly expanding labor *supply* was not matched by labor *demand*. As a result, the employment-to-population ratio declined from 40 percent in 2000 to 38 percent in 2019 (figure O.6). Although other low- to middle-income regions experienced a more severe fall, their current ratios are still higher than the Middle East and North Africa's LMIEs.

The pervasive state presence in the economy contributes to high youth unemployment. The state-led model has been the norm, with many state-owned enterprises. But governments can no longer absorb new entrants into the labor market. As a result, finding jobs for the growing youth population is a major challenge. The region ranks the highest in youth unemployment (27 percent). In 2019, youth unemployment stood at 35 percent in Tunisia, 23 percent in Morocco, and 21 percent in Egypt.[8]

Social norms and preferences create biases about the tasks that women should or should not do. The Middle East and North Africa's FLFP (7 percent)[9]—the lowest in the world—is restricted by gendered laws that constrain women to certain sectors.

FIGURE O.6

Employment-to-Population Ratios in Low- and Middle-Income Countries, by Region, 2000–19

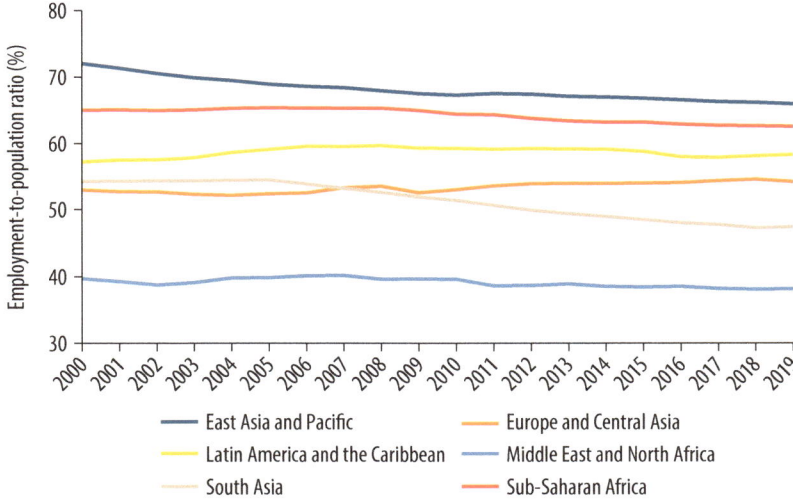

Source: World Bank based on the World Development Indicators Database, 2000–19.
Note: Values correspond to the aggregate employment-to-population ratio in each region. All regions exclude high-income economies.

A Closer Look at Exports' Role in Employment, by Country

While these three characteristics are largely present in the region as a whole, they affect individual countries to varying degrees. To assess the impact of higher exports in our case countries on labor market outcomes (like FLFP, employment, informality, and wages), we use the geography-based approach of Bartik (1991).

Our results indicate the following (table O.1):

- Informality decreased in Moroccan regions more exposed to exports relative to those less exposed, with no link detected in Egypt.

- FLFP declined in more-exposed Moroccan regions.

- Female employment decreased in more-exposed Tunisian regions, with no link detected in Egypt.

- Wages in Egypt decreased in the short run, but there was no long-run link.

Morocco

Morocco shows rapid progress on employment and formalization of the economy but mixed effects on gender and youth employment.

TABLE O.1

Estimated Short- and Long-Run Effects of Increased Export Exposure in Morocco, Tunisia, and Arab Republic of Egypt

Country, export exposure increase, and labor market indicators		Short-run effect	Long-run effect
A. Morocco: US$100 increase per worker		*2000–04*	*2000–08*
Informality	Coefficient	−0.009***	−0.006**
	t-statistic	(−2.16)	(−2.31)
FLFP	Coefficient	−0.0032*	−0.0027**
	t-statistic	(−1.91)	(−2.90)
	N	60	60
B. Tunisia: US$1 billion increase		—	*2006–16*
Female-to-male employment	Coefficient	—	−0.068**
	t-statistic	—	(−2.19)
Change in female employment	Coefficient	—	−7,904***
	t-statistic	—	(−2.59)
Change in male employment	Coefficient	—	2,418
	t-statistic	—	(0.77)
	N	—	120
C. Egypt, Arab Rep.: US$100 increase per worker		*2009–12*	*2009–17*
Wages	Coefficient	−207.85**	−0.300
	t-statistic	(−2.55)	(−0.00)
	N	250	246
Informality	Coefficient	−0.00026	−0.01514
	t-statistic	(−0.09)	(−1.09)
	N	250	246
FLFP	Coefficient	−0.00117	0.00107
	t-statistic	(−0.74)	(0.39)
	N	250	246

Source: World Bank based on data from the United Nations Comtrade database and national Labor Force Surveys for the countries and years specified in the table.
Note: The labor market indicators are chosen based on data availability. The Morocco and Egypt analyses normalized export exposure by the labor market size. The Tunisia analysis examines absolute export exposure in dollars to focus on the gender divide, which would have been harder to interpret if scaled by the labor force. Robust t-statistics are within parentheses. FLFP = female labor force participation; — = not available. Stars indicate the degree of confidence in the accuracy of the result, with more stars indicating greater confidence.
***$p < .01$ **$p < .05$ *$p < .10$.

Economic growth led by the export sector, while raising living standards overall, did not translate into enough jobs to offset the increase in population—the same as in the rest of the Middle East and North Africa region. Still, unemployment did decrease significantly from 13.4 percent in 2000 to 9.7 percent, but it benefited mostly the male population.

This occurred as the country shifted progressively from labor-intensive, female-friendly light manufacturing (like apparel and textile sectors) to capital-intensive sectors, which promote formalization and male-labor-intensive industries but tend to exclude women from the labor force. Morocco reflects an unexpected circumstance in which trade improvement lowered FLFP while contributing to formalization of the economy (box O.2).

Tunisia

Tunisia illustrates how higher exports can turn out to be the opposite of gender-neutral. Because increased exports had male-intensive employment effects, provinces with higher export exposure had relatively lower female employment growth. This change leads to a simultaneous decrease in female employment and increase in male employment.

BOX O.2

Morocco: Positive Trade Shocks Reduce Both Informality and FLFP

How do trade shocks affect labor market outcomes like the FLFP rate and the level of informality? For Morocco, we assess the impact of higher exports on these outcomes using the geography-based approach of Bartik (1991). Specifically, we estimate how more exports per worker (a trade exposure index) affect informality and FLFP rates at the province level. This "shift-share" approach looks at industry-level shocks and effects on the labor markets exposed to them to construct a region-specific export exposure shock. Our results yield the two primary findings described below.

Higher exports per worker decreases informality in regions more exposed to trade. The good news is that increasing exports reduced labor informality rates from 2000 to 2004, a correlation that weakens over the 2000–08 period. For instance, an increase

of US$100 in exports per worker decreased informality by 0.9 percentage points in the first period and by 0.6 percentage points in the second, longer period in provinces with higher trade exposure. These results are statistically significant and apply for all types of workers.

Higher exports per worker lowers the FLFP rate in regions more exposed to trade. An increase of US$100 in exports per worker reduces FLFP by 0.32 percentage points from 2000 to 2004 and by 0.27 percentage points from 2000 to 2008 in provinces more exposed to trade. Although these findings are unexpected given the standard belief that trade promotes FLFP, they are consistent with trade and labor market patterns of decreasing female participation due to specialization of capital- and male-labor-intensive ("male-intensive") industries in Morocco.

(Box continues on the following page.)

BOX O.2 (continued)

What happens at the firm level? Our microanalysis confirms that higher employment is associated with higher export sales. It also reveals that the positive impact of exports on employment has occurred mainly within the male-intensive sector.

Thus, the increase in trade due to liberalization in recent decades has had both positive and negative effects on local labor market outcomes. Although an increase in exports per worker increases formalization, it does not translate into improved FLFP owing to a combination of local and external conditions. These findings, despite being at odds with trade theory, reflect Morocco's key trade and labor market trends.

Egypt

Egypt stands out for an apparent absence of a link between trade flows and labor market outcomes. The link between trade policy and exports is solid, since trade agreements considerably boosted exports, but the rise in exports brought about only negligible changes in employment levels at the national and subnational levels. Furthermore, the country's strong *import* growth (75 percent of which is intermediate goods for production) had a negligible or short-lived impact on labor variables (such as wages, informality, and FLFP).

These findings raise the prospect that the link between exports and the labor market may be broken—or maybe the problem is that exporting firms still remain a tiny part of the labor market (box O.3).

Policy recommendation: There is strong evidence that greater trade expansion will help job creation, however small (in the case of Egypt). Moreover, if it is combined with policies to promote labor-intensive sectors, there should be even higher job creation, thereby helping Middle East and North Africa countries absorb the growing number of youth entering the labor market.

For Egypt to seize the benefits of trade, it will need to undertake deeper reforms to create incentives to substantially grow the export sector, especially in favor of labor-intensive industries, and integrate more into global value chains. This means that Egypt must improve its business environment—which can be done by lowering investment barriers (especially to foreign direct investment), cutting the costs for firms to formalize, and making the private sector more attractive than the public sector in terms of wages and job security.

BOX O.3

Egypt: A "Broken Link" between Trade Flows and Labor Outcomes?

How do we explain what appears to be Egypt's broken link between trade and local labor markets? The structure of Egyptian firms could represent one explanation. To determine whether this is the case, we dive into a firm analysis. After all, even though exports do not connect to labor markets at the macro level, as we would expect, there may be micro-level effects. Certainly, rising exports have the potential to increase employment through increased labor demand. So if that does not happen, why not? We consider four possible reasons:

- Exporting firms may be too small of a segment in the local labor market to significantly affect overall employment. For Egypt, this may be valid. Our analysis shows that only 1 percent of firms export.

- Exporting firms are often in capital-intensive sectors (like extractive industries and high-tech exports), which can expand production without significantly

increasing their workforce. This may also be valid. We find a capital–labor ratio of 31 for exporting firms and 26 for nonexporting firms.

- Exporting firms may have excess worker capacity and use the relatively idle workers to provide the additional production for exports. This does not appear to be valid. We find that a 100 percent increase in export sales would boost employment by about 20 percent.

- Firm-level production may simply shift from the domestic to the international market, without expanding production or employment. This also does not appear to be valid. We find that more export sales correlate with more employment and vice versa.

The bottom line is that there likely is not a broken link. Rather, although employment in Egypt rose in response to higher exports, it did not occur at a large enough scale to be felt at the economy-wide level.

Message 3: Trade Benefits Are Not Equally Shared

While there is ample evidence that trade spurs economic growth and reduces poverty, there is also evidence that these benefits are not equally shared. One reason why this has occurred is that as new RTAs are signed and trade flows are shifted, wealth is redistributed—meaning that there will inevitably be both winners and losers, as some sectors and regions grow and others decline. This is true even in countries that are deemed "success stories" of trade liberalization in the Middle East and North Africa, as elsewhere. Our analysis points to a few key findings on this phenomenon in the region.

Insufficient and shifting labor demand have hampered women's labor participation. Women in the Middle East and North Africa suffer more from the lack of job opportunities than do women in other low- and middle-income regions. Female unemployment in the region was close to 20 percent in 2019, far above the levels in East Asia and Pacific (3 percent), South Asia (5 percent), Europe and Central Asia and Sub-Saharan Africa (7 percent each), and Latin America and the Caribbean (10 percent) (figure O.7).

Moreover, as of 2019, the female–male unemployment rate gap in the Middle East and North Africa was the largest in the world—11 percentage points. In contrast, the East Asia and Pacific and Europe and Central Asia regions reported negative gaps of 0.7 and 0.9 percentage points, respectively, suggesting that job scarcity in these other regions affects men more than women. Latin America and the Caribbean, South Asia, and Sub-Saharan Africa had gender unemployment gaps of 3.0, 0.2, and 0.3 percentage points, respectively—all much lower than the Middle East and North Africa.

In 2000, the manufacturing sector represented 18 percent of total female employment in the Middle East and North Africa. By 2014, this figure had fallen to 15 percent.[10] As emerged from our analysis, this decline is largely due to female job loss in textiles and apparel, owing to internal industrial policies promoting male-intensive

FIGURE O.7

Unemployment Rates, by Gender and Region, 2019

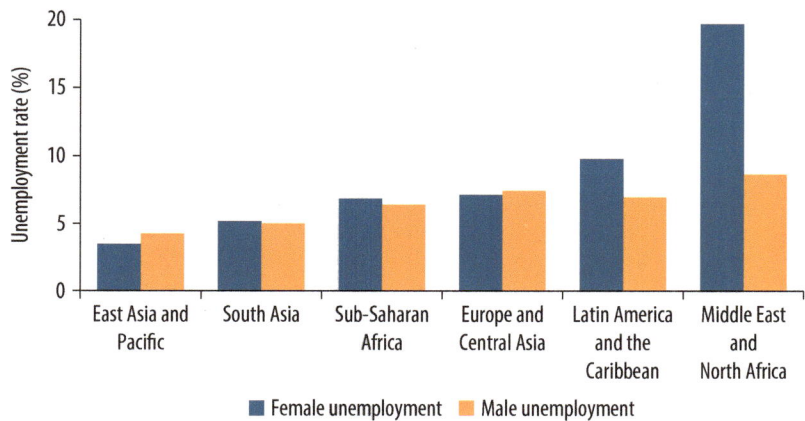

Source: World Bank based on the World Development Indicators Database.
Note: Values correspond to the aggregate unemployment rates in each region, by gender. All regions exclude high-income economies.

industries, the emergence of international competitors, and the lack of job opportunities for women in the new export sector.

Social barriers prevent many women from finding jobs outside the public sector, and most of the jobs available tend to be male labor intensive. In the 1990s, the FLFP in the Middle East and North Africa LMIEs averaged 17 percent, increasing to only 18 percent over the following decade. By comparison, FLFP reached 28 percent in South Asia, 62 percent in East Asia and Pacific, and 63 percent in Sub-Saharan Africa.[11] In particular, our case countries—Egypt, Morocco, and Tunisia—reported lower FLFP rates (with few signs of improvement over the past two decades) than the region's high-income countries (like Kuwait, Qatar, and the United Arab Emirates). Further, relative to selected countries in other world regions, the three case countries rank the lowest (figure O.8). For example, Brazil and Vietnam's FLFP rates in 2019 were 53 percent and 70 percent, respectively.

Firms that contributed the most to export growth were in male-intensive industries rather than female-intensive ones. This was the case in Morocco and Tunisia, where the FLFP rates were 23 percent and 26 percent, respectively (figure O.8). Although higher than the regional average (17 percent), when compared to the men's labor force

FIGURE O.8

Female and Male Labor Force Participation, Egypt, Morocco, and Tunisia, Compared with Selected Countries in Other Regions, 2019

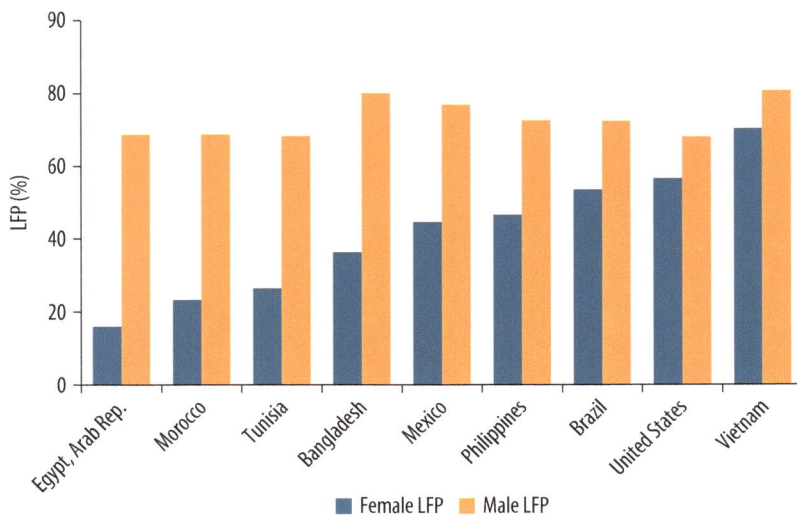

Source: World Bank based on the World Development Indicators Database.
Note: LFP = Labor force participation.

participation in each country, the gaps are 49 and 44 percentage points, respectively. As for unemployment, women are again disproportionally more affected than men. In the same period, female unemployment averaged 20 percent throughout the region's LMIEs, while men's unemployment was 9 percent.[12]

Policy recommendation: Our analysis demonstrates that promoting exports has deterred FLFP, contrary to the well-documented cases in which emerging nations' light manufacturing (such as textiles and apparel) benefit from trade openness and thus promote female employment and FLFP. In fact, we find that after a trade shock, women in the Middle East and North Africa have an especially hard time changing occupation.

To reverse this trend, steps are needed to increase female employment and close the gender gap, which has been aggravated by the recent trend toward capital-intensive and male-intensive industries. This could be done by (a) promoting high-end, high-value light manufacturing; and (b) bringing more women into traditionally male-dominated sectors and vice versa. Any trade policy package should include awareness, education, skill training, and special incentives to hire women (and youth).

Message 4: Market Segmentation by Gender Impedes Better Labor Market Outcomes

Labor frictions—such as mobility costs that inhibit workers from changing their occupational industry or geographic location—are higher in the Middle East and North Africa than in regions such as Latin American and the Caribbean and South Asia (Artuc, Lederman, and Porto 2015). This matters greatly because market segmentation hinders the benefits of trade from being shared more broadly. In fact, economists attribute many of the negative outcomes of globalization to these frictions. It is important to note here that our study considers market segmentation by gender as exogenous (external) to trade—that is, its existence is independent of the factors that influence trade. However, our findings urge the need to study this gender bias in the labor market, as specified below.

Occupational industry is segmented by gender. Biases, social norms, or individual preferences create frictions in the labor market that prevent women from moving across sectors optimally. If large enough, such frictions lead to substantial market segmentation along gender lines. For example, the textile and apparel sector has a high share of female employment, with 83.6 percent of total apparel workers globally (Lopez-Acevedo and Robertson 2012).

Gender-segmented labor markets aggravated the toll on FLFP when the Multifiber Arrangement (MFA) ended in 2004. The MFA was an international trade agreement that imposed quotas on the amount of textiles and apparel exported from low- and middle-income countries to high-income countries. Its demise triggered a net increase in global apparel exports and a reallocation of apparel production across countries, increasing apparel employment in some countries (such as Bangladesh) (Lopez-Acevedo and Robertson 2012) but reducing it in others (such as Middle East and North Africa countries).

In Morocco, women found fewer employment opportunities with the contraction of the female-dominated apparel industry. The end of the MFA—in conjunction with national economic policies that promoted formalization and high-value-added industries (which tend to be male dominated)—aggravated the decrease in FLFP. In Tunisia, women were also hardest hit. Our analysis shows that a US$1 billion increase in exposure to exports reduced the female-to-male employment ratio by 6.8 percentage points—largely driven by married women rather than single women (box O.4). Moreover, since exports are increasingly in male-intensive industries, Tunisian regions with higher exposure to exports had relatively low female employment growth.

BOX O.4

Tunisia: Trade Shocks and Labor Markets "Segmented" by Gender

Why does labor market segmentation by gender matter when trade shocks occur? This type of segmentation refers to different potential job opportunities for women and men. We explored this issue in Tunisia by leveraging the variation in exposure to exports and labor market composition across Tunisian regions. For instance, the North East and Center East regions specialize in manufacturing, while the cities in the Greater Tunis region primarily specialize in services.

Our results in chapter 4 show that between 2006 and 2016, provinces that were more exposed to higher exports saw a drop in the female-to-male employment ratio. This is not unexpected, since most foreign demand shocks (increases) were concentrated in male-labor-intensive industries, which led male employment to expand and female employment to contract.

Next, to shed light on the welfare impacts of changing trade exposure, we estimated the impact on male and female unemployment. Our analysis reveals that greater trade exposure had no significant impact on the unemployment rate of either men or women. Given the earlier finding that the employment rate of women fell, we can conclude that women (especially married ones) were dropping out of the labor force, and households seemed to be substituting female for male work. In fact, a US$1 billion increase in export exposure led to 4,605 fewer jobs among married women and 2,501 fewer jobs among single women.

Thus, geographic segmentation compounded gender segmentation to worsen FLFP.

> *Policy recommendation: Geographic and occupational market desegmentation is called for to share economic growth, reduce labor market frictions, and spread job creation to a wider population. This can be done by (a) promoting female-friendly industries; and (b) ensuring that trade expansion goes hand in hand with infrastructure and incentives that favor regions bypassed by the new industries and exports.*

> *Another issue to tackle is the existence of traditions and social norms that are well known to discourage female labor away from home. The government could help by adopting measures to favor remote work, which are likely to especially benefit women. A forthcoming study will explore the potential of the digital economy to promote home-based work and boost female employment and entrepreneurship.*

Notes

1. Data on regional trade shares of GDP from "Trade (% of GDP) – Middle East & North Africa (excluding high income)," using World Bank and Organisation for Economic Co-operation and Development (OECD) national accounts data: https://data.worldbank.org/indicator/NE.TRD .GNFS.ZS?locations=XQ.

2. In this report, the Middle East and North Africa includes only the region's low- and middle-income economies: Algeria, Djibouti, the Arab Republic of Egypt, the Islamic Republic of Iran, Iraq, Jordan, Lebanon, Libya, Morocco, the Syrian Arab Republic, Tunisia, West Bank and Gaza, and the Republic of Yemen. It excludes the region's high-income countries: Bahrain, Israel, Kuwait, Malta, Oman, Qatar, Saudi Arabia, and the United Arab Emirates.

3. Data on regional trade shares of GDP from "Trade (% of GDP) – Middle East & North Africa (Excluding High Income)," using World Bank and OECD national accounts data: https://data.worldbank.org/indicator /NE.TRD.GNFS.ZS?locations=XQ.

4. Data on aggregate GDP per capita from "GDP per Capita (constant 2015 US$) – Middle East & North Africa (Excluding High Income)," using World Bank and OECD national accounts data: https://data.worldbank.org /indicator/NY.GDP.PCAP.KD?locations=XQ.

5. These results are from the 2012–14 Arab Barometer public opinion surveys conducted in Algeria, Egypt, Iraq, Jordan, Kuwait, Lebanon, Libya, Morocco, Sudan, Tunisia, West Bank and Gaza, and the Republic of Yemen.

6. Unemployment data for 2000–19, by gender and age group, are from the World Development Indicators Database.

7. Population data for 2000–19 are from the World Development Indicators Database.

8. Youth unemployment data are from "Unemployment, Youth Total (% of Total Labor Force Ages 15–24) (Modeled ILO Estimate) – Middle East & North Africa (Excluding High Income), Egypt, Arab Rep., Morocco, Tunisia," using ILO Modelled Estimates and Projections Database (ILOEST) of the International Labour Organization (ILO) statistical database (ILOSTAT): https://data.worldbank.org/indicator/SL.UEM.1524 .ZS?end=2020&locations=XQ-EG-MA-TN&start=2019.

9. FLFP data are from "Labor Force Participation Rate, Female (% of Female Population Ages 15+) (Modeled ILO Estimate) – Middle East & North Africa (Excluding High Income), Egypt, Arab Rep., Morocco, Tunisia," using ILO Modelled Estimates and Projections Database (ILOEST), ILOSTAT: https://data.worldbank.org/indicator/SL.TLF.CACT.FE.ZS?end=2019 &locations=XQ-EG-MA-TN&start=1990.

10. Sector-specific female employment data are from "Employment in Industry, Female (% of Female Employment) (Modeled ILO Estimate) – Middle East & North Africa (Excluding High Income)," using ILO Modelled Estimates and Projections Database (ILOEST), ILOSTAT: https://data.worldbank .org/indicator/SL.IND.EMPL.FE.ZS?locations=XQ.

11. Regional FLFP data are from the World Development Indicators Database.

12. Men's and women's unemployment data are from, respectively, "Unemployment, Male (% of Male Labor Force) (Modeled ILO Estimate) – Middle East & North Africa (Excluding High Income)" (https://data .worldbank.org/indicator/SL.UEM.TOTL.MA.ZS?end=2021&locations =XQ-ZQ&start=2018); and "Unemployment, Female (% of Female Labor Force) (Modeled ILO Estimate) – Middle East & North Africa (Excluding High Income)" (https://data.worldbank.org/indicator/SL.UEM.TOTL.FE .ZS?end=2021&locations=XQ-ZQ&start=2018), both using ILO Modeled Estimates and Projections Database (ILOEST), ILOSTAT.

References

Artuc, Erhan, Daniel Lederman, and Guido Porto. 2015. "A Mapping of Labor Mobility Costs in the Developing World." *Journal of International Economics* 95 (1): 28–41.

Artuc, Erhan, Daria Taglioni, and Roman Zarate. 2022. "International Integration and Jobs in Palestine: A Review of the Experiences of Other Developing Countries." Unpublished manuscript, World Bank, Washington, DC.

Baier, Scott L., Jeffrey H. Bergstrand, and Matthew W. Clance. 2018. "Heterogeneous Effects of Economic Integration Agreements." *Journal of Development Economics* 135: 587–608. http://sites.nd.edu/jeffrey-bergstrand /files/2020/04/Heterogeneous-Effects-of-Economic-Integration -Agreements.pdf.

Bartik, Timothy J. 1991. *Who Benefits from State and Local Economic Development Policies?* Kalamazoo, MI: W. E. Upjohn Institute for Employment Research.

Lopez-Acevedo, Gladys, and Raymond Robertson, eds. 2012. *Sewing Success? Employment, Wages, and Poverty following the End of the Multi-Fibre Arrangement.* Directions in Development—Poverty. Washington, DC: World Bank. http://hdl.handle.net/10986/13137.

Lopez-Acevedo, Gladys, and Raymond Robertson, eds. 2016. *Stitches to Riches? Apparel Employment, Trade, and Economic Development in South Asia.* Directions in Development Series. Washington, DC: World Bank.

CHAPTER 1

Setting the Stage

Claudia N. Berg, Raymond Robertson,
Eddys Gonzalez, and Jaime Alfonso Roche Rodríguez

Key Messages

- The labor market is underperforming in the Middle East and North Africa's low- and middle-income economies (LMIEs), where job creation is failing to keep pace with growing working-age populations. The region's LMIEs have the lowest female labor force participation (FLFP) and the highest youth unemployment in the world.

- The weak labor picture contributes to the region's economic stagnation and low living standards—which may be a source of social and political instability, since these factors were associated with the 2010–12 Arab Spring protests.

- Trade can improve the region's labor market outcomes, but a positive link between trade and labor (in terms of employment, FLFP, wages, and informality) cannot be taken for granted, because exports did not generate the same kinds of labor market changes in our case countries as other regions experienced.

- This report investigates why better labor market outcomes in the region's LMIEs have not followed the increased exports from trade liberalization—with a focus on the Arab Republic of Egypt, Morocco, and Tunisia, all of which have significantly increased the number of active regional trade agreements since the early 2000s.

Motivation

From 2000 to 2009, many low- and middle-income countries experienced a trade-related economic boom—driven by rising exports of both raw materials and manufactured goods—that coincided with falling poverty and inequality. The economic benefits that came with higher exports were neither surprising nor new, as economists had been touting the positive labor market effects of trade for decades.

In the Middle East and North Africa, trade liberalization measures accelerated as countries tried to catch the globalization wave to integrate into global value chains and promote economic growth. Trade agreements and other reforms initially coincided with stable economic growth: gross domestic product (GDP) per capita in the region's low- and middle-income economies (LMIEs) grew at an annual average rate of 2.5 percent in 2000–04 and averaged 2.7 percent the following five years (table 1.1). These results surpassed the performance of other low- and middle-income regions, such as Latin America and the Caribbean and Sub-Saharan Africa.

However, poor labor market outcomes in the region's LMIEs—such as relatively high poverty and inequality, low average wages, high informality, and low female labor force participation (FLFP)—remained worse than in most other low- and middle-income regions. These poor outcomes helped feed the popular calls for social and political change (Ianchovichina 2018) (box 1.1).

Between 2010 and 2019, the region's LMIEs had an average annual unemployment rate of 12 percent, only a slight decrease from the previous decade. While male unemployment remained about the same—at about 9 percent—the disparity for women trended upward, with the annual average unemployment rate rising from 18 percent to 20 percent.[1] Further, youth (ages 15–24) continued to face a scarcity of jobs, and their annual average unemployment rate increased from 25 percent, already highest in the world, to 27 percent.[2]

Why did the rising trade—up from 61 percent of GDP in 2000 to 73 percent in 2008[3]—fail to produce better labor market outcomes in the LMIEs of the Middle East and North Africa? This issue is not well understood. Some experts, like Ianchovichina (2018), argue that monopolies and companies with political connections in the Arab Republic of Egypt and Tunisia hinder the growth of small and medium enterprises. Others suggest that firms with credit-access privileges may be capital intensive, thus creating fewer jobs as they substitute labor for capital (Islam, Moosa, and Saliola 2022). Still others propose that labor market rigidities create excess employment that is easily absorbed by the rising international demand (World Bank 2004).

TABLE 1.1

Average Annual Growth of Real GDP per Capita in Low- and Middle-Income Economies, by Region, in Five-Year Periods and Overall, 2000–20

Region	Trend	2000–04	2005–09	2010–14	2015–20	2000–20
Middle East and North Africa		2.0	4.2	0.6	2.4	2.3
Egypt, Arab Rep.		3.4	3.7	2.4	0.2	2.3
Morocco		3.3	3.5	1.1	−1.2	1.5
Tunisia		2.5	2.7	0.5	0.1	1.4
East Asia and Pacific		6.7	8.5	6.9	4.7	6.6
Europe and Central Asia		6.4	4.0	3.3	1.1	3.6
Latin America and Caribbean		1.0	2.0	2.5	−1.3	1.0
South Asia		2.1	2.5	2.0	−0.8	1.3
Sub-Saharan Africa		3.5	4.9	4.8	3.1	4.0

Source: World Bank based on the World Development Indicators Database.
Note: Regions exclude high-income countries.

BOX 1.1

Labor Market Concerns before and after the Arab Spring

In 2010, calls for change reverberated from Tunisia to many of its regional neighbors, including Algeria, the Arab Republic of Egypt, Iraq, Jordan, Lebanon, Libya, Morocco, the Syrian Arab Republic, and the Republic of Yemen. The protests that started in 2010 in Tunisia reflected the people's demands for increasing participation in government decision-making, basic freedoms, and overall labor market improvements. Indeed, throughout the 2000s, many low- and middle-income countries in the Middle East and North Africa reported low indicators on an index of democracy: for instance, Egypt, Morocco, and Tunisia had index values of 0.15, 0.23, and 0.09, respectively.[a] As of 2009, they also scored low in human rights protection, with Algeria, Egypt, Jordan, Morocco, and Tunisia scoring 0.26, –0.09, –0.25, 0.05, and –0.05, respectively (Herre, Ortiz-Espina, and Roser 2013).[b]

Almost two decades ago, a World Bank report, *Unlocking the Employment Potential in the Middle East and North Africa: Toward a New Social Contract*, expressed concerns about the region's labor market, warning of the potential for these problems to spill over into sociopolitical instability if not addressed (World Bank 2004). Although some of these countries undertook trade reforms starting in the early 2000s, there was still little to show in terms of labor market progress between 2010 and 2019.

a. The index of the level of liberal democracy was developed by the Varieties of Democracy (V-Dem) project (https://www.v-dem.net/). Values range from 0 (least democratic) to 1 (most democratic). It measures the extent to which political leaders are elected under the rule of political rights in free and fair elections as well as whether the rights of association and free speech are protected. It uses the Regimes of the World classification by political scientists Anna Luhrmann, Marcus Tannenberg, and Staffan Lindberg, which characterizes four types of political systems: closed autocracies, electoral autocracies, electoral democracies, and liberal democracies.
b. The human rights score measures protection of physical integrity against torture, government killing, political imprisonment, extrajudicial executions, mass killings, and disappearances.

This report tries to solve the puzzle by exploring two possibilities: First, trade agreements might not produce the same trade increases for LMIEs in the Middle East and North Africa as for peer countries in other regions. Second, exports might not generate the same kinds of labor market changes in these economies as experienced elsewhere.

The wide range of experiences across the region's countries suggests that each one must be studied individually to determine the specific link between trade and labor market. To this end, the report implements three approaches: (a) the study of trade exposure, (b) the relationship between the nature of trade shocks and job creation, and (c) a firm-level analysis. It reviews three countries in depth—Egypt, Morocco, and Tunisia—which, given their idiosyncrasies in labor markets, export diversification, and trade policy history, offer important lessons for the Middle East and North Africa's economic development.

This chapter sets the stage for our study. It begins with a snapshot of the region's labor market, then reviews its unique labor market challenges, how trade policy has influenced trade flows, and how higher exports have played out in the labor markets. It concludes with a road map for the report.

Understanding the Region's Labor Markets

Despite trade reforms, economic growth, and social demand for change, the labor markets continue to underperform in the Middle East and North Africa. To understand why, it is helpful to look at three key factors.

First, labor demand has failed to keep pace with a rapidly expanding labor supply. Between 2000 and 2019, the employment-to-population ratio—that is, the proportion of a population that is employed—has declined from an aggregate of 40 percent to 38 percent in the Middle East and North Africa's LMIEs (figure 1.1). Some other low- and middle-income regions experienced a more severe fall, but their average ratio in 2019 was 58 percent.[4] Although the total population of the Middle East and North Africa's LMIEs is smaller than their economic peer regions in absolute terms, they have one of the world's fastest annual population growth rates, averaging 1.8 percent in 2000–19. As a result, their total population has almost doubled, from 279 million in 2000 to 389 million in 2019.

Second, market segmentation—based on gender and geography—hinders trade's positive effects. For instance, social norms and preferences may create biases about the tasks that workers should or should not do, which reduces labor mobility

FIGURE 1.1

Employment-to-Population Ratios in Low- and Middle-Income Countries, by Region, 2000–19

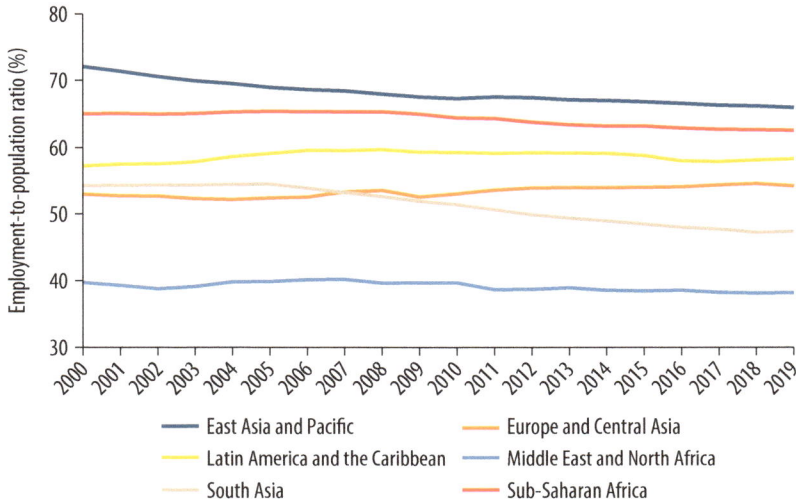

Source: World Bank based on the World Development Indicators Database, 2000–19.
Note: Values correspond to the aggregate employment-to-population ratio in each region. Regions exclude high-income countries.

across sectors. FLFP tends to be restricted by gendered laws that limit women to certain sectors. A trade shock induced by changing trade policy or a shift in foreign global demand might affect some economic sectors more than others in terms of prices, production factors, wages, and employment. Given the presence of gender-segmented sectors, it is not surprising that women and men are affected differently (box 1.2).

Third, the pervasive state presence in the economy—with limited capacity to absorb new entrants—contributes to high youth unemployment. Since the mid- to late twentieth century, when countries in the region became independent, the state-led model has been the norm. With many state-owned enterprises operating in sectors with little rationale for public activity, the education system also developed a curriculum that aimed to prepare youth for public sector careers (Arezki et al. 2018). But governments can no longer absorb new entrants into the labor market. As a result, finding jobs for the growing youth population is a major challenge. In 2019, youth unemployment stood at 21 percent in Egypt, 23 percent in Morocco, and 35 percent in Tunisia.[5]

BOX 1.2

Higher Exports in Morocco and Tunisia: Effects on the Female- and Male-Intensive Employment Sectors

The apparel sectors in Morocco and Tunisia offer good examples of the differential effects of a positive trade shock on employment. Until 2004, the Multifiber Arrangement (MFA) and the Agreement on Textiles and Clothing (ATC) imposed production quotas on countries with high capacity. After the MFA and ATC expired in 2004, the expectation was that global apparel exports would rise, prices would fall, and labor force reallocation would occur across countries (Lopez-Acevedo and Robertson 2012a). These shifts would generate winners and losers in terms of rising and declining exports and job losses.

What happened in these countries? In Morocco, the shift from female-labor-intensive ("female-intensive") to capital-intensive industries created more jobs for male workers and reduced women's labor force participation. Exports in the female-intensive apparel sector fell from 34 percent of total exports in 2000 to 12 percent in 2019.[a]

In Tunisia, the story was similar. Textile and apparel exports, which accounted for 41 percent of exports in 2000, fell to 18 percent in 2019.[b] Substituting for these leading exporting products were machinery and electronics (considered to be male-labor-intensive industries), which rose from 13 percent of total exports to 31 percent. Although this change in Tunisia's export basket may suggest global value chain upgrading, it widened the male–female employment gap.

a. Data on Moroccan exports from the World Bank's World Integrated Trade Solution (WITS) interactive online data tool: https://wits.worldbank.org/CountryProfile/en/Country/MAR/StartYear/1993/EndYear/2020/TradeFlow/Export/Indicator/XPRT-PRDCT-SHR/Partner/WLD/Product/all-group.
b. Data on Tunisian exports from the World Bank's WITS interactive online data tool: Tunisia https://wits.worldbank.org/CountryProfile/en/Country/TUN/StartYear/1993/EndYear/2019/TradeFlow/Export/Indicator/XPRT-PRDCT-SHR/Partner/WLD/Product/all-groups.

Major Labor Market Challenges

Against this backdrop—inadequate demand for a burgeoning labor supply, market segmentation, and the state's dominant role in the economy—it is not surprising that the challenges in the Middle East and North Africa's labor markets appear so daunting. Of course, this is not new. Since the early 2000s, labor market concerns such as low wages and FLFP have occupied the region's leaders, mainly because of stagnating economic performance following the high economic growth of the 1980s (World Bank 2004). Although some of these issues also exist in other low- and middle-income regions, three main problems are at the forefront of policy concerns.

An imbalance between population growth and job creation results in high unemployment. Because wages are "sticky"—that is, they tend to adjust slowly to changes in labor market conditions—unemployment is the result when demand fails to outpace the growth in supply. Between 1990 and 2010, the population of LMIEs in the Middle East and North Africa increased by 47 percent,[6] while their average unemployment rate decreased only slightly, from 12 percent in 1991 (data available) to 11 percent in 2010, the highest in the low- and middle-income world.[7] In contrast, population growth in Latin America and the Caribbean and Europe and Central Asia was 34 percent and 4 percent, respectively, while those regions' average annual unemployment rates in that period were 7 percent and 9 percent, respectively.

Women's labor market participation is lower than in other regions. Social barriers as well as country-specific policies and external international factors have prevented women from finding jobs outside the public sector. In the 1990s, FLFP in the Middle East and North Africa's LMIEs averaged about 17 percent, increasing to only 18 percent over the following decade, compared with 28 percent in South Asia, 62 percent in East Asia and Pacific, and 63 percent in Sub-Saharan Africa.[8] In particular, Egypt, Morocco, and Tunisia report lower FLFP rates, with few signs of improvement over the past two decades relative to the region's high-income countries (like Kuwait, Qatar, and the United Arab Emirates) (figure 1.2, panels a and b). Further, if compared with other world regions, the three case countries rank the lowest (figure 1.2, panel c). For example, Brazil and Vietnam's FLFP rates were 53 percent and 70 percent in 2019, respectively.

Insufficient labor demand increases especially affect women. Women in the Middle East and North Africa are more affected by the lack of job opportunities than those in other low- and middle-income regions. Female unemployment in the region was close to 20 percent in 2019, far above the levels in East Asia and Pacific (3 percent), South Asia (5 percent), Europe and Central Asia and Sub-Saharan Africa (each at 7 percent), and Latin America and the Caribbean (10 percent) (figure 1.2, panel d).

While it is evident that unemployment affects women and men differently everywhere, the female–male unemployment rate gap in these other regions is smaller than in the Middle East and North Africa. As of 2019, the gap in the region's LMIEs was 11 percentage points, whereas economic peer countries in the East Asia and Pacific and Europe and Central Asia regions reported *negative* gaps, of 0.7 and 0.9 percentage points, suggesting that men are more affected by job scarcity. Latin America

FIGURE 1.2

Labor Market Outcomes in the Middle East and North Africa

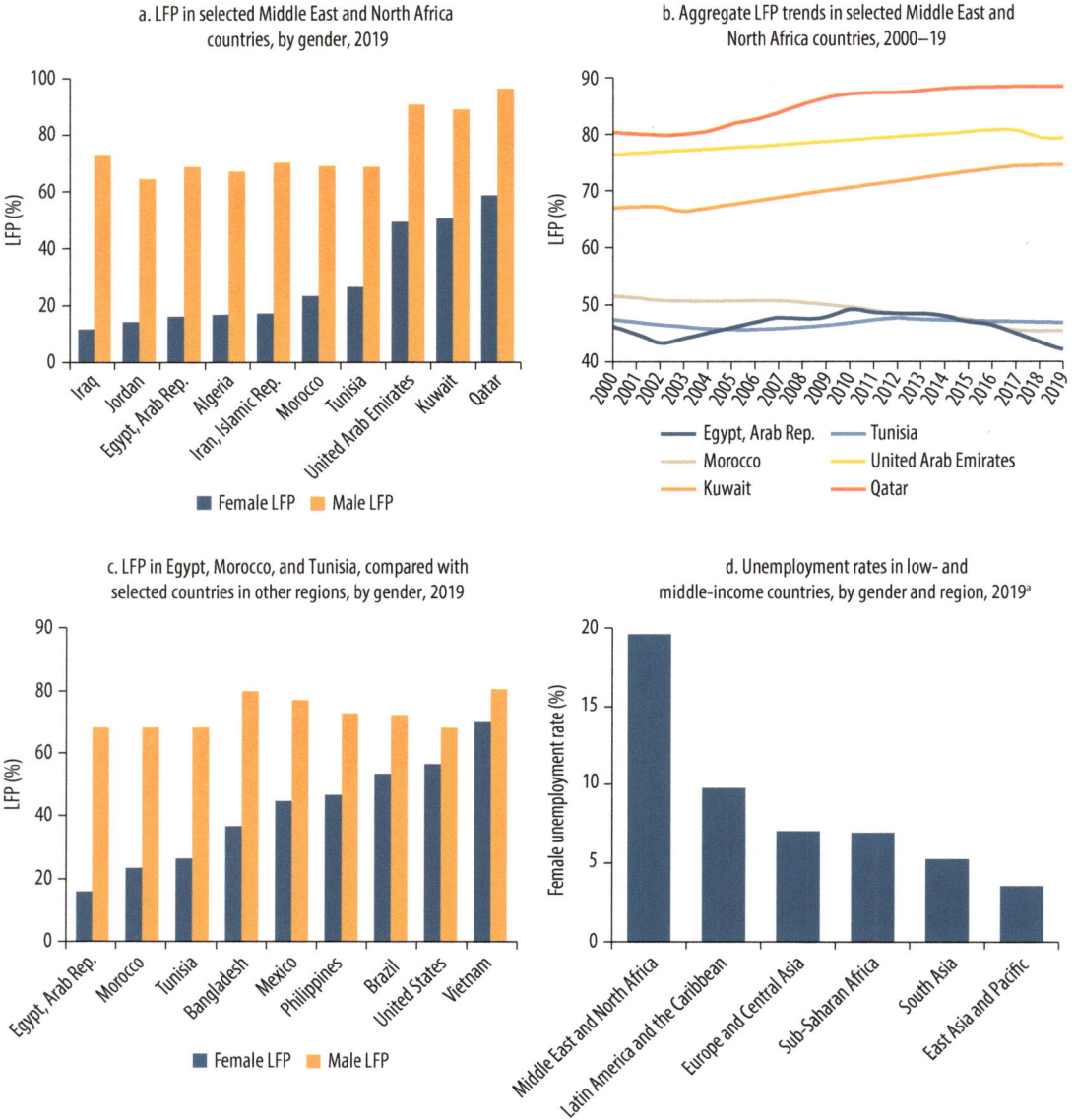

a. LFP in selected Middle East and North Africa countries, by gender, 2019

b. Aggregate LFP trends in selected Middle East and North Africa countries, 2000–19

c. LFP in Egypt, Morocco, and Tunisia, compared with selected countries in other regions, by gender, 2019

d. Unemployment rates in low- and middle-income countries, by gender and region, 2019[a]

Source: World Bank based on the World Development Indicators Database.
Note: Countries in panels a and c are shown in order of lowest to highest (left to right) female labor force participation (FLFP). LFP = labor force participation.
a. Panel d excludes data from high-income countries.

and the Caribbean, South Asia, and Sub-Saharan Africa had gender employment gaps of 3.0, 0.2, and 0.3 percentage points, respectively—all much lower than in the Middle East and North Africa.

From Trade Policy to Trade Flows

As a result of trade reforms, both Morocco and Tunisia increased their commercial exchange with the world. Moroccan exports as a share of GDP increased from 27 percent in 2000 to 35 percent in 2019, while in Tunisia they increased from 40 percent to 49 percent (figure 1.3). The upward trend for both has occurred despite security issues that disturbed the normal functioning of economic activities.

Meanwhile, Tunisian imports as a percentage of GDP rose from 43 percent in 2000 to 57 percent in 2019, driven by the rise in fuels and fall in clothing—with the latter related to the intra-industry export trade in these products (WTO 2016a). Similarly, Moroccan imports, dominated by fuel and agricultural products, grew from 33 percent in 2000 to 48 percent in 2019, according to World Development Indicators (WDI) data and the World Trade Organization (WTO) (2016b).

Egyptian trade increased in the first half of the 2000s, mainly driven by services, oil rents, apparel, and agriculture—as part of a significant effort

FIGURE 1.3

Export and Import Trends, Egypt, Morocco, and Tunisia, 2000–19

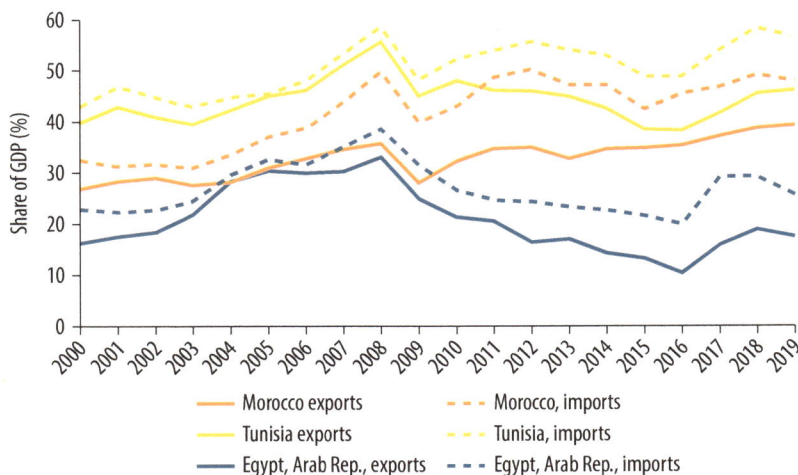

Source: World Bank based on the World Development Indicators Database, 2000–19.

to diversify its exports basket and increase overall trade (WTO 2018). Exports as a percentage of GDP averaged 25 percent before falling to an annual average of 16 percent in the 2010–19 decade (figure 1.3). However, there are some signals of recovery, mainly through natural gas production and tourism. Imports in Egypt rose from 23 percent in 2000 to 39 percent in 2008, then dropped to 26 percent in 2019, according to WDI data.

From Trade Policy to Labor Market Outcomes

The relationship between the labor market, trade, and welfare seems straightforward on a basic level. Impoverished populations obtain most of their income from jobs (Gutierrez et al. 2007). Trade is an effective tool to improve the living standards and jobs for the poor (Engel et al. 2021); it spurs economic growth while creating job opportunities and reducing the prices of goods and services that are especially beneficial to the poor (Bartley Johns et al. 2015; Lopez-Acevedo and Robertson 2012b).

In the past two decades, the Middle East and North Africa region has undergone a series of changes in its tariff and nontariff trade policies. Trade regulation in the region varies across countries, thus providing the opportunity to analyze each country case. Structural reform in the Middle East and North Africa started in the 1980s with the fall of oil prices on which some of its economies relied. This proved that prosperity in the region could not be achieved without a diversified economy, which motivated the signing of trade agreements to open commercial exchange for other products. Among the non-oil-exporting countries, the earliest trade reformers were Morocco and Tunisia.

Trade Reforms in the Three Case Countries

Morocco. In the 1980s, Morocco launched reforms with a series of measures to solve various macroeconomic problems. In 1987 it joined the General Agreement on Tariffs and Trade (GATT), and in 2003 it began gradual steps to liberalize trade and attract foreign direct investment (FDI)—which has increased at an average annual rate of 28 percent ever since. As of 2021, Morocco is a party to nine regional trade agreements, including the EU (European Union)–Morocco Association Agreement signed in 1996, the Association Agreement with the European Free Trade Association (EFTA), the Agreement on the Greater Arab Free Trade Area (GAFTA), and other bilateral agreements with countries in Sub-Saharan Africa and the Americas

(WTO 2016a). Europe is the main destination for Morocco's exports, which reached a total value of US$18.3 billion in 2020.

Tunisia. In the 1970s, Tunisia launched reforms that fostered exports and private investment, with further changes that elevated the export-oriented private sector over early import-substitution industrialization (World Bank 2003). It joined GATT in 1990 and became an original member of the World Trade Organization (WTO) when it formed in 1995. It has also signed many free trade agreements, with eight in force as of 2021. They include accession to the Association Agreement with the European Union, the Agreement on GAFTA, the free trade agreement with EFTA, the Maghreb Arab Union agreement, and a series of bilateral treaties.

Tunisia's main trade partner is the EU, with which it signed the bilateral Association Agreement in 1995 as part of the Barcelona Declaration. The EU accounts for half of its exports and half of its imports. Custom reforms have also taken place since 2001 to simplify import procedures (WTO 2005). However, further changes in Tunisia's trade policies have not occurred since 2009, when import tariffs were reduced by up to 36 percent, although 2014 legislation reaffirmed its WTO agreements (WTO 2016b).

Egypt. Following a similar path, Egypt has taken steps to stabilize the economy and attract private investment over the past decade. In 2014, it implemented the value added tax and shifted the exchange rate regime from a peg to the US dollar to a full float of the national currency. These reforms were intended to increase private sector integration, especially for micro, small, and medium enterprises (WTO 2018).

In addition, since the early 2000s, the Egyptian export basket has become moderately diversified. Back then, the main exports were services (mainly tourism, information technology, and transport), which accounted for 60 percent of total exports. That share has decreased to 43 percent as of 2019, while agriculture, chemicals, and electronics exports have increased significantly.

Persistence of High Unemployment despite Gains in Trade

Trade policies are especially important because the economic sectors affected by trade shocks often represent important sources of labor. This is the case with the apparel sector, which represented a starting point for development of today's industrialized economies. For instance, textiles and apparel accounted for 1.9 percent of total exports from the Middle East and North Africa in 2019, with more predominance in the economies of Egypt at 11 percent, Morocco at 12 percent, Tunisia at 18 percent, and Jordan at 24 percent. Notably, this sector features a high share of female employment: women make up 83.6 percent of all apparel workers in the region (Rossi 2010).

In this context, proactive policies are relevant for industries to adapt to new market trends and avoid job losses—as occurred in Morocco between 2004 and 2009, following the Multifiber Arrangement phaseout and the Global Financial Crisis, which provoked the loss of about 10,000 jobs in the country (Lopez-Acevedo and Robertson 2012b).

Nevertheless, the Middle East and North Africa's international trade integration raises the question: Why have the region's increasing exchanges with the world failed to channel enough benefits to its population? Data show a positive correlation between trade and unemployment for the region's LMIEs in general and the three case countries in particular. Despite trade liberalization, unemployment in these economies remains high (figure 1.4). Conversely, in many low- and lower-middle-income countries in other regions, increased trade has *reduced* overall unemployment.

Of course, experiences vary widely across countries of all income groups within the Middle East and North Africa. Some countries export

FIGURE 1.4

Average Unemployment Rates in Relation to Trade, Middle East and North Africa, Regionwide and Selected Countries and Economic Peers Elsewhere, 2015–19

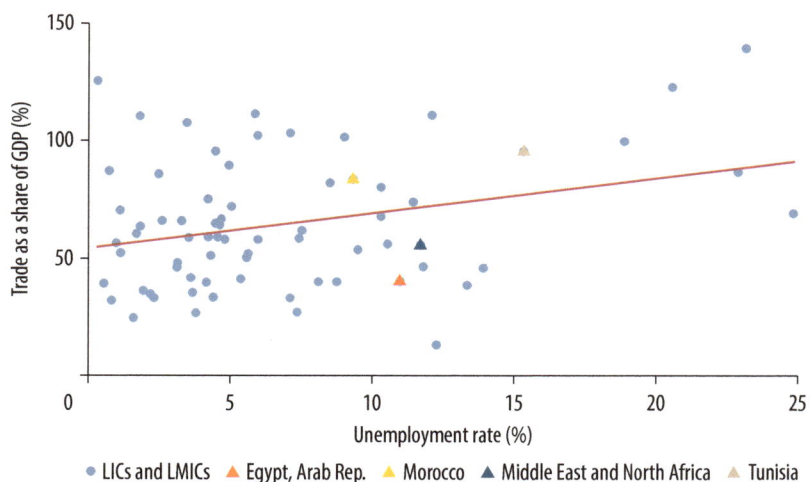

Source: World Bank based on the World Development Indicators Database, 2015–19.
Note: Values correspond to five-year averages of 2015–19 data. The red line represents the fitted trend of the data. Middle East and North Africa excludes high-income countries. Blue dots designate countries outside the Middle East and North Africa. LICs = low-income countries; LMICs = lower-middle income countries. Country income groups correspond to World Bank classifications.

oil (such as Iraq, Qatar, Saudi Arabia, and the United Arab Emirates) while others have expanded manufacturing exports, especially apparel (such as Egypt, Jordan, Morocco, and Tunisia). In the past, the concentration in labor-intensive apparel created jobs—especially for women—but changes in trade policy at home and abroad shifted the focus away from apparel toward more male- and capital-intensive sectors. This segmentation of the labor market discourages the participation of women, who contribute to 18 percent of the region's GDP. Had women fully participated in the labor market, however, they could have doubled the GDP growth rate (Mottaghi 2019).

A Road Map for the Report

To trace the relationship between trade policy and labor market outcomes, this report follows a three-pronged approach (figure 1.5).

1. As indicated on the left side of the schematic, we employ the gravity model to estimate the relationship between trade policy (in the form of trade agreements) and trade flows for our case countries relative to global averages (as further detailed in chapter 2).[9]

2. As the top right side of the schematic indicates, we estimate the relationship between trade flows and labor market outcomes at the subnational or regional level using "shift-share" analysis (following Bartik 1991)[10] to identify the distributional impacts of trade and spot which districts win or lose in response to higher export flows.

FIGURE 1.5

Approach to Examining the Link between Trade Policy and Labor Market Outcomes

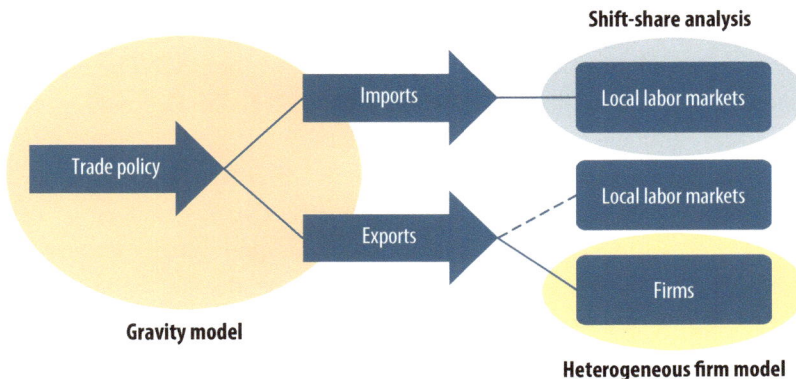

3. As the bottom right of the schematic shows, we focus on firm-level data, using the "heterogeneous firm model" to explore whether differences among firms influence the relationship between exports and labor market outcomes, as economic theory predicts. By examining the micro level, we can detect positive relationships that are not perceivable at the macro level.

One of the main ideas behind our approach is that labor markets are localized so that the effects of trade are proportional to trade-related industry employment across different cities or regions. Both imports and exports can have important labor market effects, and we apply the shift-share approach to both. We note that the increase in exports found with the gravity model is not associated with the expected increase in labor demand (higher employment and wages and lower informality), which might indicate firms are not responding to the rising demand for exports by increasing employment.

Given the nature of this report, we also briefly explore some external and internal factors that may foster or hinder the capture of export benefits. Previous World Bank reports—*Jobs for Shared Prosperity: Time for Action in the Middle East* (Gatti et al. 2013) and "Economic Growth in Egypt: Impediments and Constraints" (Beblawi 2008)—have shed light on these factors affecting economic performance and consequently labor market outcomes. Although some seem to equally affect countries in the region (such as the role of the public sector in the labor market or regulations that prevent further innovation), others appear to be unique to each country.

In Morocco and Tunisia, external factors have significantly affected the labor market. In the early 2000s, global trade regime changes, such as the MFA phaseout, reduced Morocco's share in apparel exports from 3.3 percent in 2000 to 2.8 percent in 2005. Likewise, Tunisia reported a decrease from 3.7 percent to 2.9 percent in the same period (Lopez-Acevedo and Robertson 2012b). As a result, women lost work as economies shifted to more capital-intensive industries. In the past two decades, Morocco has shifted its main share of exports toward machinery, electronics, and chemicals, which are male labor intensive. The change in international trade flows in the early 2000s and additional trade agreements have influenced Morocco's export basket.

External factors also affect Egypt, but we find that internal factors dominate. Low diversification of Egypt's export basket and little cost competition are among the explanations for a disappointing labor market despite Egypt's boost in exports. Literature on trade and the country's economic performance offers several examples of the potential roots of the broken link between trade and labor markets in Egypt. One of them is lack of competition, or—as described in a recent report, *Jobs*

Undone (Islam, Moosa, and Saliola 2022)—"market contestability." In Egypt, the state is almost omnipresent across economic sectors, and government agencies influence decision-making in state-owned enterprises. Regulation also affects internal labor markets; for example, high labor taxes increase labor costs for employers, which in turn reduces labor demand. In the Middle East and North Africa, Egypt reported the highest rate of employer contribution (40 percent) to social security (Islam, Moosa, and Saliola 2022).

The goal of this report is to understand why rising exports did not generate the same labor market improvements in the Middle East and North Africa LMIEs that many low- and middle-income countries in other regions have experienced. Recent years have seen a growing global pessimism about trade. This pessimism stems from the seeming lack of job opportunism on the export side. This report does a deep dive to understand the relationship between trade and the labor market, focusing on three countries— Egypt, Morocco, and Tunisia—all of which have significantly increased the number of active regional trade agreements since the early 2000s. What is the status of the link between exports and labor market outcomes in these three countries? Although different countries do have different experiences, our analysis points to specific policies that countries facing similar experiences may consider. Some countries might see a reduction in the relative demand for women in the workforce (as in Morocco), while other countries might see a lack of engagement with the export sector (as in Egypt).

The report begins with an overview of the gravity analysis and highlights key results (in chapter 2) before examining the three country cases (in chapters 3, 4, and 5). The report's bottom line is that trade flows increased dramatically in the Middle East and North Africa as a result of regional trade agreements, but evidence remains lacking that the population is capturing the benefits of this greater exposure to trade through better labor market outcomes.

Annex 1A. Methodology

Key Messages

- Estimating the relationship between exports and labor market outcomes is complicated by simultaneity and omitted variables.

- Our study applies the Bartik (1991) shift-share methodology: instrumenting for endogenous exports with exogenous foreign demand.

- The effects of trade differ depending on multiple dimensions—across countries, regions, industries, and workers.

The Identification Challenge

The challenge when observing simultaneous changes in exports and labor market outcomes is to establish the direction of causality. That is, does the labor market respond to a change in exports, do exports react to the labor market, or are both driven by something else (Artuc et al. 2019)? For example, omitted factors such as public investments or programs to attract foreign direct investment may be responsible for simultaneous growth in trade and changes in labor market outcomes (Vazquez and Winkler 2022). Further, exports depend partially on domestic human capital and technology use, which can be correlated with characteristics of local labor markets. Measurement error can also complicate the estimation process.

Ideally, we could observe the share of exports produced in each region ($r \in R$), but these data are typically not available.[11] Thus, an ordinary least squares regression of labor outcomes on export flows would yield biased results. This chapter annex lays out the methodology employed in the subsequent chapters to identify the causal relationship between exports and labor market outcomes (wages, employment, and informality) in the Arab Republic of Egypt, Morocco, and Tunisia.

Conceptual Underpinnings

To disentangle the causal relationship between exports from the Middle East and North Africa and local labor markets, we turn to the strategy proposed by Bartik (1991). We exploit the effects of the exogenous import demand of high-income countries on the labor markets of Egypt, Morocco, and Tunisia.

The application of the Bartik (1991) two-stage analysis is presented in figure 1A.1. In the first stage, we estimate the contribution of the US and European Union (EU) import demand on the Middle East and North Africa's exports. As the saying goes, "When the US sneezes, the world catches a cold." So, too, can we expect the US and EU—which account for a significant share of exports from each of our three case countries—to influence these Middle East and North Africa economies through trade. In figure 1A.1, this influence is represented by the arrow from the US and EU on the left to the Middle East and North Africa export market in the middle.

On the flip side, given the smaller sizes of Middle East and North Africa's economies, they do not have any reciprocal effect on the US and EU. This is represented by the vertical bar blocking the arrow from the middle bubble to the US and EU. In the second stage, we estimate the effect of an increase in exports on local Middle East and North Africa labor markets (for example, on wages, informality, and employment).

FIGURE 1A.1

Two-Stage Econometric Analysis of US and EU Import Demand Effects on Middle East and North Africa Local Labor Markets

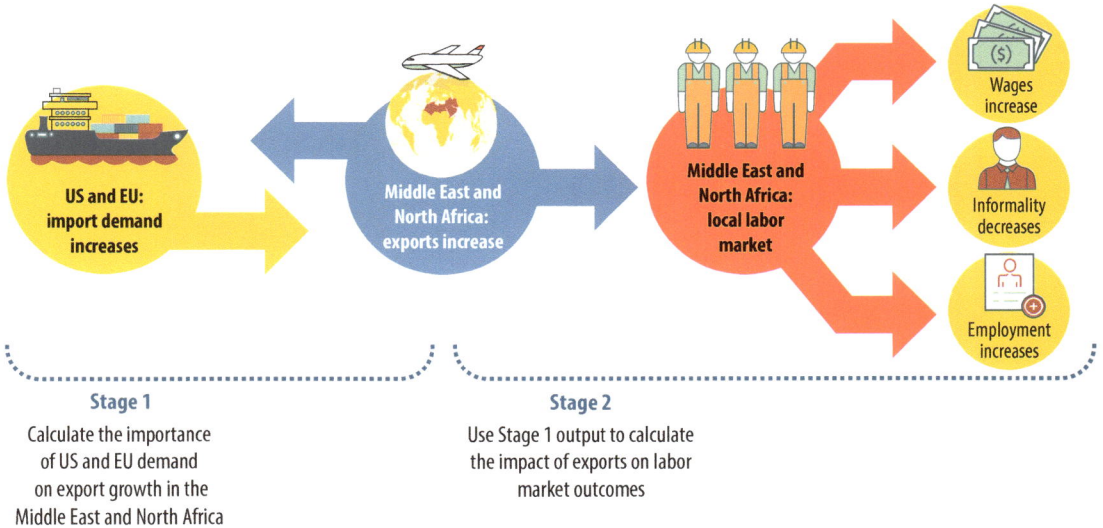

Stage 1
Calculate the importance of US and EU demand on export growth in the Middle East and North Africa

Stage 2
Use Stage 1 output to calculate the impact of exports on labor market outcomes

Source: Adapted from Artuc et al. 2019.

We expect positive export demand shocks to improve labor market outcomes. In each region, we expect regional real gross domestic product (GDP), average wages, and the number of employees to increase after a greater export-induced demand shock. The mechanism is straightforward: after a positive shock to demand for exports, prices for those exports increase. New firms then enter the market, and existing firms increase their capital through investments. As a result, output, wages, and employment are expected to increase (Artuc et al. 2019).

Trade literature and studies have widely applied the Bartik (1991) methodology. The use of import demand from high-income countries to correct for endogenous export flows is but one example of a class of instrumental variables known as Bartik-type or "shift-share instrumental." Artuc et al. (2019) present an extensive literature review of the Bartik method, together with applications to South Asian countries. Notable references include Topalova (2010), who studies the effects of tariff changes on poverty rates across India's districts. Kovak (2013) applies a similar tariff-based instrument to estimate the impact of trade liberalization on Brazil's labor markets. The "gold standard" of Bartik analysis is Autor, Dorn, and Hanson (2013), who study the impact of China's rapid growth on local US labor markets.

Under the Hood: The Mechanics of the Bartik Method

The Bartik (1991) method uses a two-stage estimation using an instrumental variable to correct for the endogeneity of our variable of interest—in our case, exports. The essence of our empirical strategy is that we use plausibly exogenous variation across industries $i \in \mathcal{J}$ interacted with differential exposure to industry-specific shocks across different local labor markets. To illustrate, consider the following regression:

$$\Delta y_{t+n}^r = \beta_0 + \beta_1 \Delta x_{t+n}^r + \beta_2 y_t^r + \varepsilon_{t+n}^r, \tag{1A.1}$$

where Δ represents the change between time t and $t+n$, y_t^r which is the labor market outcome of interest at time t in region r. By controlling for time t level of the dependent variable (y_t^r), we ensure that possible trends unrelated to export changes are purged. Our measure of trade exposure, $x_{t,t+n}^r$, is defined as follows:

$$x_{t,t+n}^r \equiv \sum_{i \in j} \frac{L_{r,i,t}}{L_{i,t}} \cdot \Delta Q_{t+n}^i = \sum_{i \in j} \frac{L_{r,i,t}}{L_{i,t}} \cdot \left(Q_{t-n}^i - Q_t^i\right), \tag{1A.2}$$

where Q_t^i is the quantity of exports of industry i at time t;[12] $L_t^{r,i}$ denotes total employment in region r and industry i; and $L_t^i \equiv \sum_{r \in \mathcal{R}} L_{r,i,t}$ is total aggregate employment in industry i. Alternatively, trade exposure can be defined in terms of industries (box 1A.1), an application of which is provided in the case of Tunisia, chapter 4.

Estimating β_1 in equation (1A.1) is consistent provided that the shifters ΔQ_{t+n}^i are as good as random (Borusyak et al. 2022)—that is, if $E\left[\Delta Q_{i,t+n} \cdot \varepsilon_{t,t+b} \mid y_t^r, L_{r,i,t}\right] = 0$ for every i and r pair. In other words,

---

BOX 1A.1

Alternative Approaches

Trade exposure can be measured in regional or industry terms. In the latter case, the trade exposure index (1A.2) would be calculated as

$$x_{t,t+n}^r \equiv \sum_{r \in \mathcal{R}} \frac{L_t^{i,r}}{L_t^i} \cdot \left(Q_{t+n}^i - Q_t^i\right). \tag{B1A.1.1}$$

Note that the summation is now over regions rather than industries. The regression equation (1A.1) would then include a dummy variable (D_t^i) on the right-hand side to indicate whether a particular industry is tradeable:

$$\Delta y_{t+n}^i = \beta_0 + \beta_1 \Delta x_{t+n}^i + \beta_2 y_t^i + \beta_3 D_t^i + \varepsilon_{t+n}^r. \tag{B1A.1.2}$$

Source: Artuc et al. 2019.

conditional on the time-trend control (y_t^r) and regional employment, share-changes in exports are uncorrelated with local labor markets characteristics. However, as discussed above, our shifters are likely endogenous to labor market dynamics.

Our instrumental variable leverages the correlation between changes in exports to destinations d and changes in foreign demand, proxied by changes in real GDP of foreign destinations. Given the gravity structure typical of international trade, and as shown in chapter 3, our instrument is strongly correlated with export flows. Formally, our instrumental variable is

$$\Delta Z_{t+n}^r \equiv \sum_{i \in j} \frac{L_t^{r,i}}{L_t^i} \cdot \sum_{d \in \mathcal{S} \setminus \{s\}} \frac{Q_t^{d,i}}{Q_t^i} \cdot \Delta Y_{t+n}^d, \tag{1A.3}$$

where $\dfrac{Q_t^{d,i}}{Q_t^i}$ denotes country d's share of industry i's exports; and ΔY_{t+n}^d is the change in real GDP in destination country d. Estimation now takes the form of two-stage least squares, with the first stage being

$$\Delta x_{t+n}^r = \alpha_0 + \alpha_1 \Delta Z_{t+n}^r + \alpha_2 y_t^r + \epsilon_{t+n}^r, \tag{1A.4}$$

and the second stage

$$\Delta y_{t+n}^r = \beta_0 + \beta_1 \Delta \hat{x}_{t+n}^r + \beta_2 y_t^r + \varepsilon_{t+n}^r, \tag{1A.5}$$

where $\Delta \hat{x}_{t+n}^r$ are the predicted values of the first stage regression equation (1A.4). Now, estimation of β is consistent if $E\left[\Delta Y_{t+n}^d \cdot \varepsilon_{t+n}^r | y_t^r, L_{r,i,t}, Q_t^{d,i}\right] = 0$ for every d and r pair—that is, if changes in foreign demand are uncorrelated with unobserved factors that drive changes in local labor markets in the exporting countries (in our case, Egypt, Morocco, and Tunisia). For an application of the Bartik method to study the labor market effects of imports, see box 1A.2.

Selecting the Ingredients: Data, Dependent Variables, and Sample Selection

The analysis presented relies on data from the United Nations (UN) Comtrade database, national Labor Force Surveys (LFS), and the World Bank's World Development Indicators (WDI). The following chapters present applications of the Bartik method in Egypt, Morocco, and Tunisia. In each case, we turn to UN Comtrade data for exports and to LFS data to calculate labor market outcomes. We source real GDP from the WDI. UN Comtrade data provide annual bilateral trade flows from 1996 to 2018 for all trading countries. The LFS is nationally representative and

---

BOX 1A.2

Modeling the Labor Market Impact of Imports

Most of the following analysis focuses on how exports affect the local labor market. For Egypt (examined in chapter 5), we also consider the effects of imports. In this case, the import exposure (m_{t+n}^r) is defined as follows:

$$m_{t+n}^r = \sum_i \frac{L_t^{i,r}\left(M_{t+n}^i - M_t^i\right)}{L_t^r L_t^{i,Egypt}}, \quad \text{(B1A.2.1)}$$

where M_t^i is the quantity of imports in industry i; L_t^r is the total number of workers

assigned to any industry in district r; and $L_t^{i,Egypt}$ is Egypt's total size of industry i. The trade exposure variable $m_{t,t+n}^r$ can be interpreted as the change in imports per worker in district r measured in real US dollars. In this case, the instrumental variable used is the predicted level of imports per industry:

$$\Delta Z_{t+n}^r \equiv \sum_{i \in j} \frac{L_t^{r,i}}{L_t^i} \cdot \sum_{d \in \mathcal{S} \setminus \{s\}} \frac{M_t^{d,i}}{M_t^i} \cdot \Delta Y_{t+n}^d .$$

$$\text{(B1A.2.2)}$$

---

allows for the calculation of labor market indicators. The WDI is a large repository of national indicators across time.

Because national statistical agencies collect different information across countries, we must use different dependent variables in each of our three case studies. In the case of Morocco, the LFS enables us to examine the impacts on informality and FLFP. In Tunisia, we consider the differing impacts on male and female employment, schooling, and firm entry and exit. In Egypt, we study the impacts of trade on wages, informality, and FLFP. Other potential outcome variables studied elsewhere include wage employment probability, informality probability, and variance of wages (Artuc et al. 2019).

Decomposing the Results

In addition to the overall impact of exports on workers, we consider the differential effects based on worker type. The rich LFS data we work with enable us to examine changes in outcomes for different types of workers. For example, we consider workers disaggregated by sex (male and female), skill (low and high), age (young and old), and residence (urban and rural).

Conclusions

The Bartik methodology enables us to analyze distributional impacts of trade across local labor markets by instrumenting for endogenous trade with exogenous foreign demand. The effects of trade differ depending on multiple dimensions—across countries, regions, industries, and workers. Significant adjustment costs imply that labor markets are segmented across regions within countries, because workers are imperfectly mobile across their regions and between industries. The Bartik approach builds on a large body of existing research. In subsequent chapters, we contribute to this research by presenting Bartik-style estimates for Egypt, Morocco, and Tunisia.

Annex 1B. Firm-Level Analysis

Key Messages

- Heterogeneity of firms is important for the relationship between trade and the labor market.

- To illustrate the role played by firms, we model an economy characterized by two sectors: one sector of homogeneous firms selling only to the domestic market and another sector of heterogeneous firms that is able to export.

- The model simulation shows that an increase in export price leads to an increase in employment in the export sector.

Introduction

Heterogeneity of firms plays an important role in the relationship between trade and labor markets within countries. Ample empirical evidence suggests that exporting firms differ substantially from firms that serve the domestic market (Bernard, Jensen, and Schott 2009; Brambilla, Chauvin, and Porto 2015). Exporters across different countries and industries employ more labor; are more productive, skill intensive, and capital intensive; and pay higher wages than nonexporting counterparts (Brambilla, Chauvin, and Porto 2015; Duda-Nyczak and Viegelahn 2018; Dutz et al. 2012). A significant positive relationship between exports and employment emerges in studies that analyze changes over time in both high-income and low- to middle-income countries (Abbey et al. 2017; Artuc et al. 2019; Fox and Oviedo 2008; Lichter, Peichl, and Siegloch 2017; Pellandra 2015).

This report demonstrates that signing trade agreements boosted trade flows in the Arab Republic of Egypt, Morocco, and Tunisia (as further discussed in chapter 2). As noted earlier in chapter 1, however, despite increased exports, these countries did not experience the same improvement in their labor markets as their economic peers in other parts of the world. To understand the link between export flows and local labor market outcomes, this report turns to firm-level data to estimate employment–export elasticity (by country, in chapters 3, 4, and 5). The empirical analysis is guided by a simple general equilibrium model inspired by Melitz (2003). What follows is this model's conceptual framework, its assumptions, and a simulation of the effects of an increase in export price on employment in the exporting economy.

Conceptual Framework

To illustrate the relationship between firm-level exporting and local labor market employment, consider a simplified general equilibrium Melitz (2003) model in which there are two sectors: The first is a "reserve" sector, like the informal or service sector, where firms are homogeneous and produce using only labor with decreasing returns-to-scale technology. The second sector is a heterogeneous sector that can export. For now, we assume that the local labor market has full employment—in the sense that, lacking unemployment or other social insurance, workers must engage with the labor market to secure an income.

For simplicity, we assume two periods of time during which firms in the heterogeneous sector have the option to shut down (or not produce), produce for the domestic market, or produce for the foreign market (export). We simulate this model to illustrate how an increase in export opportunities (represented by an increase in the export market price) affects local employment. In particular, we show that an increase in the export price of 2.3 percent would increase employment in the export sector by about 8 percent as workers shift from the reserve sector into the export sector. As such, we would expect that the increase in exports would reduce informality or employment in the reserve sector.

The 8 percent increase in employment is spread across three groups of firms in the export sector:

1. *"Always exporters"*: These firms were exporters in the first period and continue to be exporters in the second. They increase employment by about 12 percent. We refer to this effect as the "within exporter" effect because these firms slightly increase their average employment. The "within exporter" effect makes up about 4 percent of the total change in employment in the model.

2. *"Never exporters"*: These firms never export and produce only for the domestic market in both the first and second periods. The domestic firms reduce employment (a drop in average firm size of about one worker per firm). The size of this "within nonexporter" effect is about

10 percent of the total change in employment but, being negative, implies that the third type of change must explain more than 100 percent of the total change.

3. *"Mixed producers"*: These firms include those that switch from domestic commerce to exporting. We call this the "between" effect. As suggested, total employment in this group changes by more than 26 percent, about 105 percent of the total employment change. In other words, the main expected employment effect comes from firms that were producing for the domestic market and switch to exporting.

Model Details

Our model considers an economy characterized by two sectors that produce with labor as the only input. We first describe the homogeneous sector and then the heterogeneous sector before describing general equilibrium.

The homogeneous sector. The first sector produces exclusively for the domestic market, with homogeneous (same for all firms) technology. Assume that firms in the first sector produce using homogenous decreasing returns-to-scale (falling marginal product of labor) technology. These assumptions are meant to roughly emulate a "reserve" sector a, such as the informal sector found in many low- and middle-income countries. Indexing this reserve sector with a, we represent labor demand with

$$l_\alpha = f(\kappa, \lambda, w). \tag{1B.1}$$

The parameters κ and λ characterize the labor demand function. In practice we assume that labor demand in sector b is linear so that κ and λ represent intercept and slope. Firms are assumed to be small and take the market wage w as given. The market wage is set in general equilibrium, which is described in more detail after we describe the second (heterogeneous) sector.

The heterogeneous (exporting) sector. Following Melitz (2003), the second sector is characterized by heterogeneous firms differentiated by a firm-specific productivity parameter φ. After entry into the market, the firm-specific productivity parameter φ is first revealed (thus it is unknown prior to entry). The ex ante productivity parameter distribution is described by $g(\overline{\varphi}, \sigma_\varphi^2)$. In practice, we assume that the productivity parameter is drawn from an exponential distribution.[13] For simplicity, assume that production is a function of labor l_j and can be represented as $Q = \gamma l_j^\alpha$, in which $j \in (a, b)$ indicates the subsector, γ represents total factor productivity (TFP), and α (restricted to be a positive value less than 1) ensures decreasing marginal productivity of labor.

If firms are small, as we assumed for the first sector, they can affect neither the wage paid to labor w nor the domestic market price P_d. Any production (for either the domestic or export market) requires a fixed cost F_d.[14] By allowing the productivity parameter to enter the cost function, we can represent ex ante profits with the simple profit function:

$$\pi = P_d Q - \frac{wl}{\varphi} - F_d. \tag{1B.2}$$

Note that the profit-maximizing level of l is uniquely defined by P_d, φ, w, γ, and α. Perhaps trivially, the output price, TFP, and the individual-specific productivity parameter are positively correlated with firm-level labor demand. Using the asterisk to represent the optimal solution to the profit-maximization problem implied in equation (1B.2), optimal labor demand is represented as

$$l_j^* = \left(\frac{w}{P_d \alpha \gamma \varphi} \right)^{\frac{1}{\alpha - 1}}. \tag{1B.3}$$

Note that equation (1B.3) shows that more-productive firms (higher values of φ) will be larger in the sense of having higher employment, production, and profits.

Equation (1B.2) also shows that profits must be at least as large as F_d for the firm to produce a positive amount of output. Otherwise, the firm will shut down and produce nothing. Since profits are higher for higher values of φ, the model generates a cutoff value for φ that separates firms that produce from those that do not. When firms leave the market, average productivity levels increase because the lowest-productivity firms chose to exit the market.

Open Economy

In addition to producing, firms in the heterogeneous sector also have the opportunity to export. Exporting, however, requires an additional fixed cost, F_x. That is, to consider exporting, firms must first be viable domestic producers, because international transportation is costly. A common assumption is that $Q\tau$ ($\tau > 1$) goods must be exported for the quantity Q to arrive (the usual "iceberg" assumption). Under these conditions, exporting firms sell their goods for a higher price abroad than they would receive in the domestic market. In practice, the export price (P_x) is represented as a fixed markup over the domestic price. Specifically, $P_x = \tau P_d$.

The markup is related to foreign tariffs as well (τ = premium/tariff). Foreign tariffs are negatively related to the price exporters receive, and as tariffs increase, exports fall. Trade agreements decrease foreign tariffs and therefore increase the price exporters receive. As a result, we model the effects of trade agreements by raising the export price in the model. Under these conditions, firms will choose to export if

$$P_x Q - \frac{wl}{\varphi} - F_d - F_x > P_d Q - \frac{wl}{\varphi} - F_d > 0. \qquad (1B.4)$$

A key result of the model is that exporters will be more productive, larger, and have higher profits than firms in the heterogeneous sector that produce for the domestic market. As we show in the empirical work that follows, Egypt's export sectors have the same characteristics.

General Equilibrium

In this model, general equilibrium means that wages, which are exogenous to individual firms, are determined by labor demand in the two sectors. Without social insurance, the economy is assumed to be characterized by full employment, meaning that all workers have to find work somewhere—that is, in either of our two sectors—or they will have no income. Assuming no labor market adjustment costs, workers move freely between sectors to earn the highest wages. Free mobility between sectors implies that, in equilibrium, (base) wages will equalize between sectors. As in the Melitz (2003) model, total labor supply (L) is perfectly inelastic. Because our focus is mainly on trade agreements, and because the first sector is the reserve sector, we represent employment in the reserve sector to be total employment minus employment in the heterogeneous export sector:

$$l_\alpha = L - l_b. \qquad (1B.5)$$

Obviously, total employment in each sector is equal to the sum of each firm's employment. Because each firm in the export sector is unique (owing to a unique productivity parameter), each firm has a different level of employment. In the reserve sector, all firms are identical and total employment is simply the sum across all firms. Formally,

$$l_j = \sum_i l_{ij}, \qquad (1B.6)$$

in which $j \in (a,b)$ and individual firms are indexed with i. Because firms are homogeneous in the reserve sector, aggregate labor demand can be represented by a single labor demand function and all workers receive the same labor income. Given small heterogeneous firms in the export sector, small homogenous firms in the second sector, and perfect mobility between plants and sectors, wages are determined in the aggregate labor market and equalize across sectors.

Model Simulation

To simulate the model, we first have to identify parameter values and describe the initial equilibrium. Note that depending on the parameter values, the model could generate four possible outcomes (Halliday, Lederman, and Robertson 2018):

- None of the firms produces anything.

- All firms produce only for the domestic market.

- All firms produce only for the international market.

- In a mixed solution, some firms do not produce, some produce for the domestic market, and others produce for export.

We begin by picking initial parameter values so that the equilibrium falls into the mixed category. Note that the model is not calibrated. The point is to illustrate only the theoretically predicted general changes in employment patterns.

Our main variable of interest is the export price P_x. Along with other variables, the export price determines the level of employment in both sectors, which generates a feedback effect on the wage in the homogenous sector. In practice, the wage in the homogeneous sector is the worker's reservation wage—that is, the lowest wage for which someone will accept a job. The reservation wage equilibrates between the two sectors in a way that generates an equilibrium level of employment in both sectors given the export price.

Figure 1B.1 shows a typical mixed equilibrium, depicting two scenarios. Starting parameters are chosen to ensure that the (aggregate) labor demand curve in the homogenous sector is inelastic and to avoid corner solutions for observed export prices.[15] Figure 1B.1 plots profits (y-axis) against its (exponentially distributed) productivity (phi, φ) values. Firms with productivity parameters less than 1.88 do not make enough profit to cover their fixed costs and so do not produce anything. Firms with productivity greater than 1.88 can produce and sell output. These firms fall into one of two groups, depending on their level of productivity: Those with productivity between 1.88 and 9.78 cannot cover the additional fixed costs necessary to export under the original export price, and so their profit line is higher, selling only to the domestic market. The remaining firms, with productivity values higher than 9.78, find that exporting is more profitable.

Following a new trade agreement that lowers the costs of exporting, the export price that the firm receives increases by 2.7 percent. Figure 1B.1 illustrates this by a leftward shift in the export profit curve, bringing more firms into the export market. That is, the

FIGURE 1B.1

Theoretical Outcome Model in the Style of Melitz (1993)

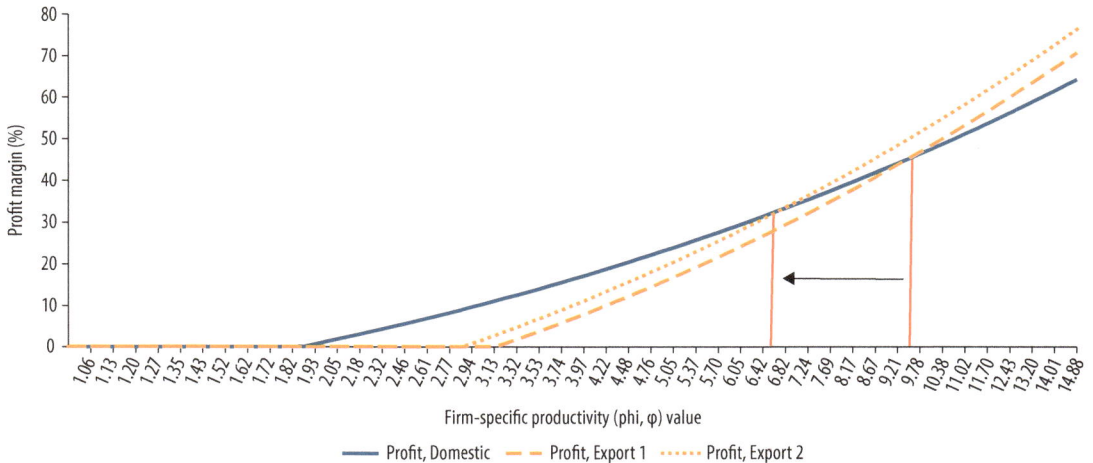

Note: The figure depicts two scenarios: one under the original international price and the other under the new, higher price enabled by a trade agreement. The domestic profit (gray) line is the same under both scenarios. Firms are sorted along the horizontal axis by increasing levels of firm-specific productivity (phi). Firms with productivity less than 1.88 produce nothing. Firms with productivity above 3.32 have the option of producing for export under the original price (their profit line designated by "Profit, Export 1"). Firms with productivity between 1.88 and 9.78 produce and sell only to the domestic market at the original price. When the international price increases by 2.7 percent, the export profit line shifts left (designated by "Profit, Export 2" line above). Under this new price, the productivity cutoff for exporting drops from 9.78 to 6.82 (illustrated by the arrow between the two red lines), thus bringing more firms into the export market.

productivity cutoff for joining the export market has fallen from 9.78 to 6.82. Note that the domestic profit curve is unaffected; firms still need to have productivity values of at least 1.88 in order to produce.

In our simulation, we fix the total number of workers at 6,000. Originally, 3,272 work in the export sector, and the rest work in the reserve sector. The model is full employment, general equilibrium. In the export sector, there are five firms selling to the international market that employ a total of 808 workers, with an average firm size of 162. The remaining 65 firms in this sector produce for the domestic market and employ a total of 2,464 workers, with an average firm size of 37.9 workers.

What happens when we model an increase in the export price of 2.3 percent? The results show that employment in the export sector increases by about 8 percent to 3,535, an increase of 263 workers. This increase is broken down into three groups of firms: (a) "always export-ers" increase employment by 11 workers; (b) "never exporters" reduce employment by 28 workers (with a drop in average firm size of about 1 worker per firm); and (c) "mixed producers" firms that switch from domestic to exporting increase employment by 280, with an increase in average firm size from 91 to 119. The change in employment in these three groups matches the overall increase in employment in the export sector.

Notes

1. The region's, men's, and women's unemployment data are modeled from the International Labour Organization Modelled Estimates and Projections (ILOEST) database, respectively, as follows: (a) https://data.worldbank.org /indicator/SL.UEM.TOTL.ZS?end=2019&locations=XQ&start=2010; (b) https://data.worldbank.org/indicator/SL.UEM.TOTL.MA.ZS?end=2019 &locations=XQ&start=2010; and (c) https://data.worldbank.org/indicator /SL.UEM.TOTL.FE.ZS?end=2019&locations=XQ&start=2010.

2. Youth unemployment data from World Bank data, modeled from the ILO Modelled Estimates and Projections (ILOEST) database, ILO Statistics (ILOSTAT) (accessed February 21, 2023), https://data.worldbank.org /indicator/SL.UEM.1524.ZS?end=2020&locations=XQ-EG-MA-TN &start=2019.

3. Data on regional trade shares of GDP from World Bank data, using World Bank and Organisation for Economic Co-operation and Development (OECD) national accounts data: https://data.worldbank.org/indicator/NE .TRD.GNFS.ZS?locations=XQ.

4. Population data from the World Development Indicators (WDI) database. Employment-to-population ratios in 2019 were estimated using WDI 2019 data.

5. Youth unemployment data from World Bank data, modeled from the ILO Statistics (ILOSTAT) Modelled Estimates and Projections (ILOEST) database (accessed February 21, 2023), https://data.worldbank.org/indicator /SL.UEM.1524.ZS?end=2020&locations=XQ-EG-MA-TN&start=2019.

6. Data on 1990–2010 population growth and unemployment rates of LMIEs, by region, are from World Bank data (https://data.worldbank.org/indicator /SP.POP.TOTL?end=2010&locations=XQ-XJ-7E&start=1990), using (a) UN DESA (United Nations Department of Economic and Social Affairs), World Population Prospects 2022; (b) census reports and other publications from national statistical offices; (c) Eurostat demographic statistics; (d) UN Statistical Division's Population and Vital Statistics Reports; (e) the US Census Bureau's International Database; and (f) Secretariat of the Pacific Community's Statistics and Demography Programme.

7. Data on the 1990–2010 unemployment rates of LMIEs, by region, are from World Bank data (https://data.worldbank.org/indicator/SL.UEM.TOTL .ZS?end=2010&locations=XQ-XJ-7E&start=1991), modeled from the ILO Statistics (ILOSTAT) Modelled Estimates and Projections (ILOEST) database.

8. Female labor force participation (FLFP) data, by region, are from World Bank data (https://data.worldbank.org/indicator/SL.TLF.CACT.FE .ZS?end=2019&locations=XQ-EG-MA-TN&start=1990), modeled from the ILO Statistics (ILOSTAT) Modelled Estimates and Projections (ILOEST) database (accessed February 21, 2023).

9. Proposed by Tinbergen (1962), the gravity model shows that bilateral trade is influenced by the economic size of each country (measured as GDP), the distance that separates them, and trade costs. Trade costs include several variables related to bilateral, multilateral, and regional trade agreements. By measuring the effect on trade of a specific trade agreement, while introducing control variables to isolate this estimation, it is then possible to determine the effectiveness of a trade agreement in fostering commercial exchange between countries, along with the significance that other variables (such as policies and trade costs) may have for improving these predictions.

10. The shift-share analysis uses the Bartik (1991) approach to look at the industry-level shocks that affect labor markets. By estimating an aggregate of these shocks, it is possible to construct an index that measures how increases in export per worker affects informality and FLFP at the province level. For more details, see annex 1A.

11. Even for countries that do report exports by region, these data typically do not account for production location but rather the location of the exporting firm—which could be an intermediary.

12. Each country exports to destination countries other than itself, $d \in S\setminus\{s\}$ where d is destinations, S is the set of all the countries in the world, and s is the source or exporting country. Thus, a country's exports are defined as
$$Q_t^i \equiv \sum_{d \in S\setminus\{s\}} Q_t^{i,r}.$$

13. Note that the exponential distribution is closely related to the Pareto distribution. For example, if x follows a Pareto distribution with a minimum of a, then $y = \log(x/a)$ (Halliday, Lederman, and Robertson 2018).

14. In other models—Bernard, Jensen, and Schott (2009), for example—the fixed cost becomes part of labor demand. Our model simplifies this by assuming fixed costs to be a pure loss. This implies that the economy's equilibrium is characterized by a small but constant trade surplus that covers its fixed costs. The conclusions of the model would not be affected if the fixed costs were instead distributed among all the workers (Halliday, Lederman, and Robertson 2018).

15. Note that modifying parameter values changes the endogenous variable values but has little impact on the qualitative path of our variables of interest, unless the export price's change drives the model into one of the two corner solutions (where either all firms export or no firms export).

References

Abbey, Emmanuel Nii, Agyapomaa Gyeke-Dako, Abena D. Oduro, F. Ebo Turkson, and Priscilla Twumasi Baffour. 2017. "The Employment Generating Effects of Exporting: Firm Level Evidence of Micro, Small and Medium Enterprises (MSMEs) in Ghana." R4D Working Paper 2017/02, Swiss Programme for Research on Global Issues for Development, Swiss National Science Foundation, Bern.

Arezki, Rabah, Lili Mottaghi, Andrea Barone, Rachel Yuting Fan, Amani Abou Harb, Omer Karasapan, Hideki Matsunaga, Ha Nguyen, and Francois de Soyres. 2018. *A New Economy for the Middle East and North Africa*. MENA Economic Monitor, October 2018. Washington, DC: World Bank. https:// documents1.worldbank.org/curated/en/331081537883965003/pdf/130143 -WP-REVISED-PUBLIC.pdf.

Artuc, Erhan, Gladys Lopez-Acevedo, Raymond Robertson, and Daniel Samaan. 2019. *Exports to Jobs: Boosting the Gains from Trade in South Asia*. South Asia Development Forum Series. Washington, DC: World Bank. https://doi .org/10.1596/978-1-4648-1248-4

Autor, David H., David Dorn, and Gordon H. Hanson. 2013. "The China Syndrome: Local Labor Market Effects of Import Competition in the United States." *American Economic Review* 103 (6): 2121–68. https://doi.org/10.1257 /aer.103.6.2121.

Bartik, Timothy J. 1991. *Who Benefits from State and Local Economic Development Policies?* Kalamazoo, MI: W. E. Upjohn Institute for Employment Research.

Bartley Johns, Marcus, Paul Brenton, Massimiliano Cali, Mombert Hoppe, and Roberta Piermartini. 2015. *The Role of Trade in Ending Poverty*. Washington, DC: World Bank; Geneva: World Trade Organization.

Beblawi, Hazem El. 2008. "Economic Growth in Egypt: Impediments and Constraints (1974–2004)." Working Paper No. 14, Commission on Growth and Development, published by World Bank, Washington, DC.

Bernard, Andrew B., J. Bradford Jensen, and Peter K. Schott. 2009. "Importers, Exporters, and Multinationals: A Portrait of Firms in the U.S. that Trade Goods." In *Producer Dynamics: New Evidence from Micro Data*, edited by Timothy Dunne, J. Bradford Jensen, and Mark J. Roberts, 513–52. Chicago: University of Chicago Press.

Borusyak, Kirill, Peter Hull, Xavier Jaravel, and Dirk Krueger. 2022. "Quasi-experimental Shift-Share Research Designs." *Review of Economic Studies* 89 (1): 181–213.

Brambilla, Irene, Nicolas Depetris Chauvin, and Guido Porto. 2015. "Wage and Employment Gains from Exports: Evidence from Developing Countries." Working Papers 2015-28, Center for Prospective Studies and International Information (CEPII) Research Center, Paris.

Duda-Nyczak, Marta, and Christian Viegelahn. 2018. "Exporting, Importing and Wages in Africa: Evidence from Matched Employer–Employee Data." Research Department Working Paper No. 26, International Labour Office, Geneva.

Dutz, Mark A., Ioannis Kessides, Stephen O'Connell, and Robert D. Willig. 2012. "Competition and Innovation-Driven Inclusive Growth." In *Promoting Inclusive Growth: Challenges and Policies*, edited by Luiz de Mello and Mark A. Dutz, 221–77. Paris: OECD Publishing.

Engel, Jakob, Deeksha Kokas, Gladys Lopez-Acevedo, and Maryla Maliszewska. 2021. *The Distributional Impacts of Trade: Empirical Innovations, Analytical Tools, and Policy Responses*. Trade and Development Series. Washington, DC: World Bank.

Fox, Louise, and Ana Maria Oviedo. 2008. "Institutions and Labor Market Outcomes in Sub-Saharan Africa." Policy Research Working Paper 4721, World Bank, Washington, DC.

Gatti, Roberta, Matteo Morgandi, Rebekka Grun, Stefanie Brodmann, Diego Angel-Urdinola, Juan Manuel Moreno, Daniela Marotta, Marc Schiffbauer, and Elizabeth Mata Lorenzo. 2013. *Jobs for Shared Prosperity: Time for Action in the Middle East and North Africa*. Washington, DC: World Bank.

Gutierrez, Catalina, Carlo Orecchia, Pierella Paci, and Pieter Serneels. 2007. "Does Employment Generation Really Matter for Poverty Reduction?" Policy Research Working Paper 4432, World Bank, Washington, DC.

Halliday, Timothy, Daniel Lederman, and Raymond Robertson. 2018. "Tracking Wage Inequality Trends with Prices and Different Trade Models: Evidence from Mexico." *Review of World Economics* 154 (1): 47–73.

Herre, Bastian, Esteban Ortiz-Espina, and Max Roser. 2013. "Democracy." Published online in Our World in Data report and database (accessed June 15, 2022), https://ourworldindata.org/democracy.

Ianchovichina, Elena. 2018. *Eruptions of Popular Anger: The Economics of the Arab Spring and Its Aftermath*. MENA Development Report. Washington, DC: World Bank.

Islam, Asif M., Dalal Moosa, and Federica Saliola. 2022. *Jobs Undone: Reshaping the Role of Governments toward Markets and Workers in the Middle East and North Africa*. Washington, DC: World Bank. https://doi.org/10.1596/978-1-4648-1735-9.

Kovak, Brian. 2013. "Regional Effects of Trade Reform: What Is the Correct Measure of Liberalization?" *American Economic Review* 103 (5): 1960–76.

Lichter, Andreas, Andreas Peichl, and Sebastian Siegloch. 2017. "Exporting and Labour Demand: Micro-Level Evidence from Germany." *Canadian Journal of Economics* 50 (4): 1161–89.

Lopez-Acevedo, Gladys, and Raymond Robertson. 2012a. "The Promise and Peril of Post-MFA Apparel Production." *Economic Premise* No. 84, World Bank, Washington, DC.

Lopez-Acevedo, Gladys, and Raymond Robertson. 2012b. *Sewing Success? Employment, Wages, and Poverty following the End of the Multi-fibre Arrangement*. Directions in Development Series. Washington, DC: World Bank.

Melitz, Marc J. 2003. "The Impact of Trade on Intra-industry Reallocations and Aggregate Industry Productivity." *Econometrica* 71 (6): 1695–1725.

Mottaghi, Lili. 2019. "Invest in Women to Boost Growth in MENA." *Arab Voices* (blog), March 6, World Bank, Washington, DC. https://blogs.worldbank.org/arabvoices/invest-women-boost-growth-mena.

Pellandra, Andrea. 2015. "Export Destinations, Employment and Wages: Firm-Level Evidence from Chile." Technical report, Economic Commission for Latin America and the Caribbean, Santiago, Chile.

Rossi, Arianna. 2010. "Economic and Social Upgrading in Global Production Networks: The Case of the Garment Industry in Morocco." Unpublished dissertation, University of Sussex, UK.

Tinbergen, Jan. 1962. *Shaping the World Economy: Suggestions for an International Economic Policy*. New York: Twentieth Century Fund.

Topalova, Petia. 2010. "Factor Immobility and Regional Impacts of Trade Liberalization: Evidence on Poverty from India." *American Economic Journal of Applied Economics* 2 (4): 1–41.

Vazquez, Emmanuel, and Deborah Winkler. 2023. "Trade and Local Labor Market Outcomes in Mexico: Disentangling the Channels and the Role of Geography, Sectors, and Trade Types." Policy Research Working Paper 10332, World Bank, Washington, DC.

World Bank. 2003. *Trade, Investment, and Development in the Middle East and North Africa: Engaging with the World*. MENA Development Report. Washington, DC: World Bank.

World Bank. 2004. *Unlocking the Employment Potential in the Middle East and North Africa: Toward a New Social Contract*. MENA Development Report. Washington, DC: World Bank.

WTO (World Trade Organization). 2005. "Trade Policy Review: Tunisia." WT/TPR/S/152, Report by the WTO Secretariat, Geneva.

WTO (World Trade Organization). 2016a. "Trade Policy Review: Tunisia." WT/TPR/S/341, Report by the WTO Secretariat, Geneva.

WTO (World Trade Organization). 2016b. "Trade Policy Review: Morocco." WT/TPR/S/329/Rev.1, Report by the WTO Secretariat, Geneva.

WTO (World Trade Organization). 2018. "Trade Policy Review: Egypt." WT/TPR/S/367, Report by the WTO Secretariat, Geneva.

CHAPTER 2

Trade Agreements and Trade Flows in the Middle East and North Africa

Claudia N. Berg and Carlos Góes

Key Messages

- Regional trade agreements signed by the Arab Republic of Egypt, Morocco, and Tunisia have boosted bilateral trade flows, typically even more so than the average trade agreement globally.

- Not every trade agreement is created equal: trade agreements have varying effectiveness in promoting trade across Egypt, Morocco, and Tunisia.

Introduction

In the late 1980s and early 1990s, many low- and middle-income countries around the world liberalized their trade regimes. Increasing numbers of them signed multiple new bilateral and regional trade agreements (RTAs) and expanded the scope of many existing ones. This process of global integration fundamentally reshaped industries and significantly realigned political dynamics within and between countries. Globally, trade as a share of gross domestic product (GDP) rose from 33 percent in 1990 to 47 percent in 2017—an increase that coincided with an unprecedented reduction in poverty from 45 percent of the global population to 11 percent (Engel et al. 2021).[1]

In the Middle East and North Africa, low- and middle-income economies (LMIEs) rode the wave of trade liberalization. Between 1998 and 2022, for example, the Arab Republic of Egypt and Morocco implemented seven RTAs each, and Tunisia implemented four, as follows (figure 2.1):

- Morocco's most important trade agreement, with the European Union (EU), entered into force in 2000. The country also implemented an RTA with the European Free Trade Association (EFTA) in 1999 and recently with the United States (2023).

- Since the mid-1990s, Tunisia has signed RTAs with the EU, EFTA, the United Kingdom, and Türkiye. It also joined Egypt and other Arab Mediterranean states through the Agadir Agreement.[2]

- Between 2004 and 2020, Egypt signed agreements with the EU, EFTA, Türkiye, and many of Egypt's regional neighbors through the Agadir Agreement.

On the flip side, significant repercussions followed the 2004 expiration of the Multifiber Arrangement (MFA)—an international trade agreement that had imposed quotas on exports of clothing and textiles from low- and middle-income countries to high-income countries. The MFA phaseout was mandated by the Uruguay Round of multilateral trade negotiations within the General Agreement on Tariffs and Trade

FIGURE 2.1

Cumulative Regional Trade Agreements, Arab Republic of Egypt, Morocco, and Tunisia, 1970–2020

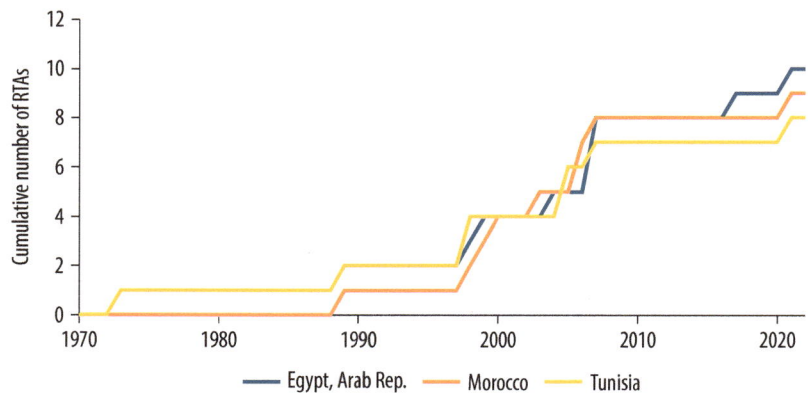

Source: World Trade Organization's Regional Trade Agreements Information System (RTA-IS), https://rtais .wto.org.
Note: "RTAs" refers to regional trade agreements currently in force.

(GATT) framework. It triggered a net increase in global apparel exports and a reallocation of apparel production across countries, increasing apparel employment in some countries but reducing it in others, such as Morocco and Tunisia (Lopez-Acevedo and Robertson 2012).

Both new trade agreements and retired ones are expected to influence trade flows, but to what extent? This report takes a twofold approach to understanding how trade affects domestic economies in the Middle East and North Africa: it relates first trade policy changes to trade flows, and then trade flows to local economic effects, particularly in labor market outcomes.

This chapter takes the first step in the investigation by asking whether trade agreements fail to produce the same trade increases for the Middle East and North Africa's LMIEs—with a focus on Morocco, Tunisia, and Egypt (as detailed in chapters 3, 4, and 5, respectively)—as they do for their economic peers in other regions. It does so by applying an empirical model with a gravity structure to assess the extent to which trade flows responded to the implementation of new trade agreements. It estimates the effect of signing new RTAs on trade flows conditional on predictive variables such as distance between trading partners as well as shared language, history, and institutions. Importantly, it starts from the assumption that not every RTA is created equal (Baier, Bergstrand, and Clance 2018; Kohl and Trojanowska 2015) and extends this research by allowing that effects may differ depending on the characteristics of contracting parties.

Understanding Gravity: Theory and Empirics

In international trade, as in astrophysics, gravity matters. By the mid-twentieth century, Tinbergen (1962) and Pöyhönen (1963) realized that a functional form resembling Newton's gravity equation could also explain bilateral trade flows between distant countries (Head and Mayer 2014). In physics, the gravitational force between two bodies increases with mass but decreases with increasing distance. So, too, in international trade: the trade flows between two countries increase with their economic mass (that is, the size of their economies) but decrease with increasing distance between them. Table 2.1 illustrates the parallels between the gravity equations in physics and trade.

The gravity model of trade became popular in empirical trade economics owing to its high predictive power in explaining the patterns of international trade flows. Indeed, economic mass and distance explain most of the variance in international trade flows. An increasing distance between trading partners decreases trade flows (figure 2.2). Other factors

TABLE 2.1

Parallels between Newton's Law of Gravity and a Gravity Equation for International Trade

Gravity in Newtonian physics	Gravity in international trade
$$F = \frac{m_i m_j}{d^2} G,$$	$$X = \frac{\left(y_i\right)^{\beta_i} \left(y_j\right)^{\beta_j}}{d^\theta} U,$$
where	where
• F is the gravitational force;	• X is the trade flow;
• m_i, m_j are the masses of two objects;	• y_i, y_j are the GDPs of two countries;
• d is the distance between the two objects; and	• d is the distance between the two countries;
• G is the gravitational constant.	• β_i, β_j, θ are elasticities; and
	• U is a residual.

Source: Adapted from Tinbergen 1962.

FIGURE 2.2

Gravity Model of Trade: An Inverse Relationship between Distance and Trade Flows

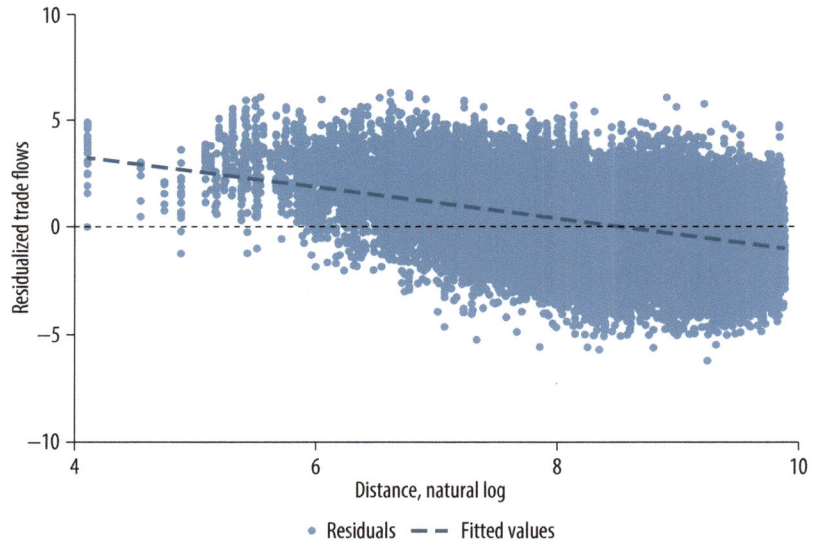

● Residuals   − − Fitted values

Note: Residualized trade flows are residuals from the regression ln $X_{sdt} = \xi_s + \delta_d + \omega_t + e_{sdt}$ where X_{sdt} are trade flows from country d to country d at period t; and $\xi_s, \delta_d,$ and ω_t are source-, destination-, and time-fixed effects, respectively. The regression line in the figure has a coefficient of −0.747 (t-statistic: −124.01).

that would typically facilitate trade include sharing a geographic border, a language, a currency, and—most relevant to our analysis—a trade agreement.

Moreover, most modern trade models present a gravity-like relationship, which implies that this empirical strategy is grounded in economic theory and can be used for both causal inference and structural estimation. This is true of essentially all modern trade models. We apply the gravity model to assess the contribution of RTAs on exports, focusing on the impacts on Egypt, Morocco, and Tunisia. (See annex 2A for derivation of the gravity equation from a version of the Eaton and Kortum [2002] model.)

Under the Hood: The Gravity Regressions

To derive our empirical specifications, we start from the structural gravity relationship of the theoretical model of annex 2A and derive the following empirical specification:

$$\ln X_{sd,t} = -\theta \ln \tilde{\tau}_{sd,t} + \xi_{s,t} + \delta_{d,t} + \tilde{\psi}_{sd} + \upsilon_{sd,t}, \tag{2.1}$$

where $\delta_{d,t}$, $\xi_{s,t}$ are the destination-year and source-year fixed effects, respectively; and $\tilde{\psi}_{sd}$ designates source-destination fixed effects. Note that the effect of distance is absorbed by the source-destination fixed effects.

The analysis below focuses on the heterogeneity of treatment effects across trade agreements by augmenting equation (2.1) in two different ways. First, we estimate a set of models that include a dummy variable for specific trade agreements that captures their average treatment effects on trade. Specifically, we specify the trade cost term as

$$\ln \tilde{\tau}_{sd,t} = \gamma \cdot TA_{sd,t} + \gamma_{sd} \cdot TA_{sd,t} \cdot I_{\left\{ TA_{sd,t} \in \mathcal{T} \right\}}, \tag{2.2}$$

where $I_{\{TA_{sd} \in \mathcal{T}\}}$ is an indicator function denoting whether the trade agreement TA_{sd} is in the agreements set $\mathcal{T}$. If one wants to capture the relative effect of a particular trade agreement, then set $\mathcal{T}$ will consist of a single trade agreement.

The term $-\theta\gamma$ captures the average treatment effect of trade agreements over bilateral trade flows. The term $-\theta\gamma_{sd}$ captures the effect of a particular trade agreement between countries s and d relative to the average effect. If this value is positive, it means the specific trade agreement boosts bilateral trade more than the average trade agreement. The total (heterogeneous) treatment effect of a particular trade agreement is $-\theta(\gamma + \gamma_{sd})$, making clear that γ_{sd} is a shifter around the average treatment effect.

Second, we focus on heterogeneous effects of trade agreements that vary according to the characteristics of country pairs. Following Baier, Bergstrand, and Clance (2018), we estimate a model that captures the heterogeneous treatment effect of trade agreements for each country pair by defining $\ln \tilde{\tau}_{sd,t}$ as follows:

$$
\begin{aligned}
\ln \tilde{\tau}_{sd,t} = {} & \gamma \cdot TA_{sd,t} + \beta_1 \cdot TA_{sd,t} \cdot d_{sd} + \beta_2 \cdot TA_{sd,t} \cdot Adj_{sd} + \\
& \beta_3 \cdot TA_{sd,t} \cdot Lang_{sd} + \beta_4 \cdot TA_{sd,t} \cdot Relig_{sd} + \beta_5 \cdot TA_{sd,t} \cdot \qquad (2.3) \\
& Legal_{sd} + \beta_6 \cdot TA_{sd,t} \cdot Colony_{sd}.
\end{aligned}
$$

In equation (2.1), $-\theta\gamma$ captures the average treatment effect of a trade agreement, just like in the preceding models. Now, however, the term $-\theta \ln \tilde{\tau}_{sd,t}$ is augmented to capture a heterogeneous treatment effect of trade agreements that depends on the characteristics of countries s and d. It captures the additional effect of the interaction of a trade agreement depending on distance (d_{sd}); border sharing (Adj_{sd}); common language ($Lang_{sd}$); common religion ($Relig_{sd}$); common legal system ($Legal_{sd}$); and historical colonial ties ($Colony_{sd}$).[3]

Note that, while the term is defined at the country-pair case, this can be interpreted as an agreement-specific treatment effect, since the variable $TA_{sd,t}$ is binary.[4] One advantage of the specification in equation (2.3) is that it allows for computing heterogeneous treatment effects for *every agreement* with a single regression. The results thus are a distribution of treatment effects for each country, which can be interpreted as the trade-promoting effects of different trade agreements such a country has signed.

We estimate the models using the definition of trade costs above as Poisson pseudo maximum likelihood (PPML) regressions. We then calculate a distribution of treatment effects by calculating the predicted treatment effect for each source-destination-year.

Our gravity analysis relies on databases from United Nations International Trade Statistics (Comtrade) and the Center for Prospective Studies and International Information (CEPII). Bilateral trade flows between 1996 and 2018 are sourced from Comtrade. Information on membership in RTAs comes from the World Trade Organization's Regional Trade Agreements Information System (RTA-IS) database. The remaining control variables are available from the CEPII gravity and language datasets.[5]

Do Trade Agreements Boost Bilateral Trade Flows?

We start by asking whether the recent trade agreements signed by Morocco, Tunisia, and Egypt have been more, less, or equally effective in promoting bilateral trade flows than the average trade agreement globally. Our results yield the three main findings presented below.

Bilateral Trade Flows Exceed Average Global Results

Figure 2.3 plots the differential treatment effect of individual trade agreements for these countries to capture the effect of a particular trade agreement relative to the average treatment effect. The positive estimates in every case suggest that the trade agreement promoted trade more intensely than the average trade agreement.

For all the countries, point estimates are positive for every trade agreement, although there is a wide dispersion in magnitudes. The agreements that include Türkiye have particularly large relative effects, while those for the EU have no differential effect—which suggests that their trade promotion effects are close to that of the average trade agreement.

All RTAs for these countries fall in the upper half of the relative treatment effects, meaning that they are at least as efficient as the average

FIGURE 2.3

Treatment Effects of Recent Trade Agreements Relative to Global Average Agreement Effects, Egypt, Morocco, and Tunisia

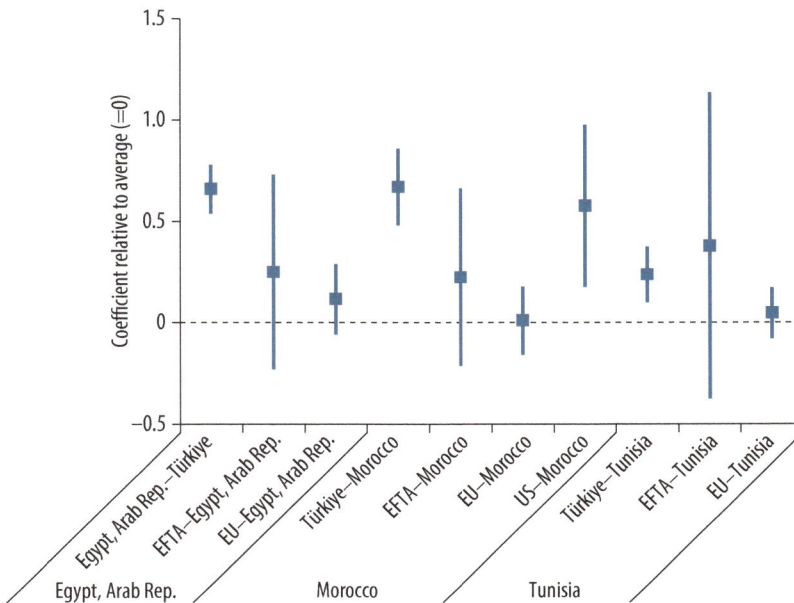

Source: World Bank estimates using United Nations Comtrade, World Trade Organization's Regional Trade Agreements Information System (RTA-IS), and Center for Prospective Studies and International Information (CEPII) datasets.
Note: Figure shows the effects of selected recent trade agreements on bilateral trade flows relative to the average treatment effect (average = 0) of bilateral trade agreements globally over the period 1996–2018. Black boxes indicate the agreement-specific treatment effects, and error bars the 95 percent confidence intervals from regressions. EFTA = European Free Trade Association; EU = European Union.

trade agreement. The most effective trade agreements for these countries (with coefficients greater than 0.5) fall in the top 10 percent of treatment effects. The moderately effective RTAs (with coefficients between 0.25 and 0.50) fall in the top quartile of relative trade effects.

Agreements Vary Greatly in Effectiveness

Next, we take a more comprehensive approach, asking about the expected additional effect on trade flows that every individual trade agreement ever signed by these countries has had.

The results confirm the high variability in effectiveness of trade agreements. This can be seen in figure 2.4, which plots the average

FIGURE 2.4

Treatment Effects of Trade Agreements, Egypt, Morocco, and Tunisia

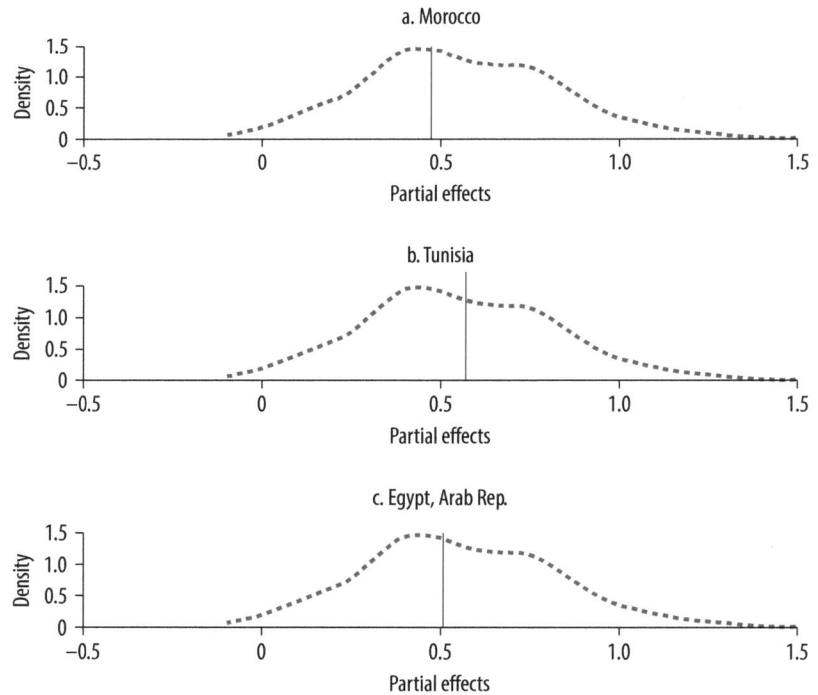

Source: World Bank estimates using data from the United Nations Comtrade database.
Note: Averages for Morocco, Tunisia, and Egypt (shown as solid vertical lines) are juxtaposed against the distribution of treatment effects for every source-destination country pair, as of 2010. Values above zero for a given trade agreement imply that such an agreement has boosted trade between those country pairs, relative to a counterfactual of absence of an agreement. Dashed lines show the distribution of estimated effects for all countries.

effect of a trade agreement for each of our sample countries against the distribution of estimated effects for all countries (shown as a dashed line). Note that these are absolute effects, meaning that positive values denote a positive effect of trade agreements on bilateral trade flows, relative to a counterfactual (absence of an agreement).

Moreover, treatment effects for Tunisia (0.57), Egypt (0.50), and Morocco (0.48) are all positive and fall close to the middle of the distribution (0.53). This suggests that their trade agreements were effective in increasing bilateral trade flows, although some agreements were more effective than others. Also, median effects are similar for both imports and exports for all three countries.

Trade Effects Are Positive but Widely Distributed by Country Pair

In the final step, we analyze every individual trade agreement signed by these countries to determine how much the additional effects vary and a possible reason for the variation. The differences between the three sample countries is shown in figure 2.5, which plots the country-specific distribution of the treatment effects of their agreements.

FIGURE 2.5

Distribution of Trade Agreements' Treatment Effects, Egypt, Morocco, and Tunisia, 2010

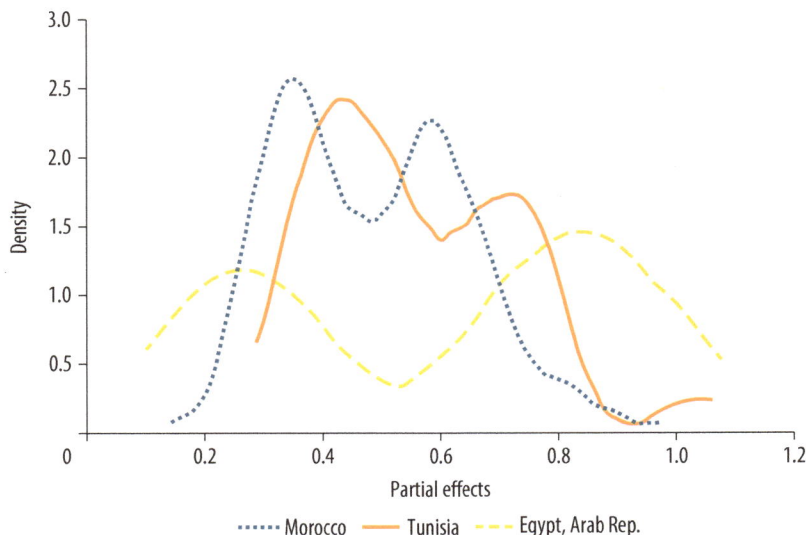

Source: World Bank estimates using data from the United Nations Comtrade database.
Note: In these distributions of treatment effects, positive values denote a positive effect in promoting trade across country pairs.

Our results show a wide distribution of the effects of trade agreements around the averages. This confirms that in Egypt, Morocco, and Tunisia, different trade agreements had quite different effects on trade flows. In fact, the range of effects varies by an order of magnitude (from 0.1 to 1.0), thereby confirming (with another methodology) the results from our first approach—that trade agreement effects are different for different country pairs. Every effect is positive, which highlights that all trade agreements seem to have been efficient in increasing trade flows in these countries.

Every effect is positive, which highlights that all trade agreements seem to have been efficient in increasing trade flows in these countries. However, the distribution of effects is bimodal for the three countries, reflecting different clusters of countries of trade agreements common to these countries. The heterogeneous estimates show that the effectiveness of trade agreements decreases with the distance between the country pair. Egypt, Morocco, and Tunisia tend to have a set of trade agreements with neighboring countries (the mode to the right) and another set of trade agreements with large countries that are more distant (the mode to the left).

Conclusion

We now return to the earlier question: Is it possible that trade agreements do not increase trade for the Middle East and North Africa's LMIEs as they have for many low- and middle-income countries in other regions? Our results show that this is not the case. In fact, the RTAs that Morocco, Tunisia, and Egypt have signed in recent decades have done a good job of boosting trade flows. Each trade agreement signed by these countries had a larger impact on trade flows than the average trade agreement globally—and each country experienced a larger increase in trade flows than the average low- to middle-income country. Thus, it is plausible that signing additional free trade agreements would further increase trade flows.

The following chapters examine the impacts of export flows on labor market outcomes at the subnational and firm levels in Egypt, Morocco, and Tunisia.

Annex 2A. Theoretical Derivation of the Gravity Model

This annex presents the theoretical derivation of the canonical Eaton-Kortum (2002) gravity model. Consider a world with $|\mathcal{K}|$ different countries. Imagine there is a representative consumer in each country,

$s \in \mathcal{K}$, who is endowed with one unit of time that she inelastically supplies to the market. She has preferences over uncountably many product varieties $\omega \in [0,1]$ and wishes to maximize her welfare subject to a budget constraint,

$$\max_{q_s(\omega)_{\omega \in [0,1]}} \left[\int_{[0,1]} q_s(\omega)^{\frac{\alpha-1}{\alpha}} d\omega \right]^{\frac{\sigma}{\sigma-1}} \quad s.t. \int_{[0,1]} p_s(\omega) q_s(\omega) d\omega \leq w_s L_s = Y_s, \quad (2A.1)$$

where $q_s(\omega)$ and $p_s(\omega)$ are, respectively, demand and prices of product variety ω in country s; w_s is the wage in country s; and $\sigma > 0$ is the elasticity of substitution across products. As it will become clear below, there will be no profits in this economy, and the existence of a single representative household implies that labor income is equal to nominal national income. Given this preference structure, demand functions for a particular product variety satisfies

$$q_s(\omega) = \left(\frac{p_s(\omega)}{P_s} \right)^{-\sigma} \cdot \frac{Y_s}{P_s}, \quad (2A.2)$$

where $P_s = \left[\int_{[0,1]} p(\omega)^{1-\omega} d\omega \right]^{\frac{1}{1-\sigma}}$ is the ideal price index in country s. That is, demand for a particular variety is decreasing in its own relative price and increasing in real income.

There are infinitely many firms producing each product variety, each endowed with a linear technology. Each of them faces the following profit maximization problem:

$$\max_{l_s(\omega)} \quad p_{ss}(\omega) z_s(\omega) l_s(\omega) - w_s l_s(\omega),$$

where $p_{ss}(\omega)$ denotes the factory gate price of variety ω produced in country s;[6] $z_s(\omega)$ is the productivity of a firm producing that variety; and $l_s(\omega)$ is the labor input. We assume there is free entry and perfect competition. Given that, the equilibrium satisfies factory gate prices equating marginal costs, or

$$p_{ss}(\omega) = \frac{w_s}{z_s(\omega)}. \quad (2A.3)$$

In this world economy, trade is not costless. If households in destination country d want to consume one unit of a given product variety imported from country s, they have source and pay for $\tau_{sd} \geq 1$ units— that is, consumers face iceberg trade costs.[7] We make the standard assumption that $\tau_{ss} = 1$ (self-trade is costless) and that $\tau_{sd} \leq \tau_{sz}\tau_{zd}$ (trade costs satisfy the triangle inequality).

Given trade costs, they will consume only the cheapest product available at a destination market $d \in \mathcal{K}$:

$$p_d(\omega) = \min_{s \in \mathcal{K}} \{\tau_{sd} \cdot p_{ss}(\omega)\} = \min_{s \in \mathcal{K}} \left\{\tau_{sd} \cdot \frac{w_s}{z_s(\omega)}\right\}. \quad (2A.4)$$

We take a firm's productivity to be the realization of a random variable with cumulative distribution function (CDF) $F_s(z) = Pr(z_s(\omega) < z) = \exp\{-T_s z^\theta\}$. We assume that this random variable is individually and identically distributed (iid) across countries and varieties. We call T_s the *scale parameter*. It is country specific and governs the overall level of technology of a given country (*absolute advantage*). By contrast, we call θ the *shape parameter*. It is common for all countries and governs the level of dispersion of the CDF across different sectors, thereby determining different levels of specialization (*comparative advantage*). The higher the θ, the smaller dispersion there is in the CDF.

Note that, given this assumption, both prices and demanded quantities are also random variables. One can show analytically that the probability of a given destination d sourcing a variety from country s is

$$Pr\left(\frac{w_s}{z_s(\omega)}\tau_{sd} < \min_{(n \neq s)}\left\{\frac{w_{n,t}}{z_n(\omega)}\tau_{nd}\right\}\right) = \frac{T_s(w_s\tau_{sd})^{-\theta}}{\sum_{n=1}^{N}T_n(w_n\tau_{nd})^{-\theta}}. \quad (2A.5)$$

Because there are infinitely many varieties w and productivities are iid random variables, by the law of large numbers, the share of varieties sourced from s to d is equal to the probability of sourcing a specific variety from s to d. That is,

$$\frac{X_{sd}}{X_d} \equiv \pi_{sd} = Pr\left(\frac{w_s}{z_s(\omega)}\tau_{sd} < \min_{(n \neq s)}\left\{\frac{w_{n,t}}{z_n(\omega)}\tau_{nd}\right\}\right) = \frac{T_s(w_s\tau_{sd})^{-\theta}}{\sum_{n=1}^{N}T_n(w_n\tau_{nd})^{-\theta}}, \quad (2A.6)$$

where X_{sd} is the expenditure in country d of goods coming from country s, and X_d is total expenditure in country d.

One can also show that $P_s^{-\frac{1}{\theta}} = \sum_{n=1}^{N}T_n(w_n\tau_{nd})^{-\theta}$. Additionally, because the utility function is locally insatiable, the household will spend all its income, such that $X_s = Y_s$. Therefore, we can write

$$X_{sd} = \frac{T_s(w_s\tau_{sd})^{-\theta}}{P_d^{-\frac{1}{\theta}}}Y_d. \quad (2A.7)$$

As a last step, note that domestic income can be pinned down by the following market-clearing condition:

$$Y_s = \sum_d X_{sd} = \sum_d \frac{T_s\left(w_s \tau_{sd}\right)^{-\theta}}{P_d^{-\frac{1}{\theta}}} Y_d \Leftrightarrow w_s^{-\theta} T_s = \frac{Y_s}{\sum_d \tau_{sd}^{-\theta} Y_d P_d^{\frac{1}{\theta}}} = \frac{Y_s}{\Pi_s}, \quad (2A.8)$$

where the last equality comes from defining $\Pi_s \equiv \sum_d \tau_{sd}^{-\theta} Y_d P_d^{\frac{1}{\theta}}$. We can then rewrite X_{sd} as

$$X_{sd} = \tau_{sd}^{-\theta} \cdot \frac{Y_d}{P_d^{-\frac{1}{\theta}}} \cdot \frac{Y_s}{\Pi_s}. \quad (2A.9)$$

Note that the term $\tau_{sd} \geq 1$ is meant to represent anything that makes trade harder between countries s and d. Importantly, trade costs are increasing in distance. This explains why this is the *gravity* equation: increasing with each country's economic mass and decreasing with distance. Nonetheless, trade costs include factors other than distance, augmenting the gravity equation. Typical variables included in τ_{sd}, which can move trade costs up or down, include common language; common legal system; common religion; historical colony–metropole relationship; and border sharing.

To derive our empirical specifications, we first take logs:

$$\ln X_{sd} = \delta_d + \xi_s - \theta \times \tau_{sd}, \quad (2A.10)$$

where $\delta_d = \ln \frac{Y_d}{P_d^{-\frac{1}{\theta}}}$ and $\xi_s = \ln \frac{Y_s}{\Pi_s}$ are, respectively, destination and source fixed effects, and τ_{sd} is some measure of trade costs. We can model τ_{sd} in different ways, but typically it is taken to be proportional to the geographic distance between countries s and d $\tau_{sd} \propto distance(s, d)$.

One of the potential components of trade costs is the existence of trade agreements between country pairs. In that case, we can model trade costs as

$$\tau_{sd} = \exp\left(\alpha \cdot d_{sd} + \gamma \cdot TA_{sd} + \sum_{k=1}^{K} \beta_k \cdot Z_{sd,k}\right), \quad (2A.11)$$

where d_{sd} is the distance between countries s and d; TA_{sd} is a dummy denoting whether there is a regional trade agreement between s and d; and $Z_{sd,k}$ are K other components of trade costs, which may or may not be observed.

We can then estimate following empirical model by Poisson pseudo maximum likelihood (PPML):

$$\ln X_{sd,t} = -\theta \, \ln \, \tilde{\tau}_{sd,t} + \xi_{s,t} + \delta_{d,t} + \tilde{\psi}_{sd} + \upsilon_{sd,t}, \tag{2A.12}$$

where $\delta_{d,t}$, $\xi_{s,t}$ are the destination-year and source-year fixed effects, respectively; and $\tilde{\psi}_{sd}$ are source-destination fixed effects. Note that the effect of distance is absorbed by the source-destination fixed effects.

To map equation (2A.12) back to the gravity equation we had specified before, note that $\ln \tau_{sd,t} = \ln \tilde{\tau}_{sd,t} + \alpha \cdot d_{sd}$. Defining $\psi_{sd} = \tilde{\psi}_{sd} + \theta \alpha \cdot d_{sd}$ and $\tilde{\upsilon}_{sd,t} = \upsilon_{sd,t} + \theta \sum_{k=1}^{K} \beta_k \cdot Z_{sd,k,t}$, equation (2A.12) becomes

$$\ln X_{sd,t} = -\theta \gamma \cdot TA_{sd,t}$$
$$-\theta \sum_{k=1}^{K} \beta_k \cdot Z_{sd,k,t} + \xi_{s,t} + \delta_{d,t} + \psi_{sd} - \theta \, \alpha \cdot d_{sd} + \tilde{\upsilon}_{sd,t}. \tag{2A.13}$$

The term $-\theta\gamma$ captures the average treatment effect of a trade agreement over bilateral trade flows. Clearly, d_{sd} is absorbed by the country-destination fixed effects, and $-\theta \sum_{k=1}^{K} \beta_k \cdot Z_{sd,k,t}$ (if time-varying) are part of the residual term in equation (2A.12).

Notes

1. It is well-documented that trade can (a) drive economic development (Bhagwati and Srinivasan 2002; Dollar and Kraay 2004; Frankel and Romer 1999; Noguer and Siscart 2005); (b) reduce poverty by generating new employment opportunities (Engel et al. 2021; Lopez-Acevedo and Robertson 2012); and (c) reduce prices of goods and services for poor consumers (Bartley Johns et al. 2015).
2. The Agreement on the Establishment of the Free Trade Area between the Arab Mediterranean States (Agadir Agreement) was signed in February 2004 by Egypt, Jordan, Morocco, and Tunisia to establish a free trade area that would increase trade both among these countries and between them and the EU.
3. To account for fixed effects, every interaction variable was demeaned.
4. This specification does not account for the quality or depth of trade agreements. Rather, it only captures the average treatment effect of the first trade agreement between s and d being active. If there are subsequent trade agreements between s and d, $TA_{sd,t}$ will not change. Therefore, this term captures the extensive margin of trade agreements (whether or not a trade agreement exists) but not the intensive margin (how deep the trade agreement is).
5. For the gravity and language datasets, see the CEPII website: http://www.cepii.fr/.
6. The subscript $_{ss}$ denotes domestic: produced and consumed in the same country s.
7. The subscript $_{sd}$ denotes traded: produced in country s and exported to country d.

References

Baier, Scott L., Jeffrey H. Bergstrand, and Matthew W. Clance. 2018. "Heterogeneous Effects of Economic Integration Agreements." *Journal of Development Economics* 135: 587–608. https://doi.org/10.1016/j.jdeveco.2018.08.014.

Bartley Johns, Marcus, Paul Brenton, Massimiliano Cali, Mombert Hoppe, and Roberta Piermartini. 2015. *The Role of Trade in Ending Poverty*. Washington, DC: World Bank; Geneva: World Trade Organization.

Bhagwati, Jagdish, and T. N. Srinivasan. 2002. "Trade and Poverty in the Poor Countries." *American Economic Review* 92 (2): 180–83. https://doi.org/10.1257/000282802320189212.

Dollar, David, and Aart Kraay. 2004. "Trade, Growth, and Poverty." *The Economic Journal* 114 (493): F22–F49.

Eaton, Jonathan, and Samuel Kortum. 2002. "Technology, Geography, and Trade." *Econometrica* 70 (5): 1741–79.

Engel, Jakob, Deeksha Kokas, Gladys Lopez-Acevedo, and Maryla Maliszewska. 2021. *The Distributional Impacts of Trade: Empirical Innovations, Analytical Tools, and Policy Responses*. Trade and Development Series. Washington, DC: World Bank.

Frankel, Jeffrey A., and David Romer. 1999. "Does Trade Cause Growth?" *American Economic Review* 89 (3): 379–99.

Head, Keith, and Thierry Mayer. 2014. "Gravity Equations: Workhorse, Toolkit, and Cookbook." In *Handbook of International Economics, Volume 4*, edited by Gita Gopinath, Elhanan Helpman, and Kenneth Rogoff, 131–95. Oxford and Amsterdam: North-Holland.

Kohl, Tristan, and Sofia Trojanowska. 2015. "Heterogeneous Trade Agreements, WTO Membership and International Trade: An Analysis Using Matching Econometrics." *Applied Economics* 47 (33): 3499–3509. https://doi.org/10.1080/00036846.2015.1016211.

Lopez-Acevedo, Gladys, and Raymond Robertson. 2012. *Sewing Success? Employment, Wages, and Poverty following the End of the Multi-fibre Arrangement*. Directions in Development Series. Washington, DC: World Bank.

Noguer, Marta, and Marc Siscart. 2005. "Trade Raises Income: A Precise and Robust Result." *Journal of International Economics* 65 (2): 447–60.

Pöyhönen, Pentti. 1963. "A Tentative Model for the Volume of Trade between Countries." *Weltwirtschaftliches Archiv* 90 (1): 93–99.

Tinbergen, Jan. 1962. *Shaping the World Economy: Suggestions for an International Economic Policy*. New York: Twentieth Century Fund.

CHAPTER 3

Morocco Case Study: Trade Expansion with Mixed Results

Jaime Alfonso Roche Rodríguez and Daniela Ruiz Zárate

Key Messages

- Although Morocco's trade openness policies of the past two decades have lowered labor informality, they have also reduced employment opportunities for women.

- These results reflect a shift from labor-intensive to capital-intensive sectors, which promotes labor formalization but tends to favor men over women in the labor force.

- At the firm level, the positive impact of exports on employment has occurred mainly in male-labor-intensive sectors—with the likelihood of exporting going hand in hand with a higher male-to-female employment ratio.

- Morocco is an example of an economy where both internal factors (like industrial policies) and external ones (like trade accords and the emergence of export competitors) have left light manufacturing (apparel and textiles sectors) behind—unlike the well-documented cases of countries where trade promoted apparel and hence female labor participation.

Introduction

Over the past two decades, Morocco's economic progress has been impressive. Between 2000 and 2019, living standards registered a big improvement, per capita income almost doubled, the overall poverty rate fell to almost one-third of its 2000 level, literacy rates and health outcomes improved, and access to basic utilities (such as water and electricity) increased. Moreover, the expansion of the working-age population (ages 15 and older) offers a potential "demographic window" to support a jobs-led growth policy for the next two decades (Lopez-Acevedo, Devoto et al. 2021).

However, higher economic growth—in part fueled by trade liberalization and the resulting greater trade flows—has not created enough jobs to offset the increase in population or improve some important labor market outcomes. Morocco's labor informality rate, although decreasing, still ranks among the highest in the Middle East and North Africa. The industrial and services sectors in Moroccan cities have not completely absorbed the agricultural job losses in rural areas. And female labor force participation (FLFP) is lower than it was two decades ago, with a persistent 50 percentage-point gender gap (Lopez-Acevedo, Betcherman et al. 2021).

A big problem is that the business environment is seen as "unpredictable and bureaucratic," which has constrained investment despite significant policy changes to boost efficiency. Other major impediments to doing business include judicial shortcomings and regulatory ambiguity, poor competition, market concentration issues, and corruption (World Bank 2018).

Could stepped-up trade flows put Morocco on a better path to sustainable, inclusive growth? This chapter tackles this question by exploring why past efforts on the trade front have failed to improve labor market outcomes. It builds on the bilateral trade flow results discussed in chapter 2, which show that Morocco's free trade agreements boosted its trade flows. It asks how these flows affected local labor markets, focusing on informality and FLFP rates. It also analyzes the role of domestic factors (industrial policies) and external ones (international and bilateral trade accords). It then explores the relationship between export sales and labor demand at the firm level.

Our study adds value by presenting the case of a country whose export promotion decreased FLFP—contrary to the well-documented cases of emerging nations where light manufacturing (such as textiles and apparel) benefit from trade openness and thus promote female employment and participation.

Morocco's Trade Flows and Labor Markets: A Snapshot

Since the early 2000s, the living conditions of Morocco's population have improved greatly in several respects:

- The national poverty rate fell from 15.3 percent to 4.8 percent in 2014 (Lopez-Acevedo, Betcherman et al. 2021).

- Per capita income almost doubled, from US$4,112 to US$8,218 (in purchasing power parity [PPP], constant 2017 international $) in 2018.[1]

- Life expectancy increased from 67 years in 2000 to 74 years in 2020.

- Net primary school enrollment rose from 77 percent in 2000 to 99 percent in 2020.

However, this brighter economic picture has not been labor intensive enough to absorb its working-age population. As a result, Morocco still struggles to overcome the "middle-income trap"—that is, the difficulty in boosting its gross domestic product (GDP) per capita (US$8,058 in 2021) above the upper-middle-income level of about US$18,000 (in PPP constant 2017 international $), largely because it lost its competitive edge in exporting manufactured goods yet cannot keep up with higher-income economies in the high-value-added market (Lopez-Acevedo, Betcherman et al. 2021).

That said, Morocco has reformed institutional and regulatory frameworks to boost specific sectors. It has implemented several industrial policies—the Emergence Program (2000–07), the National Pact for Industrial Emergence (2009–14), and the Industrial Acceleration Plan (2014–20)—to promote foreign direct investment (FDI), boost exports, increase formalization, and reposition manufacturing sectors into new segments with more value added. The latter especially benefited the automobile, aeronautics, and electronics sectors as well as offshoring.

Key Trade Flow Trends

Morocco has pursued a policy of trade liberalization in recent decades. It has signed nine trade agreements since 1988 (table 3.1)—the most important being one with the European Union (EU), which accounts for nearly 70 percent of Morocco's total exports. This pact was signed in 1996 and entered into force in 2000, committing Morocco to reduce tariffs to zero on imports of manufactured goods from the EU. Moreover, the emergence of China as an export power, followed by the end of the Multifiber Arrangement in 2004, meant greater competition in the European market, especially in textiles and apparel (Lopez-Acevedo and Robertson 2012).

TABLE 3.1

Trade Agreements Signed by Morocco, 1988–2019

Agreement name	Coverage	Signature	Entry into force	Partners
Global System of Trade Preferences (GSTP) among Developing Countries	Goods	April 13, 1988	April 19, 1989	Forty-two countries spanning all income groups
Pan-Arab Free Trade Area (PAFTA)[a]	Goods	February 19, 1997	January 1, 1998	Nineteen Middle East and North Africa economies
European Free Trade Association (EFTA) Agreement	Goods	June 19, 1997	December 1, 1999	Morocco and the EFTA member states: Iceland, Liechtenstein, Norway, and Switzerland
EU–Morocco	Goods	February 26, 1996	March 1, 2000	European Union (EU), Morocco
Morocco–United Arab Emirates	Goods	May 25, 2001	July 9, 2003	Morocco, United Arab Emirates
Turkey–Morocco	Goods	April 7, 2004	January 1, 2006	Morocco, Türkiye
Unites States–Morocco	Goods	June 15, 2004	January 1, 2006	Morocco, United States
Agadir Agreement[b]	Goods	February 25, 2004	March 27, 2007	Egypt, Arab Rep.; Jordan; Morocco; Tunisia
United Kingdom–Morocco	Goods	October 26, 2019	January 1, 2021	Morocco, United Kingdom

Source: "Morocco and the WTO." Member information page, World Trade Organization website: https://www.wto.org/english/thewto _e/countries_e/morocco_e.htm.
a. The Pan-Arab Free Trade Area (PAFTA) is also known as the Greater Arab Free Trade Area (GAFTA).
b. The Agadir Agreement is also known, more formally, as the Agreement on the Establishment of the Free Trade Area between the Arab Mediterranean States.

As a result of these developments, Morocco's tariff rates have dropped sharply and its trade openness has almost doubled, although the trade balance remains in the red, as these data indicate:

- *The mean tariff rate* has declined from 45.4 percent in 1993 to 3.6 in 2020 (figure 3.1, panel a).[2]

- *Trade openness* (imports plus exports as a percentage of GDP) has risen from 52.1 percent in 1993 to 77.5 percent in 2020, with the only down period being after the 2008 Global Financial Crisis (figure 3.1, panel b).

- *Total exports* have increased by 307 percent from 1993 to 2019, decreasing in 2020 because of the shocks of the COVID-19 (coronavirus) pandemic (figure 3.1, panel c).

- *The trade balance* (exports minus imports) has remained negative (and worsening), in part reflecting a high dependence on fossil fuel imports (figure 3.1, panel d).

Among several trade flow trends that stand out, Morocco's trade basket remains undiversified in terms of partners, while the number of products exported has moderately increased. In 2018, nearly 70 percent

FIGURE 3.1

Key Trade Trends, Morocco, 1993–2020

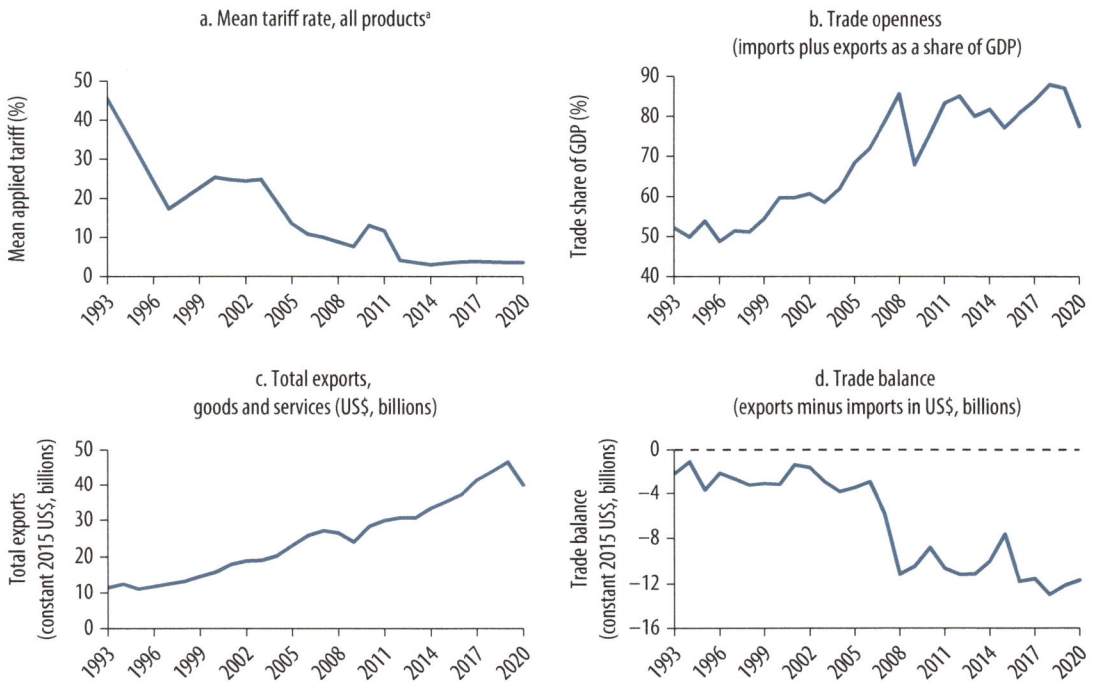

a. Mean tariff rate, all products[a]

b. Trade openness
(imports plus exports as a share of GDP)

c. Total exports,
goods and services (US$, billions)

d. Trade balance
(exports minus imports in US$, billions)

Sources: World Bank based on data from Our World in Data (panels a and b) and World Development Indicators (panels c and d) databases.
a. The weighted mean applied tariff is the average of effectively applied rates weighted by the product import shares corresponding to each partner country.

of Moroccan exports went to high-income countries—including about 22 percent to France and 24 percent to Spain. And between 2001 and 2019, especially in the later years, Morocco increased the number of products it exported from 2,704 different products to 3,133.[3]

In addition, trade patterns have shifted from labor-intensive to capital-intensive industries in the past two decades. In 2000, Morocco was largely an exporter of textiles and apparel—a sector typically characterized by a female workforce. More recently, machinery and electronics, transportation, and chemicals have surpassed textiles in the country's share of total exports (figure 3.2). This shift means that typically labor-intensive, female-dominated industries lost share relative to sectors that are mainly capital-intensive and tend to employ mainly male workers. A big factor may be an increase in relative prices for capital-intensive goods, reflecting both external factors (like trade accords) and internal ones (like industrial policies).

FIGURE 3.2

Shares of Exports, by Industry, Morocco, 2000–20

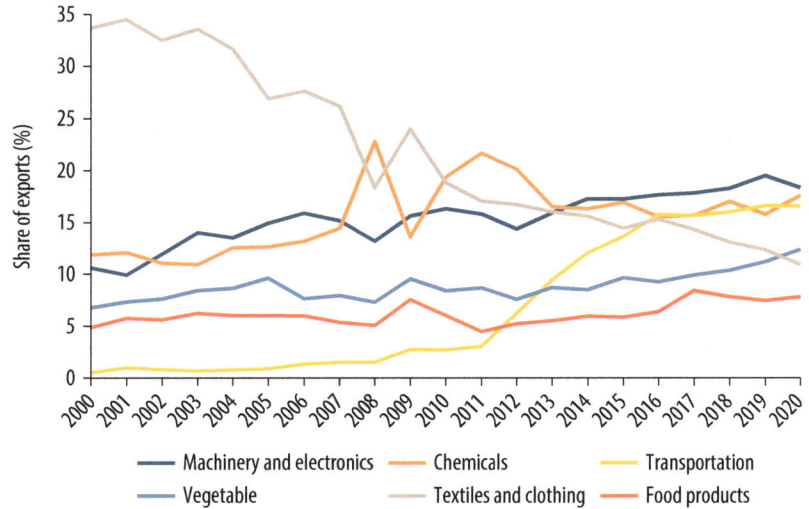

Source: World Bank based on data from the World Bank's World Integrated Trade Solutions (WITS) interactive database tool.
Note: Product groups appear as reported by WITS.

The textiles and apparel sector, which represented nearly 40 percent of Moroccan exports in 2000, fell to 10.8 percent in 2020. At the same time, internal Moroccan policies have incentivized FDI in specific capital-intensive sectors.

Key Labor Market Trends

Working-age population growth. Several labor market trends stand out as well. Perhaps most notably, the fast growth of Morocco's working-age population (ages 15 and older) has not been offset by sufficient job creation. While the rural working-age population increased by 14.2 percent between 2000 and 2018, the urban working-age population shot up by 49.9 percent in the same period, with both genders following the same trends (figure 3.3, panel a).[4]

Employment growth, rural versus urban. In addition, rural employment has increased by only 1.9 percent between 2000 and 2018, while urban employment grew by 45.8 percent, mainly driven by male jobs (figure 3.3, panel b). More drastically, while 3.4 million women became part of the working-age population, just 117,800 new jobs were created, increasing the gap between male and female employment.

FIGURE 3.3

Working-Age and Employed Populations, by Gender and by Urban or Rural Location, Morocco, 2000–18

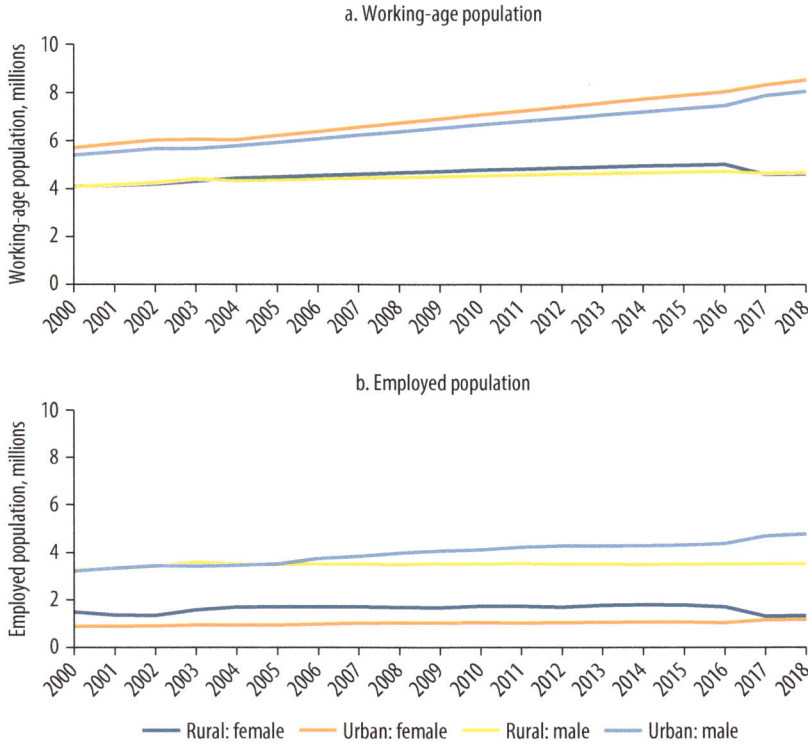

a. Working-age population

b. Employed population

Rural: female   Urban: female   Rural: male   Urban: male

Source: Estimates based on Morocco Labor Force Surveys, 2000–18.
Note: "Working-age population" refers to ages 15 and older. Employment data include both formal and informal employment.

Unemployment rates. As for unemployment, it has slightly decreased, especially for men in the years preceding the COVID-19 pandemic. The overall unemployment rate declined from 13.4 percent in 2000 to 9.75 percent in 2018—reaching an all-time low in 2011 (8.91 percent) (figure 3.4).[5] This drop was driven mainly by the lower rate for men, in contrast to the higher rate for women, which started to rise in 2009.

Labor force participation. Especially for women and youth, labor force participation has been low. The overall labor force participation rate edged down from 53 percent in 2000 to 46 percent in 2018—with a minor drop for both men (from 79 percent to 71 percent) and women (from 28 percent to 22 percent) (figure 3.5). At this point, women

FIGURE 3.4

Unemployment Rates, by Gender, Morocco, 2000–18

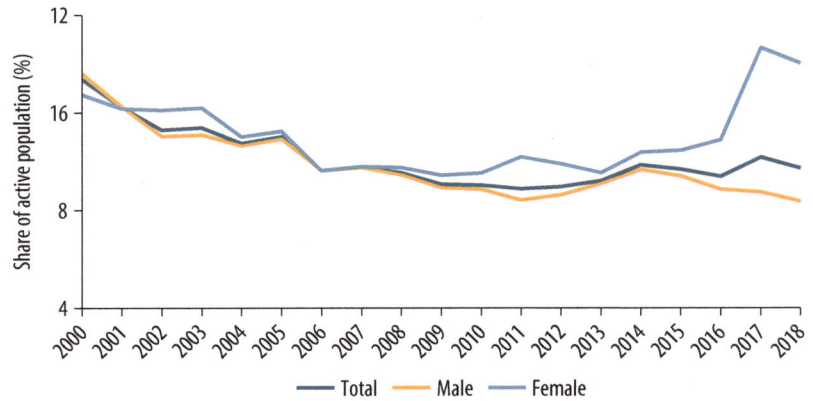

Source: Estimates based on the Morocco Labor Force Surveys, 2000–18.
Note: The unemployment rate is calculated by dividing the total unemployed working-age population (ages 15 and older) by the active working-age population ("active" comprising both the employed and the unemployed who are looking for work).

FIGURE 3.5

Labor Force Participation Rates, by Gender, Morocco, 2000–18

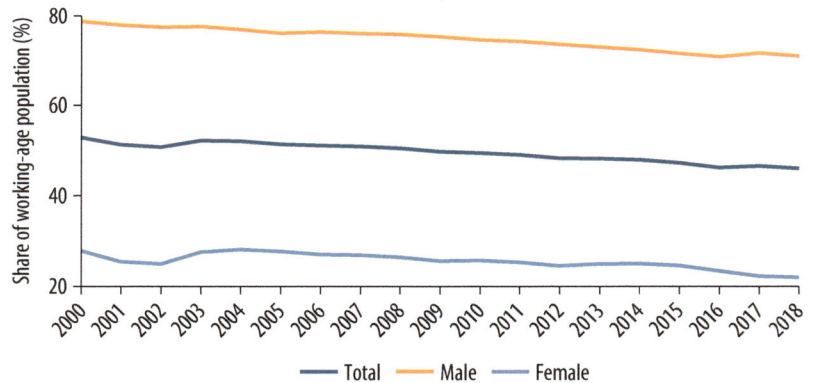

Source: Estimates based on the Morocco Labor Force Surveys, 2000–18.
Note: Labor force participation rates are for the working-age population (ages 15 and older) and include both formal and informal labor. They are calculated as the active working-age population (the employed plus the unemployed who seek work) divided by the total working-age population.

constitute most of the "inactive"—those who are not only unemployed but also so discouraged about the prospect of finding a job that they have stopped looking. This attitude is on top of domestic duties and childcare, which are among the main reasons that women cite for not working (Lopez-Acevedo, Betcherman et al. 2021).

Another problem group is that the youth population (ages 15–24) exhibits higher inactivity and unemployment rates than other age groups. Morocco's "not in education, employment, or training" (NEET) rate— that is, not in the labor force—has remained among the highest in the Middle East and North Africa. Moroccans in the NEET category in 2010 were still NEET even 10 years later (Alfani et al. 2020).

Female employment, by sector. The FLFP decline might reflect the changing structure of female employment. Whereas the manufacturing sector represented 18 percent of total female employment in 2000, it accounted for just 11 percent in 2014—largely because of female job loss in the textiles and apparel sector (figure 3.6).[6] At the same time, the share of female employment in agriculture remained steady (59 percent in 2000 and 61 percent in 2014), whereas the share of services rose from 18 percent to 25 percent.

FIGURE 3.6

Decomposition of Female Employment, by Sector, Morocco, 2000–14

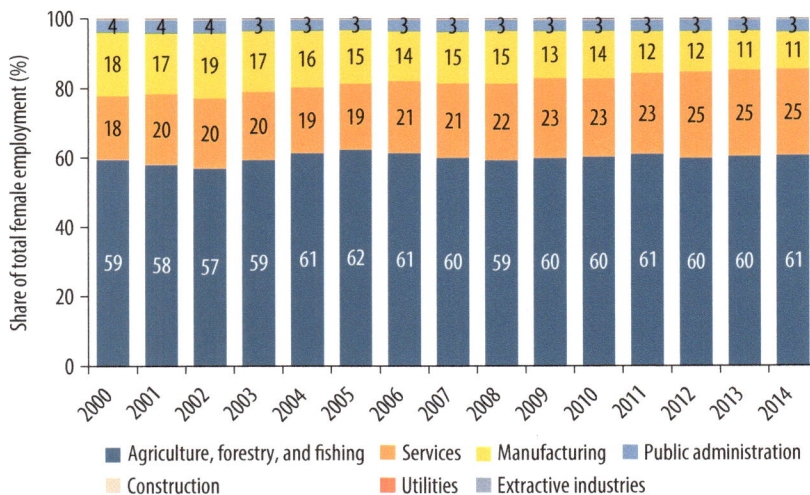

Source: Estimates based on the Morocco Labor Force Surveys, 2000–14.
Note: Employment shares are those for working-age females (ages 15 and older). The data include both formal and informal employment. Shares in some years may not add up to 100 because the labeling does not include certain small sectors.

This realignment of sector shares for female employment is atypical and differs from theory in the sense that increases in trade are expected to promote the manufacturing sector in the economy (Artuc et al. 2019). It reinforces the idea of a premature "deindustrialization" process, in which urban job creation has not been enough to offset migration from rural areas and the increase in the working-age population—discouraging women but, at the same time, promoting male employment in just a few capital-intensive sectors.

Unique Labor Effects from Trade Expansion

Labor market outcomes in Morocco reflect a unique circumstance in which positive trade shocks lower FLFP while contributing to less informality. For the past 15 years, both female and male labor force participation have been decreasing, in contrast to the trends in other low- and middle-income countries after trade growth.[7] At the same time, informality rates (the percentage of workers without access to social security) for both men and women have also decreased—meaning a smaller share of people work in informal jobs and a larger share in formal jobs.

These trends result in part from policies that promote formalization but also tend to constrain female participation in specific sectors. Informality rates in the top exporting sectors (figure 3.7, panel a) are low relative to Morocco's overall informality rate of 74 percent in 2018.[8] At the same time, the female share of employment is higher in industries that are losing the most jobs (figure 3.7, panel b), compared with the 23 percent overall female share of employment in 2018.

However, these labor market variables differ depending on geography. Employment distribution varies greatly across regions. For example, 58 percent of total employment was in agricultural jobs in 2014, but in the Oriental Region this share was just 30 percent, with 45 percent in services (figure 3.8). At the same time, those regions with the highest shares in agricultural jobs (Béni Mellal-Khénifra, Drâa-Tafilalet, and Marrakech-Safi) have the lowest unemployment rates. The regions with the lowest FLFP rates are also those with the highest unemployment (the Oriental Region and Guelmim-Oued Noun and parts of Laayoune-Sakia El Hamra).[9]

Informality rates. In addition, the informality rate varies across regions. Guelmim-Oued Noun and parts of Laayoune-Sakia El Hamra have the lowest informality rate (about 53 percent), driven by their high employment share in public administration. It is no surprise that Drâa-Tafilalet's rate is the highest (about 80 percent), because most of its jobs are in agriculture (map 3.1). These regional variations can also be observed to vary over time in both informality and FLFP rates (see the supplementary figures in annex 3A).

FIGURE 3.7

Informality Rates and Female Shares of Employment in Morocco, Nationally and by Selected Sector, 2000–18

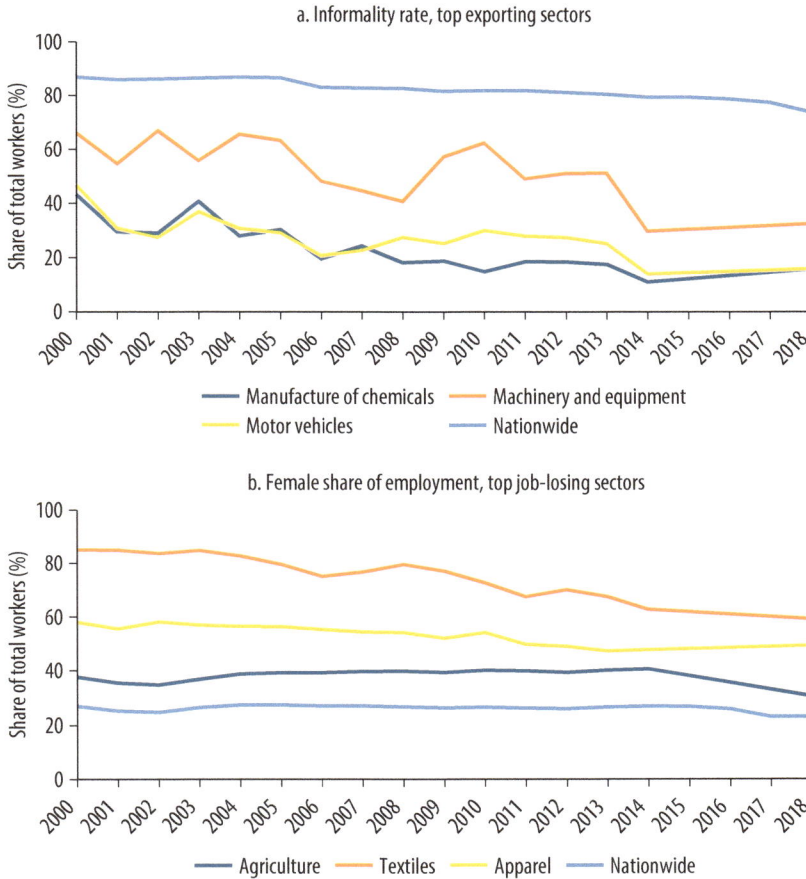

a. Informality rate, top exporting sectors

— Manufacture of chemicals   — Machinery and equipment
— Motor vehicles   — Nationwide

b. Female share of employment, top job-losing sectors

— Agriculture   — Textiles   — Apparel   — Nationwide

Source: Estimates based on the Morocco Labor Force Surveys, 2000–18.
a. The informality rate is defined as the percentage of workers without access to social security.
b. Employment shares are those for working-age females (ages 15 and older), and they include both formal and informal employment.

How Trade Affects Local Labor Markets

In sum, the labor market backdrop is one where (a) informality rates in the top exporting sectors (which are also the main jobs-creating sectors) are considerably lower than in other sectors and continuing to decrease; and (b) the female share of total jobs is higher in job-losing industries and relatively low in the top exporting industries. Against this backdrop, it is important to ask what the impact of higher exports would be.

FIGURE 3.8

Sectoral Decomposition of Employment across Morocco, by Region, 2014

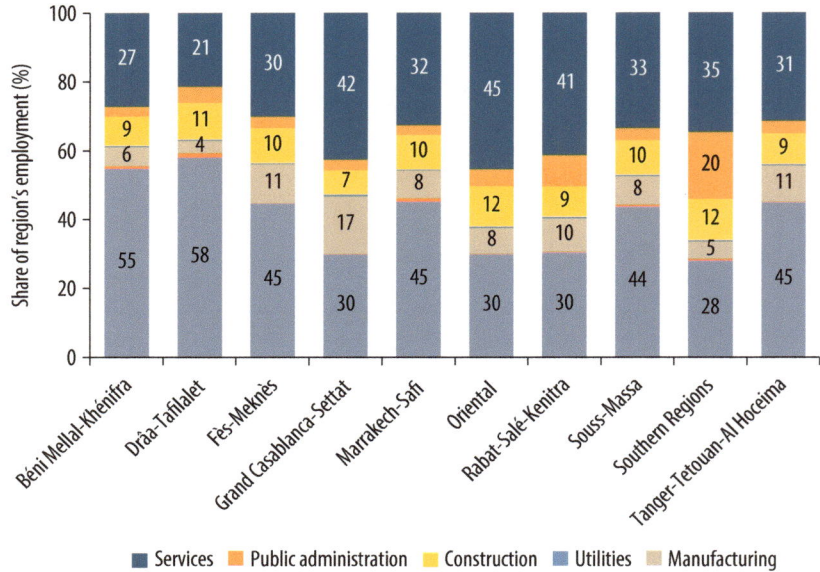

Source: Estimates based on the 2014 Morocco Labor Force Survey.
Note: "Southern regions" refers to Guelmin-Oued Noun and part of Laayoune-Sakia El Hamra. The shares displayed in most regions do not add up to 100 because certain extremely small sectors are not included.

Methodology, Data, and Constraints

Here, we use a Bartik (1991) approach (box 3.1) to estimate how more exports per worker (trade exposure index) affects informality and FLFP rates at the province level (as discussed in detail in chapter 1, annex 1A). This "shift-share" approach looks at industry-level shocks and effects on labor markets exposed to them to construct an aggregate shock regional labor force exposure index. Our assumption is that shares are not random, while the shifters are, after proper instrumentation, as good as random with respect to local labor markets.

Our Bartik analysis draws on labor market indicators from the Morocco Labor Force Survey (LFS) and on trade flows from the United Nations (UN) Comtrade database. The LFS, a nationally representative survey conducted by Morocco's Higher Planning Commission, includes detailed information on the active population's main demographic and professional characteristics, enabling the study of Moroccan labor market trends.[10] It provides employment, formality, and participation data from 2000 to 2018.

MAP 3.1

Informality Rates, by Region, Morocco, 2018

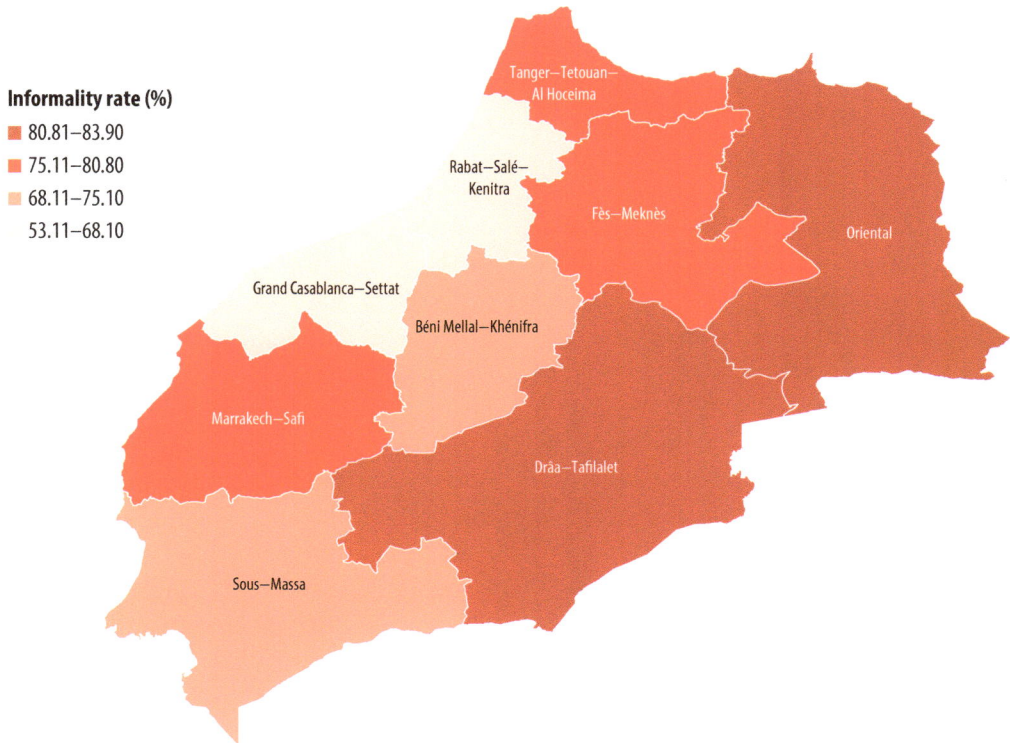

Informality rate (%)
- 80.81–83.90
- 75.11–80.80
- 68.11–75.10
- 53.11–68.10

Tanger–Tetouan–Al Hoceima

Rabat–Salé–Kenitra

Fès–Meknès

Oriental

Grand Casablanca–Settat

Béni Mellal–Khénifra

Marrakech–Safi

Drâa–Tafilalet

Sous–Massa

Source: Estimates based on the 2018 Morocco Labor Force Survey.
Note: The informality rate is the percentage of workers without access to social security. The darker the color, the higher the informality rate.

However, the lack of homogeneous regional variables over time constrains some estimates. Only 10 regions can be homogenized across the 2000–18 period—a low number of observations for econometric analysis. Given that the LFS's "province" variable for the period between 2000 and 2009 contains 60 consistent observations, our analysis relies on these (excluding 2009 because of postcrisis shocks from the Global Financial Crisis). The LFS also lacks industry codes for 2015–17 and has a different classification system in 2018. Annual bilateral trade flows from 2000 to 2018 come from the UN Comtrade database. We focus on exports from Morocco or analogous world imports from Morocco—and then merge these trade data with labor market indicators, using the concordance between International Standard Industrial Classification of All Economic Activities (ISIC) Revision 3.1 (from the LFS) and the Harmonized System trade classification code HS0 (1988/92) (used by UN Comtrade).

BOX 3.1

Empirical Estimation

We estimate the following equation:

$$y_{t+n}^d - y_t^d = \beta_0 + \beta_1 x_{t,t+n}^d + X_c'\beta_c + \epsilon_d, \quad \text{(B3.1.1)}$$

where

$y_{t+n}^d - y_t^d$ is the change in the dependent variable (informality and female labor force participation rates);

$x_{t,t+n}^d$ is the change in the export exposure index (change in exports from Morocco to the Organisation of Economic Co-operation and Development [OECD] weighted by sectoral employment); and

X_c refers to control variables (y_t^d to control for trends).

For the instrument, we estimate

$$x_{t,t+n}^d = \pi_0 + \pi_1 z_{t,t+n}^d + X_c'\pi_c + e_d, \quad \text{(B3.1.2)}$$

where $z_{t,t+n}^d$ refers to predicted values from a time-series regression of Morocco's exports to the OECD on the OECD gross domestic product by industry, as a proxy for Moroccan exports to the OECD solely explained by external aggregate demand.

We chose the instrument using the following assumption (Artuc et al. 2019): local market conditions in a district of Morocco do not affect total OECD imports from other countries (excluding Morocco). Thus, if exports of a given district in Morocco show a correlation to total OECD imports, we attribute it to a shock originating from OECD countries—which account for more than 75 percent of Moroccan exports—rather than to a shock from the given district.

Analysis

Our results show both pluses and minuses for the Moroccan local labor markets.

On the plus side, higher exports per worker decreases informality. The good news is that increasing exports reduced informality rates from 2000 to 2004, a correlation that dissipates somewhat over the 2000–08 period. For instance, an increase of US$100 in exports per worker led to decreases of 0.9 percentage points in informality in the first period (2000–04) and 0.6 percentage points in the second period (2000–08) in provinces with higher exposure to trade. These results are statistically significant and apply for all types of workers (table 3.2).

On the minus side, higher exports per worker lowers the FLFP rate. Our results show that the same increase of US$100 in exports per worker reduces FLFP by 0.32 percentage points from 2000 to 2004 and by 0.27 percentage points in 2000–08 in provinces more exposed to trade (table 3.3). Although this finding is unexpected given the standard belief that trade promotes FLFP, it is consistent with trade and labor market

TABLE 3.2

Estimated Effect on the Labor Informality Rate of a US$100 Increase in Exports per Worker in Morocco

Type of worker		Exports	
		2000–2004	2000–2008
All	Coefficient	−0.009**	−0.006**
	t-statistic	(−2.16)	(−2.31)
	N	60	60
Males	Coefficient	−0.007**	−0.005***
	t-statistic	(−2.05)	(−2.90)
	N	60	60
Females	Coefficient	−0.016**	−0.007
	t-statistic	(−2.14)	(−1.46)
	N	59	58
Low skill	Coefficient	−0.010***	−0.005***
	t-statistic	(−2.59)	(−2602)
	N	60	60
High skill	Coefficient	−0.010	−0.007***
	t-statistic	(−1.60)	(−3.49)
	N	45	45
Young	Coefficient	−0.014***	−0.006***
	t-statistic	(−2.86)	(−2.62)
	N	60	59
Old	Coefficient	−0.006	−0.005**
	t-statistic	(−1.44)	(−2.07)
	N	60	60
Rural	Coefficient	−0.005	−0.003**
	t-statistic	(−1.48)	(−2.39)
	N	53	53
Urban	Coefficient	−0.010***	−0.007***
	t-statistic	(−3.48)	(−2.90)
	N	58	58

Source: World Bank based on data from United Nations Comtrade database and Morocco Labor Force Surveys.
Note: "Low skill" refers to primary or less education and "high skill" to secondary or above. "Young" refers to ages 35 or younger, and "old" to ages above 35. Stars indicate the degree of confidence in the accuracy of the result, with more stars indicating greater confidence.
***$p < 0.01$ **$p < 0.05$ *$p < 0.10$.

patterns of decreasing FLFP due to the export-led specialization of capital- and male-labor-intensive industries in Morocco.

In sum, the increase in trade due to liberalization in recent decades has had both positive and negative effects on local labor market outcomes in Morocco. Although an increase in exports per worker

TABLE 3.3

Estimated Effect on the FLFP Rate of a US$100 Increase in Exports per Worker in Morocco

Type of worker		Exports	
		2000–2004	2000–2008
All	Coefficient	−0.0032*	−0.0027***
	t-statistic	(−1.91)	(−2.90)
	N	60	60
Low skill	Coefficient	−0.0032*	−0.0027***
	t-statistic	(−1.88)	(−2.88)
	N	60	60
High skill	Coefficient	−0.0031**	−0.0017**
	t-statistic	(−2.11)	(−2.66)
	N	57	56
Young	Coefficient	−0.0033*	−0.0027***
	t-statistic	(−1.87)	(−2.83)
	N	60	60
Old	Coefficient	−0.0031**	−0.0027***
	t-statistic	(−1.97)	(−3.01)
	N	60	60
Rural	Coefficient	−0.0038	−0.0020
	t-statistic	(−0.74)	(−1.42)
	N	53	53
Urban	Coefficient	−0.0025	−0.0019***
	t-statistic	(−1.63)	(−2.75)
	N	58	58

Source: World Bank based on data from United Nations Comtrade database and Morocco Labor Force Surveys.
Note: "Low skill" refers to primary or less education and "high skill" to secondary or above. "Young" refers to ages 35 or younger, and "old" to ages above 35. Stars indicate the degree of confidence in the accuracy of the result, with more stars indicating greater confidence. FLFP = female labor participation rate.
***$p < 0.01$ **$p < 0.05$ *$p < 0.10$.

increases formalization (as expected), it does not translate into an improvement in the FLFP rate, owing to a combination of local and external conditions. These findings, despite being at odds with trade theory, reflect Morocco's key trade and labor market trends.

The Role of Firms

Could the role of firms in Morocco's local labor markets help to explain this rather unexpected outcome—that higher exports reduce informality but actually worsen the FLFP rate? Here, we turn to microeconomic firm data to analyze the relationship between exports and employment. One possibility is that it depends on the differences among firms, given that simple models of firm-level heterogeneity and exports suggest that changes in employment are concentrated along the extensive margin (new firms entering export markets). We therefore draw upon rich firm-level data to complement the previous Bartik analysis.

At the firm level, there are two ways to analyze the relationship between exports and jobs:

- *Cross section analysis*, which means comparing firms at one point in time. The model predicts that being an exporter is associated with higher firm-level productivity, a higher price of exported goods, and a fixed cost of exporting. It shows that exporters tend to be larger (in terms of employment and sales) and that the larger firms tend to export more.

- *Time series analysis*, which means comparing the same firm over time. The model suggests that if the price of an exported good rises, existing exporters will expand somewhat, but the largest employment gains will come from firms entering the export market.

Although it might seem intuitive that expanding exports requires more workers, firms might just export goods that they used to sell to the domestic market and not increase production. Or if they have excess capacity, they might produce more by, say, expanding hours instead of employment. Understanding how firms adjust employment when exports increase is critical for understanding the relationship between trade policy and labor market outcomes. A further wrinkle is how to adjust employment in a way that also boosts FLFP (box 3.2).

To evaluate the link between exports and employment at the firm level, we use the World Bank Enterprise Surveys, which are representative samples of an economy's private sector firms based on interviews with business owners and top managers about topics like trade and jobs. In Morocco, the Enterprise Surveys conducted in 2007, 2013, and 2019[11] covered firms in the manufacturing, construction, motor vehicle sales and repair, wholesale, retail, hotels and restaurants, storage, transportation, communications, and information technology sectors. They include only firms with more than five workers and a minimum of 1 percent of private ownership.[12]

The Enterprise Surveys reflect significant firm-level differences. Of the 1,096 Moroccan firms interviewed in 2019, 37 percent (405 firms) were small, 35 percent (384 firms) were medium, and 28 percent (307 firms) were large.[13] By sector, 11 percent operated in the food sector, 16 percent in garments, 16 percent in other manufacturing,

BOX 3.2

Finding a Way to Boost Both Exports and FLFP

For exports to increase female labor force participation (FLFP), female-labor-intensive ("female-intensive") firms need to either enter the export market or increase production. Indeed, two-sector trade models with heterogeneous firms and differences in factor intensity across sectors (Bernard, Redding, and Schott 2011) predict that rising export demand in one sector will increase the demand for the workers intensively employed in that sector throughout the economy.

Although most manufacturing exports tend to be male-labor-intensive ("male-intensive"), exports from female-intensive sectors could increase the demand for women and hence expand female employment.

However, in this case, they must also increase the demand for women *more* than the demand for men—which implies that exports of female-intensive goods will only increase FLFP if rising exports represent an increase in labor demand and are a significant fraction of economic activity.

The problem is that, in Morocco, male-intensive exports have increased relative to female-intensive exports owing to a combination of internal and external factors—such as higher international prices for capital-intensive goods, incentives to promote capital-intensive industries, and rising competition in the (female-intensive) apparel sector.

17 percent in retail, and 41 percent in other services. By age, the surveyed firms present a right-skewed distribution. In fact, 63 percent of firms have been in operation for less than 20 years. As for trade, only 20 percent of firms export more than 10 percent of their sales directly, but this is higher than the Middle East and North Africa average (excluding high-income countries) of 17 percent. However, the proportion of firms that use foreign inputs for production is 42 percent, considerably lower than region's average of 64 percent.

Characteristics of Exporters

Our results highlight several major characteristics of Moroccan exporting firms.

Exporters are typically the largest firms. This result is not novel: in many countries, exporting firms tend to be larger, more productive, and more skill- and capital-intensive than those that sell only to the domestic market (Bernard, Redding, and Schott 2011). Morocco is no exception. Larger firms in Morocco are more likely to export than medium and smaller firms (figure 3.9). That the Enterprise Surveys show a similar pattern in Morocco suggests the surveys are reliable.

FIGURE 3.9

Kernel Density Functions of Employment among Moroccan Exporting and Nonexporting Firms, 2013 and 2019

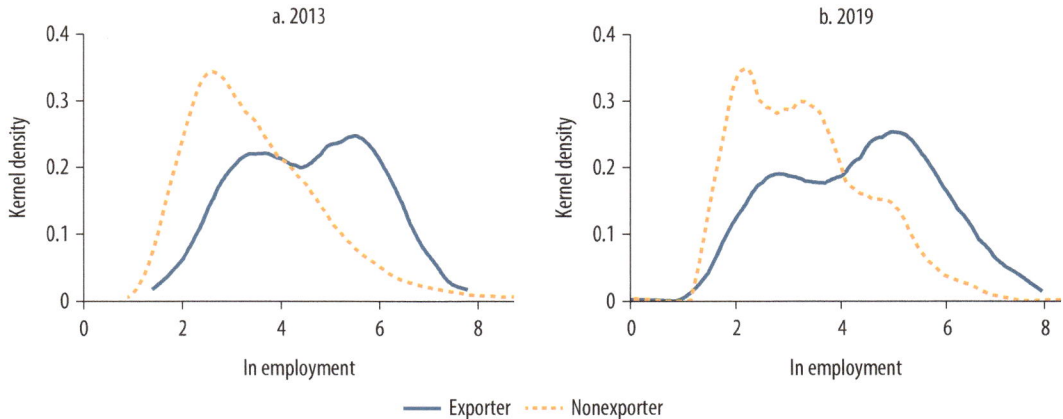

Source: World Bank based on World Bank Enterprise Survey data.
Note: "Exporters" are those firms that export at least 10 percent of their sales directly. All other firms are classified as "nonexporters." The numbers on the x-axis show the natural logarithm (ln) of employment.

Export sales are higher among larger firms. There is a positive correlation between total employment and the amount of export sales, assuming all other variables are held constant (figure 3.10). Larger firms could export more because of productivity differences, scale economies, or other factors affecting employment.

Exporting firms tend to be male-intensive. The number of exporting firms is lower among female-labor-intensive ("female-intensive") firms than male-labor-intensive ("male-intensive") ones (figure 3.11). Moreover, the average export sales amount is considerably higher among male-intensive firms than female-intensive firms (defined as those with a higher share of female workers than the average of all Moroccan firms).

Male-intensive firms, on average, also employ more total workers than female-intensive firms. This fact is also evident from the employment distributions of male- and female-intensive firms. In figure 3.12, exporters (dashed lines) are generally on the left side of the distribution of female-intensive firms (panel a), showing that these firms employ fewer workers. Meanwhile, exporters have a more similar distribution among male-intensive firms (panel b).

The female labor share is higher, and rising, in the agriculture and services sectors. The share of total female workers is highest in retail (45.7 percent) and in food, beverages, and agricultural products (34.4 percent). In addition, the share of female workers rose in both "other services" and agriculture between 2013 and 2019, during which

FIGURE 3.10

Relationship between Export Sales and Size of Exporting Firms, Morocco, 2019

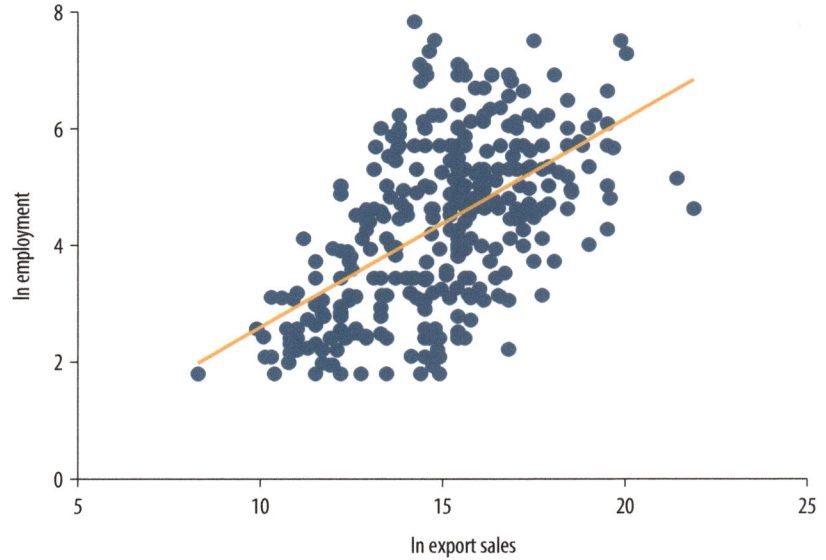

Source: World Bank based on World Bank Enterprise Survey data.
Note: "Exporting firms" are those that export (directly or indirectly) at least 10 percent of sales. Values along the y-axis show the natural logarithm (ln) of employment, and those along the x-axis the ln of export sales. The diagonal line designates the linear relationship between both.

FIGURE 3.11

Employment and Export Indicators in Female-Intensive and Male-Intensive Firms, Morocco, 2019

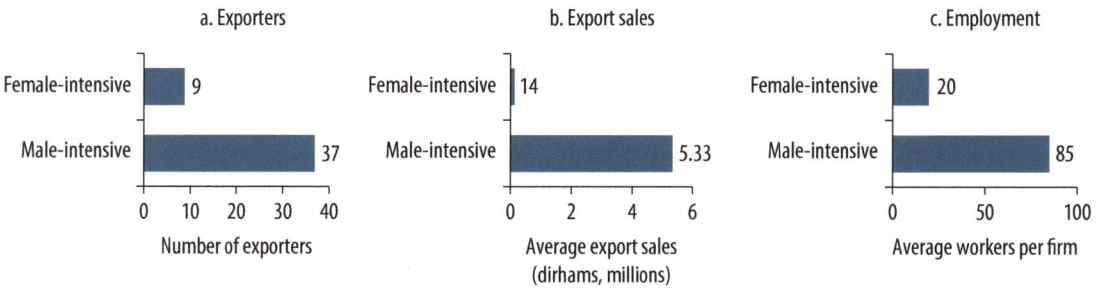

Source: World Bank based on World Bank Enterprise Survey data.
Note: The figure shows results from "exporters"—firms that export (directly or indirectly) at least 10 percent of sales. "Female-intensive firms" are those with a higher share of female workers than the average among all Moroccan firms.

FIGURE 3.12

Employment Kernel Density Functions of Moroccan Firms, by Female and Male Labor Intensity, 2019

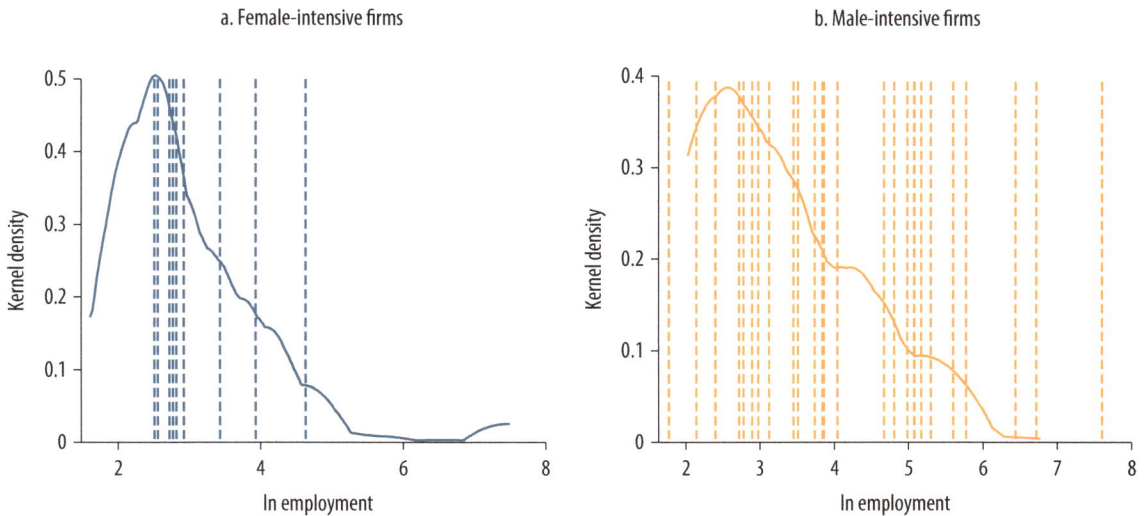

a. Female-intensive firms

b. Male-intensive firms

Source: World Bank based on World Bank Enterprise Survey data.
Note: Values along the x-axis show the natural logarithm (ln) of employment. Solid lines represent the entire sample of female- or male-intensive firms—defined as those whose shares of female and male workers, respectively, are higher than the average of all Moroccan firms. Each dashed line represents an exporter—that is, a firm that exports (directly or indirectly) at least 10 percent of sales.

the share in "other manufacturing" remained steady (table 3.4). While the female labor share is much higher among exporting firms in other manufacturing (43.6 percent) and retail industries (35.8 percent), it is significantly higher among nonexporting firms in the agriculture sector (37.8 percent) (table 3.5).

Analysis of Firm Dynamics

Firm dynamics reflect changes within existing exporters (the "intensive" margin) and changes in the number of exports (the "extensive" margin). Our study highlights a few key trends.

Entries and exits of exporting firms may significantly affect employment. A static number of exporters from 2013 to 2019 does not consider that some firms began exporting while others stopped exporting. This is more relevant in the Moroccan context, where an external shock (the combination of a rise in capital-intensive prices, strong Chinese competition in textile industries, and the end of the Multifiber Arrangement) and an internal shock (public policies that promoted capital-intensive industries) might have motivated important changes

TABLE 3.4

Average Share of Female Workers in Selected Moroccan Industries, 2013 and 2019

Industry panel data	2013	2019
Food, beverages, and agricultural products (% female workers)	32.5	34.4
Textiles and garments (% female workers)	13.3	—
Other manufacturing (% female workers)	22.2	22.7
Retail (% female workers)	28.7	45.7
Other services (% female workers)	21.7	29.9

Source: World Bank based on World Bank Enterprise Survey data.
Note: Included firms are those with data in both 2013 and 2019. — = not available for the panel database.

TABLE 3.5

Average Share of Female Workers in Selected Moroccan Industries, by Exporting and Nonexporting Firms, 2019

Industry cross-sectional data	Exporters	Nonexporters
Food, beverages, and agricultural products (% female workers)	31.1	37.8
Textiles and garments (% female workers)	33.7	34.2
Other manufacturing (% female workers)	43.6	23.5
Retail (% female workers)	35.8	28.6
Other services (% female workers)	28.5	27.0

Source: World Bank based on World Bank Enterprise Survey data.
Note: "Exporters" are firms that export (directly or indirectly) at least 10 percent of sales.

in the structure of the market at a firm level. One would expect lower employment if the economy shifted to less labor-intensive sectors.

The number of exporting firms increased, but the average workers per firm decreased. We would expect this result from a shift to capital-intensive industries. Although the share of total exporting firms increased in Morocco from 17 percent in 2013 to 35 percent in 2019, the average number of workers employed by all firms decreased from 70 to 62 (table 3.6). Moreover, average export sales fell in real terms because, as predicted, smaller firms entered the export market. In addition, the average annual employment growth rate slowed from 2013 to 2019, consistent with a shift from labor- to capital-intensive sectors.

Lower export sales and average employment reflects the patterns of female-intensive firms. From 2013 to 2019, the share of exporters increased among both male-intensive and female-intensive firms. But whereas average export sales increased among the male-intensive firms, average export sales and employment both fell significantly among the female-intensive firms—a result consistent with smaller firms entering the export market (table 3.7).

TABLE 3.6

Sales and Employment Indicators among Exporters in Morocco, 2013 and 2019

Variable (panel data)	2013	2019
Exporters (% of total firms)[a]	17	35
Real export sales (DH, millions, per firm)	3.86	3.64
Employment (average workers per firm)	70	62
Employment growth (average annual %)[b]	5.60	3.06

Source: World Bank based on World Bank Enterprise Survey data.
Note: DH = dirhams.
a. "Exporters" are firms that export (directly or indirectly) at least 10 percent of sales.
b. "Employment growth" refers to average annual growth of permanent employment in the past three fiscal years.

TABLE 3.7

Sales and Employment Indicators among Exporters in Morocco, by Male or Female Labor Intensity, 2013 and 2019

Variable (panel data)	Male-intensive firms		Female-intensive firms	
	2013	2019	2013	2019
Exporters (number of firms)[a]	17	29	2	7
Real export sales (DH, millions, per firm)	4.26	5.33	2.25	0.14
Employment (average workers per firm)	83	85	24	20
Employment growth (annual %)[b]	4.7	2.2	8.9	4.6

Source: World Bank based on World Bank Enterprise Survey data.
Note: Firms are either "male-intensive" or "female-intensive" if their shares of male and female workers, respectively, are higher than the average of all Moroccan firms. DH = dirhams.
a. "Exporters" are those firms that export (directly or indirectly) at least 10 percent of sales.
b. "Employment growth" refers to average annual growth of permanent employment in the past three fiscal years.

The reduction in average employment can also be seen in table 3.8, which shows that average employment per firm is lower among new exporters than those existing in 2013. This shows that the exporting firms on average employ fewer workers in 2019 than in 2013 and that this decrease has been more evident for female-intensive than for male-intensive exporters.

Lower employment, on average, reflects the trend of exporters rather than nonexporters. From 2013 to 2019, average employment among exporters dropped, in contrast to a slight increase among non-exporters (figure 3.13). Moreover, the distribution of nonexporter firms has remained almost the same, while the distribution of exporters has shifted to the left.

Average employment is higher for firms that have "always" exported than for new exporters. Almost 60 percent of the surveyed

TABLE 3.8

Average Employees of New Moroccan Exporters in 2019 versus Existing Exporters in 2013, by Male or Female Labor Intensity

Gender intensity (panel data)	Average employees of exporters (2013)	Average employees of new exporters (2019)
Male-intensive firms	163.8	51.5
Female-intensive firms	50.9	6.8

Source: World Bank based on World Bank Enterprise Survey data.
Note: "Exporters" are firms that export (directly or indirectly) at least 10 percent of sales. "New exporters" are those that entered the category in 2017–19. Firms are either "male-intensive" or "female-intensive" if their shares of male and female workers, respectively, are higher than the average of all Moroccan firms.

FIGURE 3.13

Employment Kernel Density Functions of Moroccan Exporters and Nonexporters, 2013 and 2019

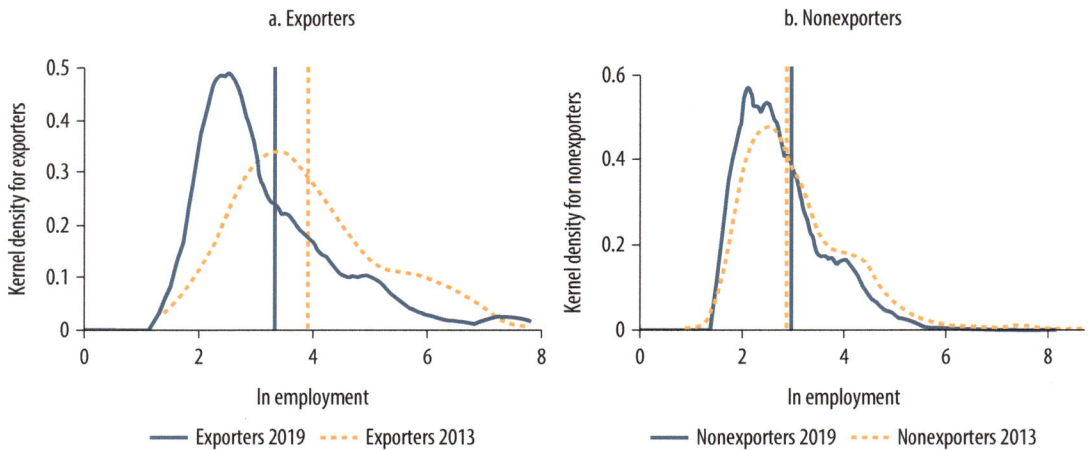

Source: World Bank based on World Bank Enterprise Survey data.
Note: "Exporters" are firms that export (directly or indirectly) at least 10 percent of sales. Values along the x-axis show the natural logarithm (ln) of employment. Vertical blue (solid) and orange (dashed) lines designate the mean of the distribution in 2019 and 2013, respectively.

firms never exported either directly or indirectly. Among those that do export, however, most are "new exporters." The average volume of exports and the average number of employees are considerably higher for firms that had "always" exported than for "new exporters," which is consistent with our model predicting that new exporters will be smaller than existing exporters (see chapter 1, annex 1B, on "Firm-Level Analysis"). In addition, those that stopped exporting had, on average, more employees than those firms that had just entered the market (new exporters), because those that had stopped exporting are likely to be less productive (and smaller) than existing exporters but larger than the new exporters (figure 3.14).

FIGURE 3.14

Employment Kernel Density Functions of Moroccan Firms, by Exporting Status, 2019

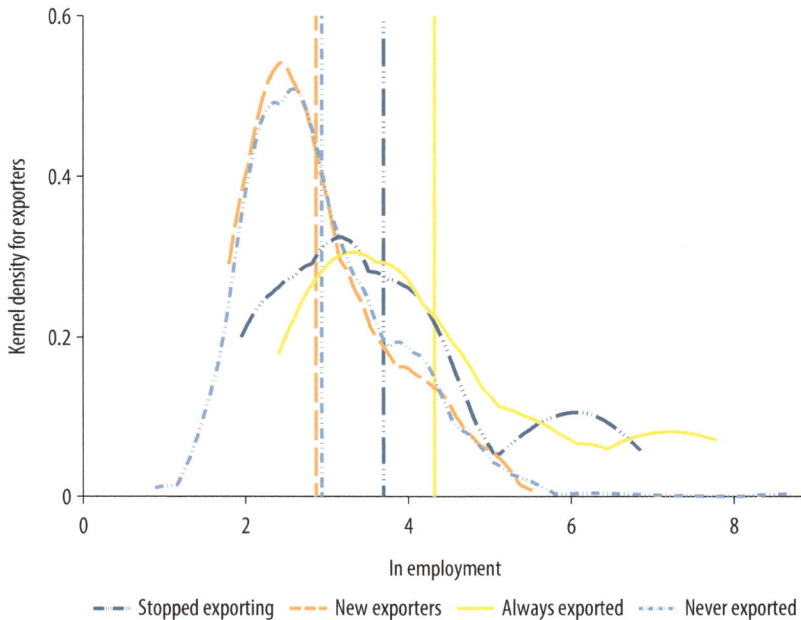

Source: World Bank based on World Bank Enterprise Survey data.
Note: "New exporters" are firms that exported in 2019 but not in 2013. "Always exported" are firms that exported in both 2013 and 2019. "Never exported" are firms that exported in neither 2013 nor 2019. "Stopped exporting" are firms that exported in 2013 but not in 2019. Values along the x-axis show the natural logarithm (ln) of employment. Vertical lines designate the means of the distribution of each respective group.

Conclusion

Morocco's economic policies have promoted a shift from female-, labor-intensive sectors to male-, capital-intensive sectors, thereby reducing the positive effects of trade liberalization on employment. The Bartik analysis indicates that trade liberalization in Morocco reduces informality. Contrary to expectations, it also decreases FLFP. Our analysis of firm-level data confirms these trends.

Employment has decreased on average for exporting firms between 2013 and 2019. This could be because new exporters are typically smaller than those firms that always exported or stopped exporting. Or it could reflect a shift to capital-intensive sectors. Or it could reflect Morocco's simultaneous pursuit of other domestic reforms to promote high-value-added sectors.

However, because these industries were also male- and capital-intensive ones, the shift to these activities reduced job opportunities for women in the exporting sectors. In fact, FLFP increased in sectors like retail and other services, while it decreased in manufacturing (except in the food and textile industries). In addition, average employment decreased more in the female-intensive exporting firms than in the male-intensive ones.

Thus, Morocco's experience offers important lessons for policy makers to consider when promoting capital-intensive sectors in low- and middle-income countries without also supporting female-intensive industries—a tactic that could undercut female employment. A policy recommendation in this case would be to reduce fixed costs for female-intensive firms by lowering barriers or giving incentives. Our study shows that labor-abundant countries might want to provide incentives to labor-intensive industries rather than only supporting capital-intensive ones—especially in industries where females typically perform the labor-intensive jobs. Here, it is important to note that we focus mainly on the labor demand side. Policies related to the supply side should also be weighed to create incentives for females to join the labor force, such as those related to social norms, regulation, and barriers to job mobility.

Annex 3A. Supplemental Figures

FIGURE 3A.1

Informality Rates, by Region, Morocco, 2000–18

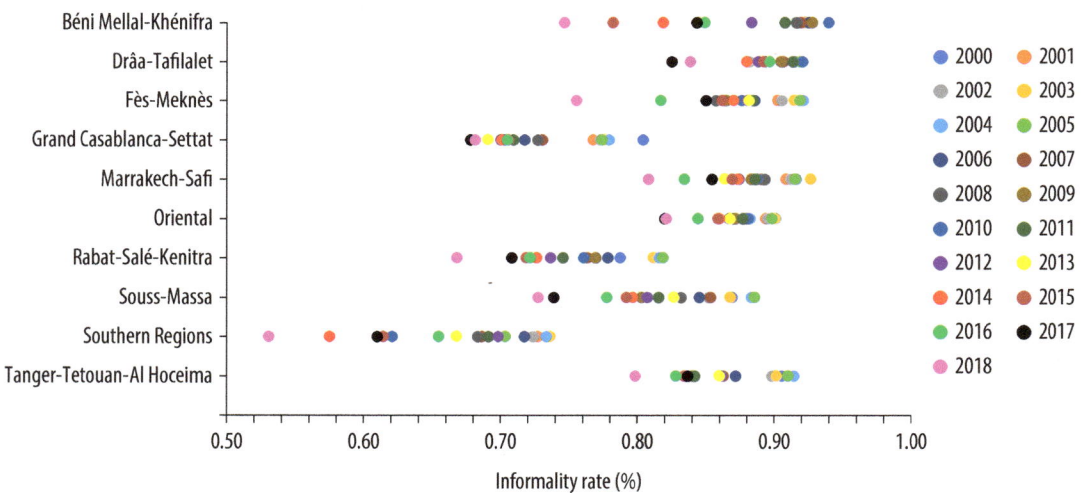

Source: Estimates based on the Morocco Labor Force Surveys, 2000–18.
Note: The "informality" rate is defined as the percentage of workers without access to social security. "Southern regions" refers to Guelmin-Oued Noun and part of Laayoune-Sakia El Hamra.

FIGURE 3A.2

Female Labor Force Participation Rates, by Region, Morocco, 2000–18

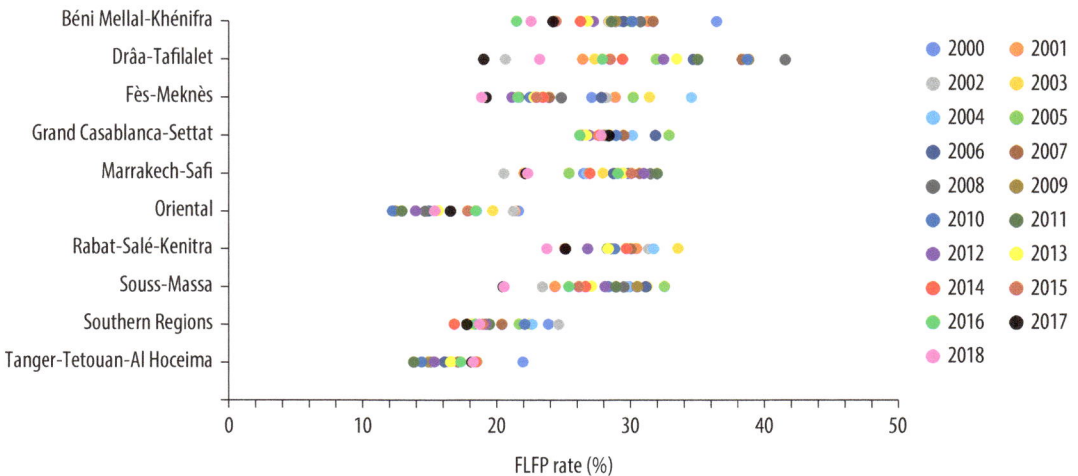

Source: Estimates based on the Morocco Labor Force Surveys, 2000–18.
Note: Female labor force participation (FLFP) is calculated as the active (the employed plus the unemployed who seek work), working-age (ages 15 and older) female population divided by the total female working-age population. The data cover both formal and informal labor. "Southern regions" refers to Guelmin-Oued Noun and part of Laayoune-Sakia El Hamra.

Annex 3B. Extended Firm-Level Analysis

Firm heterogeneity suggests that many factors contribute to exports at the firm level. There is significant variation across firms—both within exporters and those that sell to the domestic market. The model in chapter 1, annex 1B, suggests that this variation can be explained by firm-level productivity differences. Many factors might be correlated with firm-level productivity. To understand the variation across firms, we first estimate the firm's probability of being an exporter conditional on several variables that might be associated with firm-level productivity: the value of assets, technology, global integration, female intensity, innovation, age, and formality. We then estimate the *conditional* relationship (holding these factors constant) between exporter status, export sales, and employment.

The probability of being an exporter is positively correlated with a firm's age; innovation; formality status (being in the formal or informal sector); and global integration (foreign participation, foreign technology use, and use of imported inputs). To measure factors that determine the probability of being an exporter, we apply a probit model. The probit model has a binary dependent variable that takes the value "1" when the firm is an exporter and "0" otherwise. For independent variables, we constructed proxies for several factors commonly mentioned in the literature using the information contained in the World Bank Enterprise Surveys.

In table 3B.1, column 1 presents a model for the probability of being an exporter, considering only the dummies for female intensity, region, and years. We focus specifically on female intensity to establish a benchmark for later analysis. As illustrated previously, the association between female-intensive firms and exports tends to be negative, although not statistically significant. The results from column 2 show that the probability of exporting is higher among firms that have foreign participation in assets and use imported inputs—factors that are reasonably thought to be associated with firm-level productivity. A firm is also more likely

TABLE 3B.1

Probit: Marginal Effect of Extensive Margin

Dependent Variable: Exporter (yes =1)

Variables	(1)	(2)
New products (yes=1)		−0.042
		(−0.14)
Value of machinery[a]		−0.015
		(−0.67)
Cost per worker[a]		0.083
		(0.96)
Firms' age[a]		0.493**
		(2.24)
Foreign ownership (yes=1)		0.866***
		(2.96)
Registered at the beginning (yes=1)		1.749***
		(2.67)
Foreign technology (yes=1)		0.088
		(0.25)
Imported inputs (yes=1)		1.572***
		(5.50)
Female labor intensity (yes=1)	−0.185	0.777***
	(−0.86)	(2.88)
Year dummies	Yes	Yes
Sector dummies	No	Yes
Region dummies	Yes	Yes
Constant	−0.308	−4.408***
	(−1.36)	(−3.01)
Observations	240	236

Note: Robust z-statistics in parentheses. Column 1 includes only dummies for female-intensity, year, sector, and region.
a. Measured in logarithms.
***p < 0.01 **p < 0.05 *p < 0.10.

to export if it started in the formal sector, which might indicate a lower fixed cost of exporting if formality comes with any government support (for example, technical assistance). Results also show that the probability of exporting is higher for older firms, which reflects market experience that might reflect higher productivity owing to both a survival effect and learning by doing. Once controlling for other factors related to global integration, value of assets, foreign technology, and others, being female-labor-intensive becomes positive and statistically significant at a 99 percent confidence level. This might mean that female-labor-intensive firms would be more eager to export if they have similar characteristics in terms of experience, capital, and foreign participation.

Comparing the cross section and time series results shows that existing exporters do not significantly expand employment over time. To contrast the relationship between exporting and employment between the cross section and the time series, we apply two models using the panel dataset (table 3B.2).

The dependent variable in both models is total employment. The independent variables are the same as those we presented previously. Column 1 (the "cross section" results) shows that exporters, older firms, and firms that use foreign technology tend to be larger in the cross section. Female-intensive firms tend to be smaller, holding all else constant. In column 2, we focus on the "time series" firm results, which show the characteristics associated with employment growth over time within firms. Column 2 shows that exporters tend to grow slightly more (in terms of employment) than nonexporters. More capital and lower labor costs are also associated with employment growth, which is not surprising. None of the other explanatory variables seem to be significantly related with employment growth because they explain exporter status in the cross section, but, as the model in chapter 1, annex 1B, shows, the expansion of employment among exporters is limited compared with those entering the export market.

Employment is associated with higher firm export sales. We apply two other models to measure the relationship between the amount of export sales and employment at a firm level. The models in table 3B.3 are similar to table 3B.2 but include real export sales instead of the exporter dummy. As we would expect, results show a positive correlation between export sales and employment given that firms that export the most are in general the largest. The relationship of export sales to total employment is weaker than the one presented in table 3B.2, which is consistent with the model presented in chapter 1, annex 1B, in the sense that the variation among exporters (shown in column 1 of table 3B.3) is smaller than the comparison between exporters and nonexporters (shown in column 1 of table 3B.2).

TABLE 3B.2

Estimated Results of Employment and Export Status

Dependent Variable: Total Employment[a]

Variables	(1) Cross section	(2) Time series
Exporter (yes=1)	1.026**	0.222*
	(2.30)	(1.66)
Value of machinery[a]	0.045	0.040***
	(1.43)	(3.16)
Cost per worker[a]	−0.029	−0.084**
	(−0.25)	(−2.14)
Firms' age[a]	0.567**	−0.135
	(2.28)	(−1.36)
Foreign ownership (yes=1)	0.232	0.192
	(0.52)	(1.13)
Registered at the beginning (yes=1)	−0.061	−0.086
	(−0.10)	(−0.44)
Foreign technology (yes=1)	0.998**	0.025
	(2.37)	(0.13)
Imported inputs (yes=1)	−0.108	−0.210
	(−0.25)	(−1.27)
Female intensity (yes=1)	−1.067***	0.037
	(−2.68)	(0.36)
Constant	1.127	4.886***
	(0.72)	(8.34)
Year dummies	No	Yes
Region dummies	Yes	No
Sector dummies	Yes	No
Observations	252	252
R-squared	0.480	0.148
Number of panelid	126	126

Note: t-statistics in parentheses.
a. Measured in logarithms.
***$p < 0.01$ **$p < 0.05$ *$p < 0.10$.

Column 2 shows that exporters have a very limited employment response to increases in exports, which is also consistent with the model presented in chapter 1, annex 1B. As in table 3B.2, the other explanatory variables that are reasonably thought to represent firm-level technology are correlated with exports in the cross section but not in the time series results, because technology determines export status more than how exporters will adjust employment in response to rising exports.

TABLE 3B.3

Estimated Results of Employment and Export Sales

Dependent Variable: Total Employment[a]

Variables	(1) Cross section	(2) Time series
Export sales[a]	0.083***	0.017*
	(3.15)	(1.87)
Value of machinery[a]	0.043	0.040***
	(1.40)	(3.18)
Cost per worker[a]	−0.036	−0.088**
	(−0.32)	(−2.19)
Firms' age[a]	0.502**	−0.133
	(2.04)	(−1.36)
Foreign ownership (yes=1)	0.129	0.181
	(0.29)	(1.07)
Registered at the beginning (yes=1)	−0.021	−0.096
	(−0.04)	(−0.50)
Foreign technology (yes=1)	0.896**	0.023
	(2.16)	(0.12)
Imported inputs (yes=1)	−0.190	−0.214
	(−0.46)	(−1.30)
Female intensity (yes=1)	−1.057***	0.034
	(−2.74)	(0.33)
Constant		−0.015
		(−0.16)
Year dummies	No	Yes
Region dummies	Yes	No
Sector dummies	Yes	No
Observations	(0.87)	(8.38)
R-squared		
Number of panelid	252	252

Note: t-statistics in parentheses.
a. Measured in logarithms.
***$p < 0.01$ **$p < 0.05$ *$p < 0.10$.

Annex 3C. Supplemental Firm-Level Results

To complement the understanding of the link between exports and employment in Morocco from a dynamic perspective, we estimated several models for new exporters. First, we estimate the firm's probability of becoming an exporter, conditional on the same variables as before. Second, we evaluate the impact of becoming an exporter on employment. Finally, we include a model to evaluate whether the change in employment from 2013 to 2019 was associated with the change in exports.

Probability of Becoming an Exporter

The probability of a firm becoming an exporter is higher when the firm uses imported inputs, which might capture higher technology or a lower (fixed) cost of exporting. Using a probit model and as dependent variable a dummy that takes a value of "1" when the firm is a new exporter and "0" otherwise, we observe that the probability of becoming an exporter is higher among firms that use imported inputs (table 3C.1). Meanwhile, the probability of becoming a new exporter is higher among firms with

TABLE 3C.1

Probability of Becoming an Exporter

Dependent Variable: New Exporter (yes = 1)

Variables	(1) New exporters
New products (yes=1)	−0.586
	(−1.57)
Value of machinery[a]	−0.084***
	(−3.29)
Cost per worker[a]	0.074
	(0.84)
Firms' age[a]	−0.140
	(−0.69)
Foreign ownership (yes=1)	−0.089
	(−0.30)
Registered at the beginning (yes=1)	0.382
	(0.72)
Foreign technology (yes=1)	0.566
	(1.54)
Imported inputs (yes=1)	1.593***
	(5.30)
Female labor intensity (yes=1)	0.152
	(0.56)
Year dummies	Yes
Sector dummies	Yes
Region dummies	Yes
Constant	−0.766
	(−0.55)
Observations	184

Note: Robust z-statistics in parentheses.
a. Measured in logarithms.
***$p < 0.01$ **$p < 0.05$ *$p < 0.10$.

lower value of machinery. This might reflect that new exporters have a lower level of capital than exporters operating in the market for years. This fact could also reflect some of the distortions generated by public incentives for investments, which might not be translating into competitiveness and therefore into exports. Interestingly, very few of the other variables presented previously seem to have a statistically significant correlation with the fact of becoming an exporter.

Impact of Becoming an Exporter on Employment

New exporters and nonexporters tend to be smaller than firms that have always exported. As we can see in the next table, the level of employment is negatively associated with the fact that the firm started exporting. This is because new exporters are smaller than those that have always exported, as suggested by the model in chapter 1, annex 1B. Other factors previously mentioned also played a role, such as the firm's age and foreign technology, while, as in previous models, female intensity is associated with a lower level of employment (table 3C.2).

TABLE 3C.2

Employment and New Exporters

Dependent Variable: Total Employment[a]

Variables	(1)
	Time series
Always exported (yes=1)	0.366
	(1.12)
New exporters (yes=1)	−0.927***
	(−2.87)
Never exported (yes=1)	−0.882***
	(−3.21)
Value of machinery[a]	0.025
	(1.62)
Cost per worker[a]	−0.053
	(−0.97)
Firms' age[a]	0.293*
	(1.94)
Foreign ownership (yes=1)	0.226
	(1.02)
Registered at the beginning (yes=1)	0.091
	(0.33)

(Continued)

Employment and New Exporters *(continued)*

Dependent Variable: Total Employment[a]

Variables	(1) Time series
Foreign technology (yes=1)	0.546**
	(2.53)
Imported inputs (yes=1)	0.077
	(0.38)
Female labor intensity (yes=1)	−0.451**
	(−2.25)
Sector dummies	Yes
Region dummies	Yes
Constant	3.136***
	(3.50)
Observations	252
R-squared	0.424

Note: Robust z-statistics in parentheses.
a. Measured in logarithms.
***p < 0.01 **p < 0.05 *p < 0.10.

Association between Change in Employment and Change in Exports

The change in employment is associated with a higher amount of exporting sales and more capital. When we run the model to the time-differences, the change in employment from 2013 to 2019 seems to be positively associated with the changes in the value of firms' assets and amount of export sales, and negatively correlated with labor costs (table 3C.3). As we would expect, the change in employment is not associated with becoming an exporter.

Estimated Relationship between Changes in Employment and Exports

Dependent Variable: Change in Total Employment[a]

Variables	Export sales	New exporters
Change in export sales[a]	0.014**	
	−2.33	
New exporter (yes=1)		0.137
		(0.92)

(Continued)

TABLE 3C.3

Estimated Relationship between Changes in Employment and Exports *(continued)*

Dependent Variable: Change in Total Employment[a]

Variables	Export sales	New exporters
Change in value of machinery[a]	0.033***	0.032***
	−3.06	(2.98)
Change in cost per worker[a]	−0.084**	−0.073*
	(−2.17)	(−1.93)
Change in female workers share[a]	−0.001	−0.000
	(−0.24)	(−0.09)
Constant	0.027	0.012
	−0.33	(0.13)
Observations	127	127
R-squared	0.123	0.107

Note: Robust t-statistics in parentheses.
a. Measured in logarithms.
***p < 0.01 **p < 0.05 *p < 0.10.

Notes

1. Data on per capita income, life expectancy, and primary school enrollment are from 2021 World Development Indicators (WDI) data.
2. The weighted mean applied tariff is the average of effectively applied rates weighted by the product import shares corresponding to each partner country.
3. Moroccan export data are from the World Bank's World Interactive Trade Solution (WITS) interactive data tool (https://wits.worldbank.org/).
4. All working-age and employed population data are estimated based on Morocco Labor Force Surveys, 2000–18.
5. All unemployment and labor force participation data are estimated based on Morocco Labor Force Surveys, 2000–18.
6. Data on female employment, by sector, are estimated from Morocco Labor Force Surveys, 2000–14.
7. Labor force participation rates are calculated as the active population (the employed plus the unemployed seeking work) divided by the total working-age population.
8. The informality rate and female employment rate are estimated based on the Morocco Labor Force Surveys, 2000–18.
9. The "Southern regions" in this chapter refer to Guelmin-Oued Noun and part of Laayoune-Sakia El Hamra.
10. The "active" population refers to those of working age (ages 15 and older) who are either (a) employed or (b) unemployed but seeking work.
11. For the evolution of the same firms (panel), we analyze the trends from 2013 to 2019.

12. The Enterprise Surveys exclude firms from agriculture, fishing, mining, public utilities, financial intermediation, public administration, education, health, and social work. They exclude businesses with fewer than five workers, informal firms, and firms that are 100 percent state owned.

13. In the Enterprise Surveys, "small" firms employ 5–19 workers; "medium" firms, 20–99 workers; and "large" firms, 100 or more workers.

References

Alfani, Federica, Fabio Clementi, Michele Fabiani, Vasco Molini, and Enzo Valentini. 2020. "Once NEET, Always NEET? A Synthetic Panel Approach to Analyze the Moroccan Labor Market." Policy Research Working Paper 9238, World Bank, Washington, DC.

Artuc, Erhan, Gladys Lopez-Acevedo, Raymond Robertson, and Daniel Samaan. 2019. *Exports to Jobs: Boosting the Gains from Trade in South Asia*. South Asia Development Forum Series. Washington, DC: World Bank. https://doi.org/10.1596/978-1-4648-1248-4.

Bartik, Timothy J. 1991. *Who Benefits from State and Local Economic Development Policies?* Kalamazoo, MI: W. E. Upjohn Institute for Employment Research.

Bernard, Andrew B., Stephen J. Redding, and Peter K. Schott. 2011. "Multiproduct Firms and Trade Liberalization." *Quarterly Journal of Economics* 126 (3): 1271–1318.

Lopez-Acevedo, Gladys, Gordon Betcherman, Ayache Khellaf, and Vasco Molini. 2021. *Morocco's Jobs Landscape: Identifying Constraints to an Inclusive Labor Market*. International Development in Focus Series. Washington, DC: World Bank. https://doi.org/10.1596/978-1-4648-1678-9.

Lopez-Acevedo, Gladys, Florencia Devoto, Matías Morales, and Jaime Roche Rodríguez. 2021. "Trends and Determinants of Female Labor Force Participation in Morocco: An Initial Exploratory Analysis." Policy Research Working Paper 9591, World Bank, Washington, DC.

Lopez-Acevedo, Gladys, and Raymond Robertson. 2012. *Sewing Success? Employment, Wages, and Poverty following the End of the Multi-fibre Arrangement*. Directions in Development Series. Washington, DC: World Bank.

World Bank. 2018. "Kingdom of Morocco Systematic Country Diagnostic: Governing towards Efficiency, Equity, Education and Endurance." Report No. 123653, World Bank, Washington, DC.

CHAPTER 4

Tunisia Case Study: How Gender Segmentation Shapes Local Effects of Trade

Carlos Góes

Key Messages

- Over the past decade, the Tunisian economy has faced both domestic and international economic shocks—ones that have affected, and sometimes reshaped, a domestic labor market characterized by gender imbalances.

- These imbalances take the form of higher female unemployment, lower female labor force participation, and labor markets with a high gender segmentation—with virtually no female workers in some industries and nearly exclusively female workforces in others.

- Following the Arab Spring, positive foreign demand shocks have been concentrated primarily in male-labor-intensive industries— the biggest contributors to export growth.

- Our study shows that a US$1 billion increase in export exposure leads to an average decrease of 6.8 percentage points in the female-to-male employment ratio—that is, a reduction in female employment relative to male employment.

- Policies that reduce gender segmentation in labor markets can promote more gender equity in the present—and indirectly induce more equitable effects in the future whenever economic shocks (like higher exports) affect the local economy.

Introduction

In recent decades, Tunisia has experienced major social, political, and economic changes—with a notable inflection point being the Arab Spring, which began in 2010. In its aftermath, Tunisia reformed many of its legal and political institutions to create a more inclusive, democratic society. But at the same time, the economy stalled owing to a combination of both domestic and global shocks. Between 2012 and 2018, average growth in gross national income was 1.31 percent per year, down from 3.14 percent per year between 1991 and 2010 (figure 4.1, panel a).[1] Similarly, the growth in the value of exports dropped to 1.85 percent per year between 2012 and 2018, down from 5.77 percent per year between 1991 and 2010, stopping a decades-long growth trend (figure 4.1, panel b).

FIGURE 4.1

Trends in Income and Export Growth, Tunisia, 1990–2020

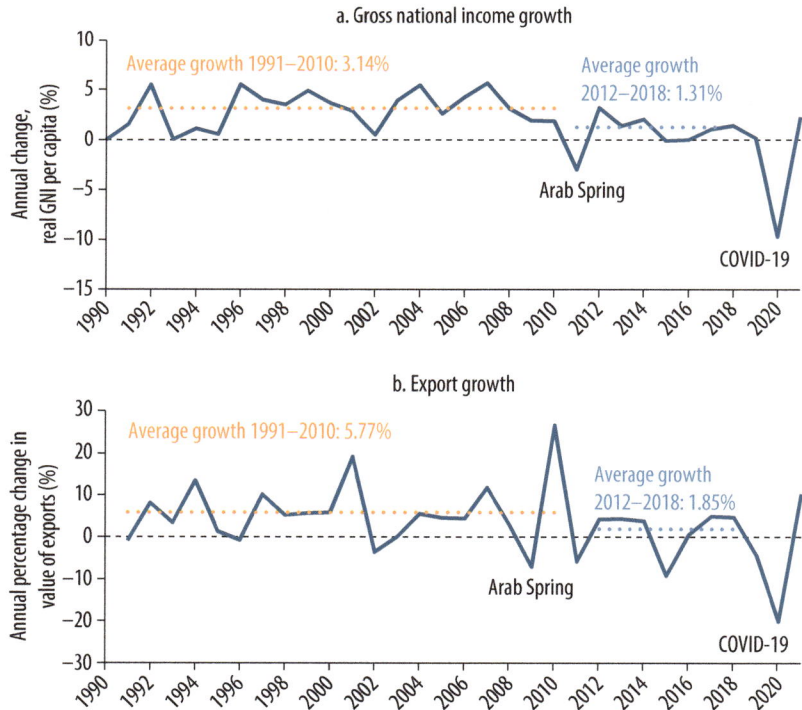

Source: Calculations based on World Development Indicators data.
Note: Dotted lines (orange and blue) designate the annual average growth during their respective periods. Solid lines designate the growth in each particular year. In panel b, the annual percentage change reflects the change in total value (in US$, billions) of exports (both goods and services). GNI = gross national income.

Various sectors have contributed to the decrease in economic activity and external trade. For some of them, such as tourism services, the setback can be more directly traced to the past decade's political unrest. For others, such as oil, mining, and textiles, drivers are more related to other global shifters (like commodity prices and trade diversion). Given that domestic institutions and social norms play a big role in how these shifters affect the local economy, it is vital to understand what occurred in Tunisia's gender-segmented labor markets. For instance, immediately after the Arab Spring, both male and female unemployment increased, but female unemployment, unlike male unemployment, never came back to pre–Arab Spring levels.

Gender inequality in labor markets is a widely discussed phenomenon, both among researchers and the public. Even in countries that rank high in gender equality indicators, female workers tend to earn less than males with the same observable characteristics.[2] This suggests that biases, social norms, or individual preferences create frictions in the labor market that prevent workers from moving across sectors optimally. If large enough, such frictions can lead to substantial market segmentation—whereby male and female workers are more likely performing tasks predetermined as "male" or "female," respectively, than the tasks each individual may be more productive in.

How does trade fit into this segmentation of the labor market? Trade shocks induced by changes in policy or foreign demand alter domestic relative prices (in product and factor markets) and will likely affect employment and wages. Therefore, if the domestic market has a high degree of gender segmentation, it would not be surprising if trade shocks affected males and females differently.

The empirical evidence does suggest that trade reforms correlate with more gender equality, but the mechanisms are almost always context specific. First, in many low- and middle-income countries, trade liberalization induced sectoral shifts toward industries and tasks that are more female labor intensive ("female intensive") in a gender-segmented labor market. Second, stepped-up foreign competition can temporarily displace male workers, reduce household incomes, and induce females to supply labor out of the household—an added worker effect.[3]

These factors highlight that the nature of both the trade shocks and the domestic labor market institutions matter for determining the impact of trade on gender inequality. However, the literature on the impact of increased exports induced by foreign demand shocks on labor market gender inequality is smaller than the one that relates trade liberalization to gender inequality.[4]

This chapter sheds light on the relationship between exports and gender-segmented labor markets by examining the effects of increased foreign demand on local labor markets in Tunisia—which is a good case to study. Tunisia has higher female labor force participation (FLFP) than other Middle East and North Africa countries, underscoring the relevant role that female workers play in Tunisia's domestic labor markets. However, those markets still exhibit a substantial degree of gender segmentation, with some industries having virtually no female workers and others being nearly exclusively female.

This study makes two main contributions: It documents that, in Tunisian industries, foreign demand shocks were more strongly positive in male-dominated industries after the Arab Spring. It also shows that these foreign demand shocks caused a decrease in female employment relative to male employment during this period, which is consistent with some specific theoretical mechanisms.

A Profile of Tunisia's Trade Flows and Labor Markets

Tariffs and Trade Flows

The value of Tunisian exports as a share of its economy was roughly constant between 1990 and 2000, an indication that trade was growing at the same pace as the overall economy. After 2000, Tunisia started liberalizing trade, with average tariffs dropping from 20 percent in 2000 to 5–10 percent in 2015 (figure 4.2, panel a).[5] A major milestone was the European Union–Tunisia Association Agreement (signed in 1995 and entered into force in 1998), which liberalized manufactured products between the two trade partners and set forth a framework for liberalizing agricultural products in the future.

In the immediate aftermath of this policy change, both imports and exports increased as a share of gross domestic product (GDP), suggesting that the country was going through a process of trade deepening (figure 4.2, panel b).[6] However, since 2006, imports have outpaced exports, creating what is turning out to be an increasing trade deficit. The decrease in trade as a share of GDP was stronger during the 2008–09 Global Financial Crisis and after the Arab Spring.

Sectoral Shares of Labor and Exports

Among the key trends in trade flows and labor markets that stand out, the services sector is Tunisia's largest employer, but manufacturing accounts for most of the country's exports. Services accounts for 40 percent of employment, agriculture and manufacturing for 20 percent each, and public administration for 19 percent (figure 4.3).[7] By far, however, it is

FIGURE 4.2

Trends in Tariffs and Trade Flows, Tunisia, 1990–2020

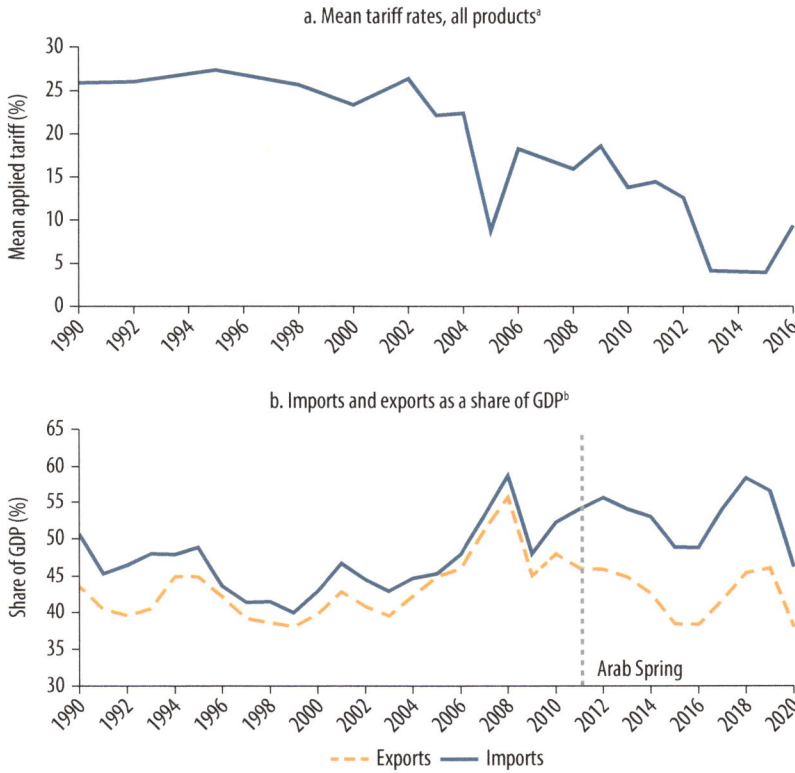

a. Mean tariff rates, all products[a]

b. Imports and exports as a share of GDP[b]

- - - Exports   ——— Imports

Sources: Calculations based on data from the World Bank's World Development Indicators (WDI) Database and World Integrated Trade Solutions (WITS) interactive data tool; United Nations Comtrade merchandise database; and the Balanced Trade in Services (BaTiS) dataset of the World Trade Organization and Organisation for Economic Co-operation and Development.
a. Tariff rates are the applied, weighted mean for all products as a percentage, ad valorem. Trade data for 2017–20 were unavailable at the time of writing.
b. The vertical dotted line designates the beginning of the Arab Spring.

manufacturing that accounts for the largest share of total exports (60 percent), followed by services (26 percent) (figure 4.4).[8] The industries with the largest exports are electrical parts (US$4.2 billion), banking and insurance (US$3.9 billion), textiles and garments (US$3.5 billion), manufacturing not elsewhere classified (US$3.4 billion), and tourism (US$2.3 billion).

As for overall trade, the two largest industries are electrical parts and textiles; combined, they account for about a third of imports and half of exports. Because Tunisia imports a large quantity of inputs for new exports, it appears that one of the country's trade patterns is to insert itself at this point in the global value chain.

FIGURE 4.3

Decomposition of the Tunisian Labor Force, by Industry, 2006–16

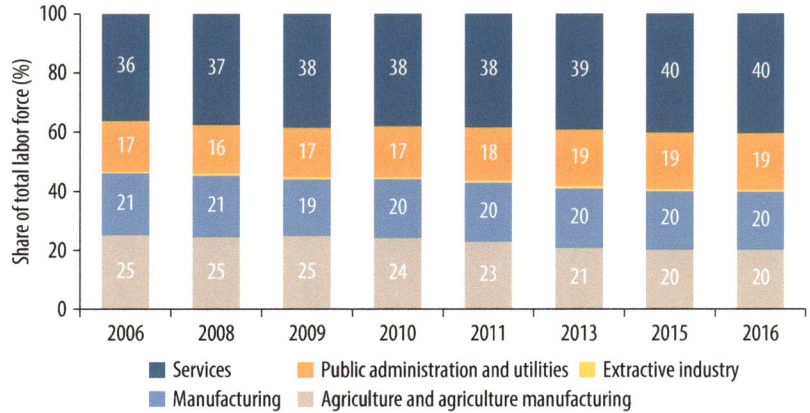

Source: World Bank calculations using data from the National Survey on Population and Employment, National Institute of Statistics, 2006–16.
Note: Percentages do not add up to 100 because the labeling does not reflect certain small sectors.

FIGURE 4.4

Decomposition of Tunisian Exports, by Industry, 2006–16

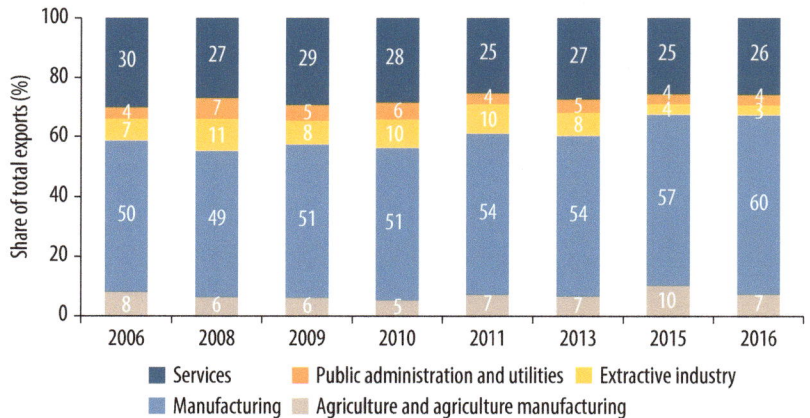

Sources: World Bank calculations using United Nations Comtrade merchandise data and the Balanced Trade in Services (BaTiS) dataset of the World Trade Organization and Organisation for Economic Co-operation and Development.
Note: Percentages in some years do not add up to 100 due to rounding.

Labor Force Participation

Female labor force participation (FLFP) in Tunisia is low relative to most countries in other regions. The country's FLFP as a share of the working-age female population (ages 15–64)—remaining at about 25 percent from 2005 to 2017—is higher than in other Middle East and North Africa countries.[9] However, it is about half of the rate of Organisation for Economic Co-operation and Development (OECD) countries and much lower than other low- and middle-income regions such as Latin America and the Caribbean (figure 4.5).

Men's labor force participation has been much higher than women's during this time. On average, between 2006 and 2016, labor force participation was about 25 percent for women and 69 percent for men, according to data from the Tunisian Labor Force Survey. Overall labor force participation is about 51 percent.

Unemployment remains a big problem in Tunisia, especially for women. From 2006 to 2011, unemployment rose by 6 percentage points, to 18 percent, before dropping to around 15.5 percent in 2016, which is still a high level compared with 2006.[10] Women have consistently had higher unemployment rates than men, but the gender gap in unemployment has increased substantially since the Arab Spring—and female unemployment rates have never returned to pre–Arab Spring levels (figure 4.6).

FIGURE 4.5

Female Labor Force Participation and Comparator Country Groups, Tunisia, 2005–17

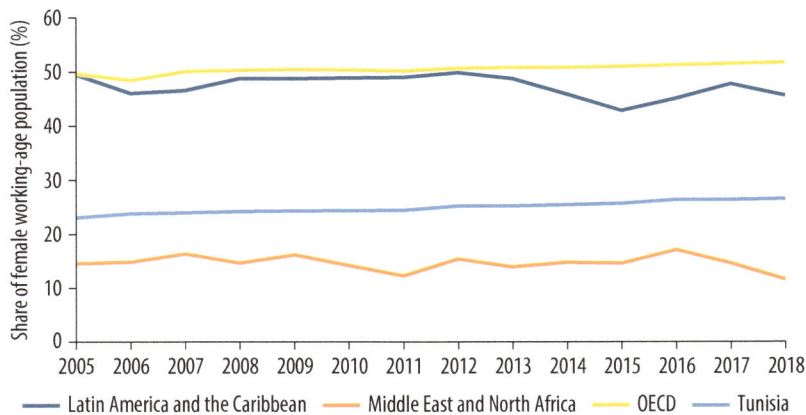

Source: World Bank calculations using International Labour Organization Statistics (ILOSTAT) data.
Note: Female labor force participation is calculated as the total female labor force divided by total female population (ages 15 and above). OECD = Organisation for Economic Co-operation and Development.

FIGURE 4.6

FIGURE 4.6

Unemployment Rates, Total and by Gender, Tunisia, 2006–16

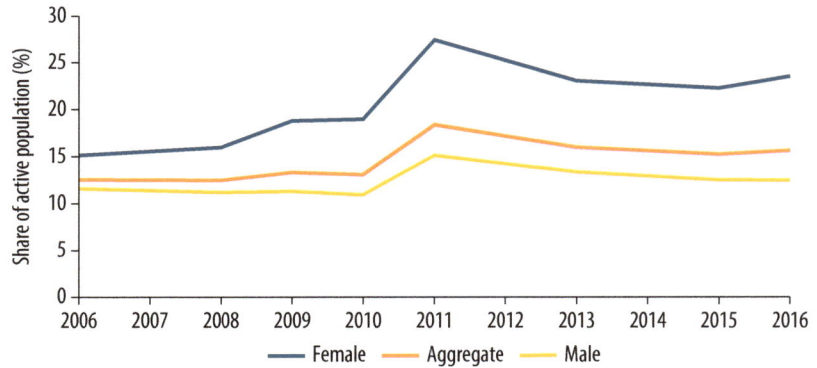

Source: World Bank calculations using data from the National Survey on Population and Employment, National Institute of Statistics.
Note: Unemployment rates are calculated as the shares of the total, male, and female active population who are unemployed. "Active" refers to people who are either working or looking for a job.

Gender Segmentation of Labor

Sectoral employment is very segmented across gender lines, and exports grew less in more-female-intensive sectors. In 2016, the female share of sectoral employment ranged from 2 percent to 73 percent, with the most female-intensive industries being textiles, social and cultural services, education, and banking and insurance (figure 4.7).[11] But World Bank Enterprise Survey data show that the male-intensive industries—not the female-intensive ones—contributed most to export growth over the 2006–16 period (figure 4.8).

High gender segmentation in the labor market suggests the existence of frictions that prevent females from moving across industries. Formal or informal institutions—such as social norms—can advance the perception that males and females are "different kinds of workers" who contribute in different proportions as factors of production in the labor market. One way to rationalize this framework is to assume that social norms dictate that some tasks are exclusively "female tasks" (such as sewing for garments) while other tasks are exclusively "male tasks" (such as operating an oil rig). Thus, if industries use tasks in different proportions, they will consequently be either female- or male-intensive industries.

FIGURE 4.7

Share of Female Employment, by Industry, Tunisia, 2016

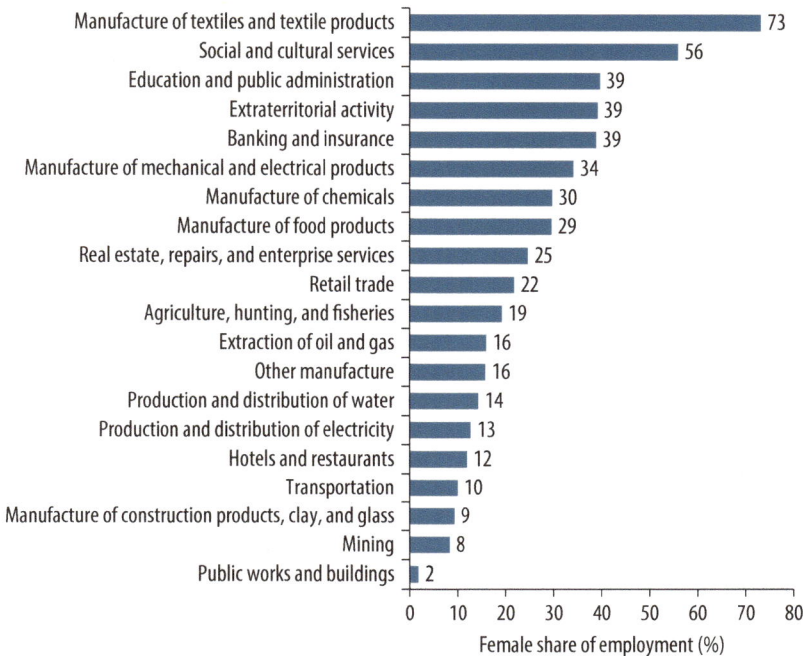

Source: World Bank calculations using data from the 2016 National Survey on Population and Employment, National Institute of Statistics.

Gender segmentation in the labor market implies that households now face a decision regarding whether to substitute male for female labor supply after facing a shock. For instance, if a male worker is laid off in a household, the female worker might want to increase her labor supply outside of the household to supplement the household's budget. Conversely, if wages in male-intensive industries increase, females might be induced to work less outside of the household, since the relative opportunity cost of housework has fallen.

Firm-Level Trends

Larger firms are more likely to export. Exporting firms in Tunisia are larger, more productive, and more skill and capital intensive than those that sell only in domestic markets, consistent with economic theory and empirical evidence from other countries.[12] In 2013 and 2020, exporting firms in Tunisia were larger (figure 4.9). We also observe a positive

FIGURE 4.8

Relationship between Export Growth Contribution and Initial Female Labor Intensity, by Industry, Tunisia

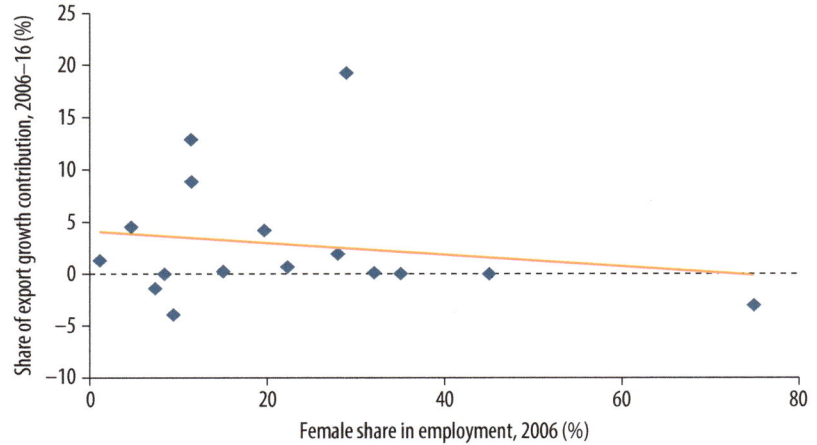

Source: World Bank based on World Bank Enterprise Survey data.
Note: The figure shows selected industries (blue diamonds) in terms of their initial (2006) share of female employment in relation to their eventual (2006–16) contribution to export growth. The slanted solid line designates the linear relationship between both variables. "Export growth contribution" is calculated as the industry's share of the 2006–16 change in total value of exports of goods and services (in constant 2015 US$, billions).

FIGURE 4.9

Employment Kernel Density Functions of Exporters and Nonexporters, Tunisia, 2013 and 2020

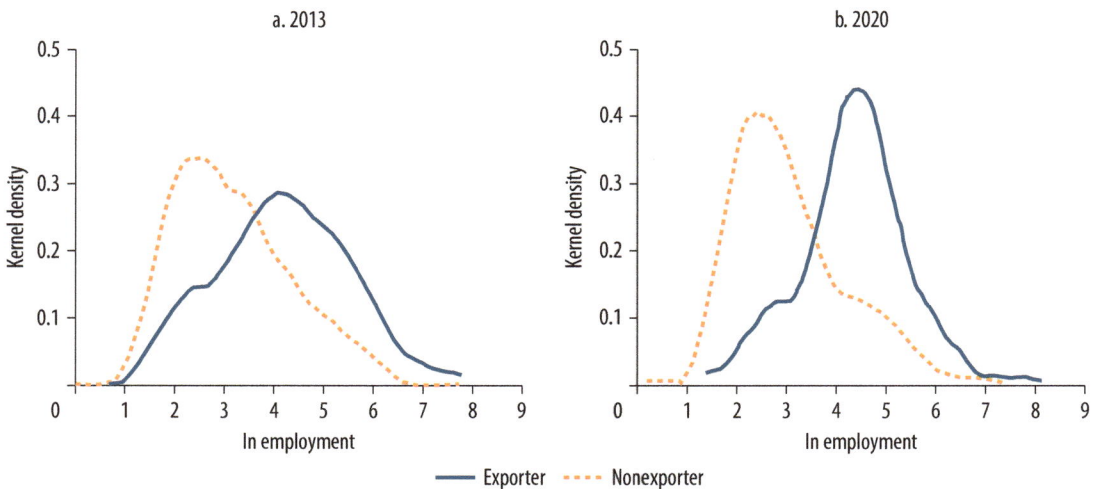

Source: World Bank calculations using World Bank Enterprise Survey data.
Note: ln = natural log.

correlation between export sales and total employment (figure 4.10).[13] These findings are consistent with the results presented in this report's case studies of Morocco (chapter 4) and the Arab Republic of Egypt (chapter 5).

Exporting firms tend to be female intensive, according to calculations from World Bank Enterprise Survey data. On average, Tunisian firms that employ more females as a share of their workforce have a larger share of exports in their total sales (figure 4.11). Firms with a higher-than-average share of female workers have substantially higher nominal exports than those below the average.

At the firm level, exports are likely a key driver of female employment dynamics. Larger (and presumably more productive) firms tend to be those that export more as well as those that hire more females as a share of their workforce. Therefore, on average, female workers are likely to have higher exposure to exports than male workers. This highlights the importance of estimating the effect of foreign demand shocks on female employment in Tunisia.

FIGURE 4.10

Relationship between Rising Export Sales and Employment in Tunisian Firms

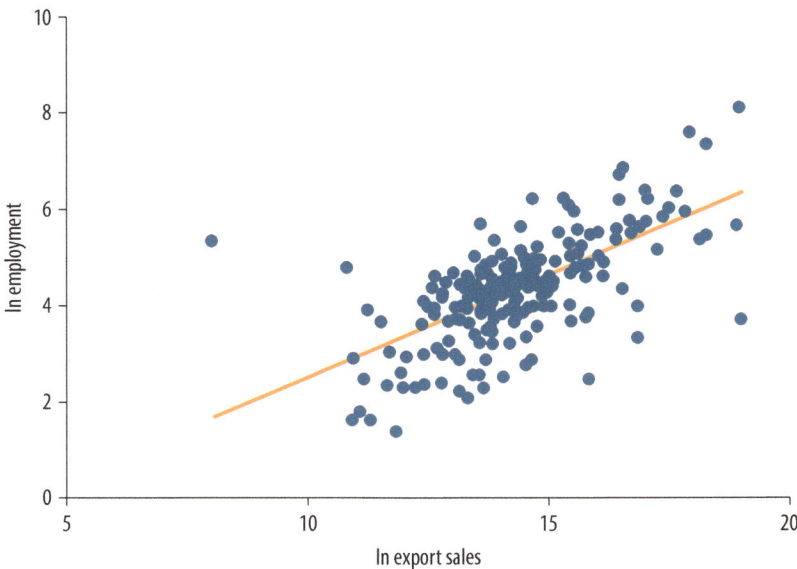

Source: World Bank based on World Bank Enterprise Survey data, 2013–20.
Note: The scatterplot shows the correlation and ordinary least squares (OLS) regression line between log of exports and log employment at the firm level. ln = natural logarithm.

FIGURE 4.11

Relationship between Shares of Exports and Shares of Female Workers in Tunisian Firms, 2020

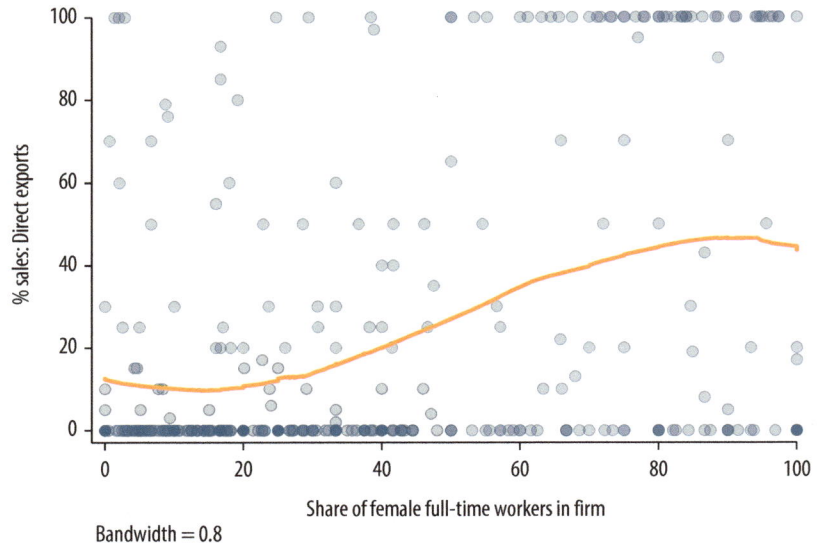

Bandwidth = 0.8

Source: World Bank based on World Bank Enterprise Survey data.
Note: The graph shows the relationship between the share of female workers in Tunisian firms and the percentage of the firms' total sales from direct exports. The red line denotes the predicted values of a local band regression (LOWESS). It shows that, on average, firms with higher female share also tend to have a higher percentage share coming from exports, but this relationship is nonlinear. The darker the circle, the higher the overlap in the number of firms.

Gender-Segmented Labor Markets and Trade

Foreign demand shocks can either increase or decrease female employment relative to male employment. The response depends crucially on (a) the sectoral composition of the demand shock, and (b) the relative market shares of each industry at the destination market. The former determines whether the demand shock translates into a higher demand for goods whose production is either female intensive or male intensive. The latter controls how intensely the demand increases from the foreign to the domestic market.

Intuitively, an increase in foreign demand for female-intensive goods will increase the labor demand for females relative to males. All else being equal, this will increase the relative wages of female workers. In equilibrium, households respond by increasing the female-to-male labor supply ratio up to the point in which the labor market clears. Given the large degree of gender segmentation in the labor market and the variation in industries' levels of exposure to exports, Tunisia is a good country to evaluate how gender-segmented labor markets respond to trade shocks.

Methodology and Data

To test this hypothesis, we leverage the variation in exposure to exports and labor force composition across Tunisian regions. For instance, the North East and Center East regions specialize in manufacturing, whereas the cities in the North East's Grand Tunis area primarily specialize in services. By interacting (a) the labor force composition of each region across different sectors and (b) the growth in exports in each sector, one can calculate each region's degree of export exposure.[14]

Tunisia exhibits a large degree of regional variation in exposure to exports (map 4.1). Exposure to exports is particularly large in those regions that have a large share of their labor force in manufacturing, such as the North East and the Center East regions. By contrast, the South East and South West regions, where large shares of the workforce are mainly employed by the public administration and utilities sectors, have little exposure to exports.

This report relies on multiple data sources. Labor market indicators come from the Tunisian government's National Survey on Population and Employment (ENPE). Among other information, the ENPE reports employment by industry, gender, and province for intermittent years between 2006 and 2016. Trade data come from two sources: merchandise trade data come from the United Nations Comtrade database, while services trade numbers are from the Balanced Trade in Services (BaTiS) dataset of the World Trade Organization and OECD. We then mapped Harmonized System (HS) and Balance of Payments Statistics (BOPS) trade product codes onto International Standard Industrial Classification of All Economic Activities (ISIC) industry codes, using concordance tables from the World Bank's World Integrated Trade Solution (WITS) interactive data tool. Finally, we mapped ISIC industry codes onto the Tunisian Nomenclature of Activities, which is a domestic economic activity classification based on Statistical Classification of Economic Activities in the European Community (NACE) Revision 3.

The main empirical model is to regress the change in regional female-to-labor employment ratios on the change in regional exposure to exports.[15] However, because exports depend partially on domestic human capital and technology use, which can be correlated with characteristics of local labor markets, they are likely not exogenous. For that reason, exposure to exports is instrumented with changes in exposure to foreign demand, proxied by changes in real GDP in foreign destinations.[16] (For more details on the methodology, see annex 1A on shift-share methodology.)

MAP 4.1

Exposure to Exports, by Governorate, Tunisia, 2016 (in US$, billions)

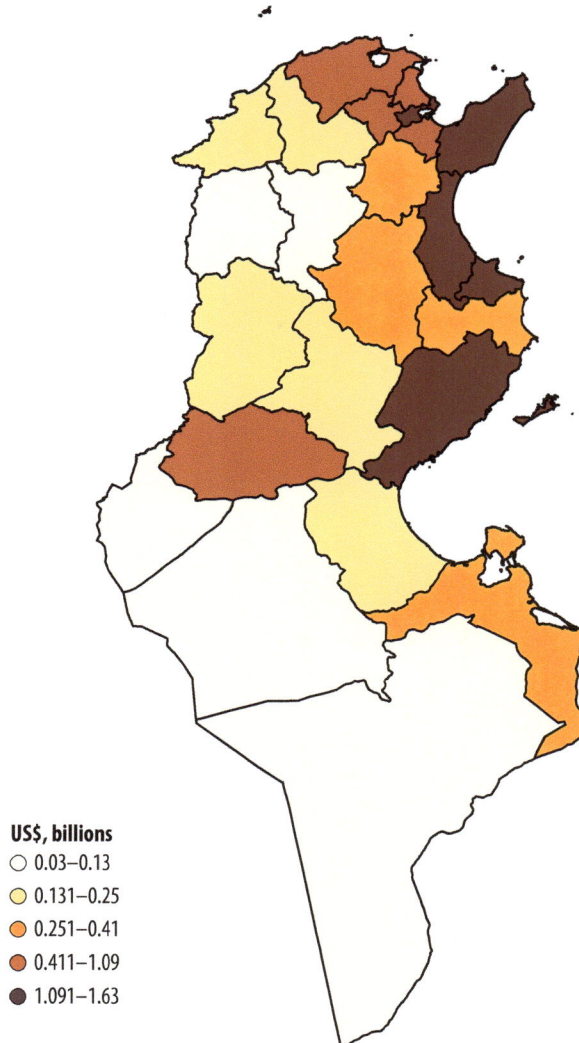

US$, billions
- ○ 0.03–0.13
- ○ 0.131–0.25
- ● 0.251–0.41
- ● 0.411–1.09
- ● 1.091–1.63

Source: World Bank calculations.

Note: Exposure to exports is defined as $\tilde{X}_{r,t+h} = \sum_i \frac{L_{r,i,t}}{L_{i,t}} \cdot \tilde{X}_{i,t}$, where $\tilde{X}_{i,t}$ denotes total exports of industry i at period t; $L_{r,i,t}$ denotes total employment in region r and industry i; and $L_{i,t} \equiv \sum_{r \in R} L_{r,i,t}$ is total aggregate employment in industry i.

Analysis and Findings

Effects of Increased Exports on Labor Demand

Our results show that the increase in exports has been the opposite of gender neutral.

First, because recent increases in exports have been from male-intensive industries, regions with higher export exposure had relatively lower female employment growth. Specifically, a US$1 billion increase in export exposure led to an average decrease of 6.8 percentage points in the female-to-male employment ratio, which is statistically significant at the 5 percent confidence level and in the same direction (that is, negative) as predicted by the theoretical mechanism (table 4.1, panel a). To better understand the economic magnitude of these results, one can normalize these coefficients (put them in the same scale) by dividing them by standard deviations of each variable. We find that an increase in export exposure of 1 standard deviation decreases the female-to-male employment ratio by 0.137 standard deviations.

Second, this change is likely driven by a simultaneous decrease in female employment and increase in male employment. This can be seen in table 4.1 (panels b and c), where the effects of increased exports induced by foreign demand shocks have opposite signs on female and male employment. In response to a US$1 billion increase in export exposure, the point estimate for female employment is of 7,903 *fewer* jobs, whereas the point estimate for male employment is of 2,418 *additional* jobs.

Normalizing in terms of standard deviations highlights that female employment is more responsive to trade at the extensive margin. An increase in exposure to exports of 1 standard deviation decreases the female employment ratio by 0.062 standard deviations but increases male employment by 0.009 standard deviations.

Effects of Increased Exports on Labor Supply

So how did labor respond to the foreign demand shocks? The results suggest that households are substituting male for female labor supply. Even though the ENPE has no information on wages, estimating the effect of the change in exposure to exports on the change in female and male unemployment can shed some light on the welfare effects of foreign demand–induced exports on domestic welfare. A few key findings stand out.

First, female workers drop out of the labor force rather than move into unemployment. Specifically, on average, a US$1 billion increase in export exposure displaced 272 women *into* unemployment and 1,280 males *out of* unemployment, although neither estimate is statistically

TABLE 4.1

Effects of Increased Export Exposure on Female and Male Employment, Tunisia

a. Response variable: Change in female-to-male employment ratio[a]

	(1)	(2)	(3)
Change in exports exposure (US$1 billion)	0.002	−0.068*	−0.068**
	(0.018)	(0.035)	(0.031)

b. Response variable: Change in female employment

	(1)	(2)	(3)
Change in exports exposure (US$1 billion)	−1,929.460	−8,173.887**	−7,903.951***
	(2,257.502)	(2,257.502)	(3,048.396)

c. Response variable: Change in male employment

	(1)	(2)	(3)
Change in exports exposure (US$1 billion)	1,756.212	1,140.393	2,418.129
	(1,842.006)	(3,026.194)	(3,133.433)

d. First-Stage Regression. Response variable: Change in exports exposure (US$1 billion)

	(1)	(2)	(3)
Change in foreign demand exposure (US$1 billion)	.0058***	.0046***	.0045***
	(.0006)	(.0008)	(.0004)
F-statistic	77.82	30.25	139.95
Time fixed effects		✓	✓
District fixed effects		✓	✓
Sociodemographic controls			✓
N	120	120	120

Note: District cluster robust standard errors in parenthesis.
a. Panel a shows the results of the two-stage least squared regression of the change in female-to-male employment ratio on the change in exposure to exports instrumented by the change in exposure to foreign demand. The preferred specification, which includes time and district fixed effects, as well sociodemographic controls, is column 3.
*$p < 0.1$ **$p < 0.05$ ***$p < 0.01$.

significant (table 4.2, panels a and b). From our previous estimates, male workers moved from unemployment into jobs, alongside other male workers who joined the labor force to occupy new trade-induced jobs.

Second, effects are driven primarily by married women rather than single women. Another important insight comes from comparing the responses of married versus single female workers. If households are substituting male for female labor supply, then one would expect the effect to be stronger among married women. This is indeed the case, with most of the variation in female employment after a foreign demand shock coming from married female workers (table 4.2, panels c and d).

Third, a US$1 billion increase in export exposure, on average, led to 4,605 fewer jobs among married female workers and 2,501 fewer jobs among single female workers. The underlying question here is whether these changes are a result of household optimization in a gender-segmented labor market. If yes, they are likely welfare improving, although we cannot say definitively whether that is the case.

TABLE 4.2

Effects of Increased Export Exposure on Unemployment, by Gender and Women's Marital Status, Tunisia

a. Response variable: Change in unemployed females			
	(1)	(2)	(3)
Change in exports exposure (US$1 billion)	−1,387.8	147.3	272.0
	(1,617.9)	(2,611.8)	(2,749.1)
b. Response variable: Change in unemployed males			
	(1)	(2)	(3)
Change in exports exposure (US$1 billion)	−1,750.4	−602.6	−1,279.6
	(1,680.8)	(2,243.9)	(2,156.9)
c. Response variable: Change in female employment, married women			
	(1)	(2)	(3)
Change in exports exposure (US$1 billion)	−343.177	−4,540.806**	−4,605.166**
	(1,348.004)	(1,993.872)	(1,897.571)
d. Response variable: Change in female employment, single women			
	(1)	(2)	(3)
Change in exports exposure (US$1 billion)	−1,446.643	−2,750.395*	−2,501.416
	(1,127.362)	(1,549.210)	(1,429.758)
e. First-Stage Regression. Response variable: Change in exports exposure (US$, billions)			
	(1)	(2)	(3)
Change in foreign demand exposure (US$1 billion)	.0058***	.0046***	.0045***
	(.0006)	(.0008)	(.0004)
F-statistic	77.82	30.25	139.95
Time fixed effects		✓	✓
District fixed effects		✓	✓
Sociodemographic controls			✓
N	120	120	120

Note: District cluster robust standard errors in parentheses.
*$p < 0.1$ **$p < 0.05$ ***$p < 0.01$.

These results are statistically significant at the 5 percent confidence level for married female workers but statistically insignificant for female workers, indicating that the relationship is much tighter for married women. They also suggest that the empiric response is consistent with the theoretical mechanism.

Fourth, households appear to be optimizing quantities of female and male labor supply in a gender-segmented labor market. If there were large increases in unemployment, it would suggest that female workers would be looking for jobs but could not find them because of labor market failures. The results instead suggest that female workers who stop working outside the household after a negative trade shock are choosing to leave the labor force, which is consistent with a household jointly optimizing labor supply decisions.

Conclusion

As Tunisia regroups to boost growth—and in a sustainable, inclusive manner—trade policy is an important lever. Our study shows that because the effects of trade are mediated by domestic institutions and social norms, as well as by the sectoral composition of the local labor force, the effects of increased foreign demand on local labor markets will always depend on the domestic characteristics.

For Tunisia, a key issue is the substantial degree of gender segmentation, along with much greater female intensity in some sectors (like textiles and textile products) than others. Policy makers must then take this aspect into account when anticipating the domestic consequences of trade policy.

This chapter highlights the importance of gender segmentation in labor markets in shaping the local effects of international trade. In theory, foreign demand shocks may either increase or decrease the female-to-male employment ratio. It depends crucially on the sectors that face the foreign demand shock and the relevance of the countries from which the demand shocks originate.

In Tunisia, positive foreign demand shocks have been relatively larger in male-intensive sectors, which induced a decrease in the female-to-male employment ratio. Because male-intensive sectors had relatively more favorable foreign demand shocks, the equilibrium response is that households likely substituted female for male labor supply. Estimates using data from 2006 to 2016 confirm the theoretical mechanism postulated in this chapter.

One important policy implication of our study is that less gender segmentation in labor markets will dampen the effect of foreign demand shocks on gender inequality. Taking foreign demand shocks as exogenous, the policy maker can only induce changes on the institutions that generate domestic gender segmentation in labor markets. If every sector had no gender segmentation, however, any foreign shocks would be distributionally neutral across genders—that is, males and females would be equally affected.

Thus, as Tunisia increases its exports, it might want to consider policies that reduce gender segmentation in labor markets. Policies that promote gender equity have the immediate benefit of more gender equity in the present—but they can also have the unintended benefit of inducing more equitable effects in the future whenever economic shifters (like commodity prices and trade diversion) affect the local economy.

Annex 4A. Supplementary Data

TABLE 4A.1

Summary Statistics on Effects of Increased Exports Exposure, Tunisia

Variable	N	Mean	Std. dev.	Min	Max
Change in exports exposure (US$1 billion)	120	−.052	.374	−1.546	1.376
Change in female-to-male employment ratio	120	−.004	.072	−.386	.277
Change in female employment	120	592.7	6,152.9	−20,144.3	17,400.2
Change in male employment	120	1,592.5	5,740.2	−12,011.2	15,507.2
Change in education (high school or higher share)	120	−.008	.014	−.048	.023
Change in urban share	120	−.0002	.063	−.248	.267

FIGURE 4A.1

Decomposition of Sectoral Workforce, by Region, 2016

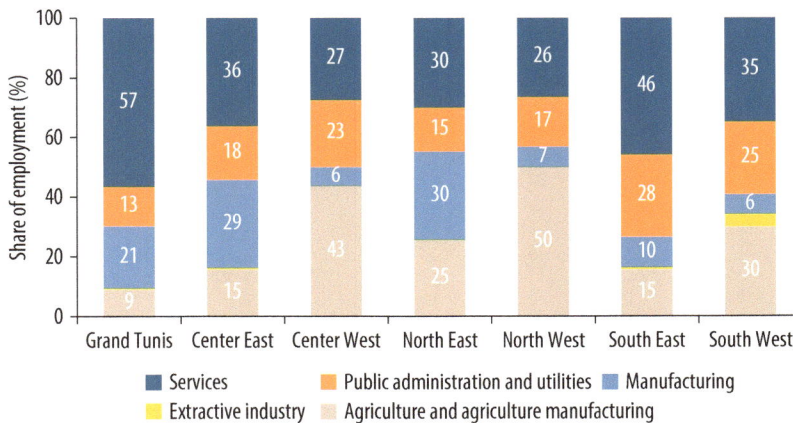

Source: World Bank calculations using data from the National Survey on Population and Employment, National Institute of Statistics.

FIGURE 4A.2

Decomposition of Male and Female Workforce, by Region, Tunisia, 2016

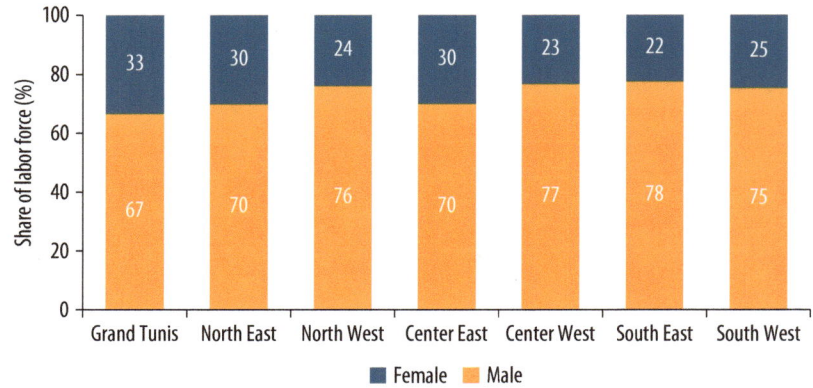

Source: World Bank calculations using data from the National Survey on Population and Employment, National Institute of Statistics.

FIGURE 4A.3

Female Labor Force Participation Rates, by Region, Tunisia, 2006–16

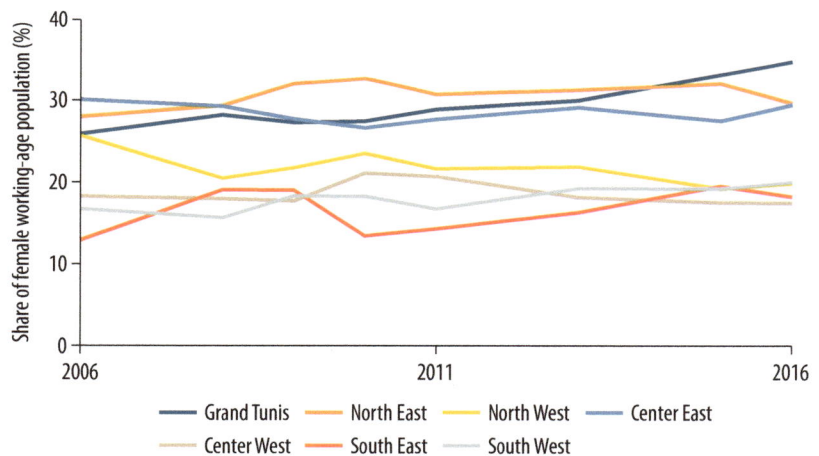

Source: World Bank calculations using data from the National Survey on Population and Employment, National Institute of Statistics.
Note: Female labor force participation is calculated as the total female labor force divided by total female working-age population (ages 15 and above).

FIGURE 4A.4

Unemployment Rates, by Region, Tunisia, 2006–16

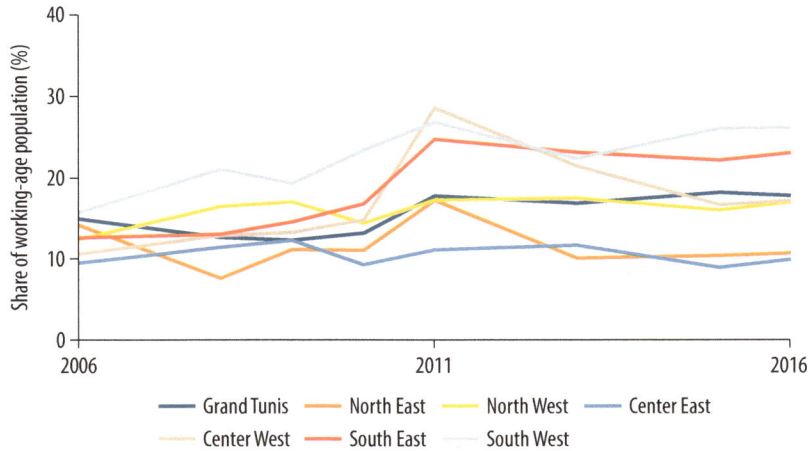

Source: World Bank calculations using data from the National Survey on Population and Employment, National Institute of Statistics.
Note: Unemployment rates are calculated as the shares of the total, male, and female active, working-age (ages 15 and above) populations who are unemployed. "Active" refers to people who are either working or looking for a job.

Notes

1. Data on Tunisian gross national income and export growth are from the World Development Indicators (WDI) Database.
2. See, for instance, the report on the gender pay gap in high-income economies published by the Organisation for Economic Co-operation and Development (OECD 2012).
3. Across different low- and middle-income countries, trade liberalization is linked to increased gender equity. Using Brazilian data, Gaddis and Pieters (2012) show that following trade liberalization, there was a relative increase in female labor force participation and a relative decrease in female unemployment in more-trade-exposed states compared with less-exposed states. Two forces contributed to this increased female participation in the labor market: (a) large reallocations both within and between sectors, particularly an increased shift of the total labor force from manufacturing to services, in line with the idea that structural transformation increases female participation; and (b) income effects for those households whose male worker transitioned into unemployment or the informal sector after trade liberalization. In a related finding, Kis-Katos, Pieters, and Sparrow (2018, 763) study Indonesia and show that "female work participation increased and participation in domestic duties declined in regions that were more exposed to input tariff reductions" but not to output markets liberalization. Juhn, Ujhelyi, and Villegas-Sanchez (2013) reach a similar conclusion, using US data to analyze the effects of the North American Free Trade Agreement (NAFTA)

on gender inequality. They argue that tariff reduction induces technological upgrading to less physically demanding tasks, which explains the increase in the relative female wage in blue-collar but not in white-collar tasks. In another work, they find similar effects and mechanisms using firm-level data from Mexico (Juhn, Ujhelyi, and Villegas-Sanchez 2014). Finally, Ben Yahmed and Bombarda (2020, 259) study labor markets in Mexico using individual survey data and show that "tariff cuts increase the probability of working formally for both men and women within four-digit manufacturing industries" and find no differential impact across genders.

4. De Hoyos, Bussolo, and Núñez (2012) show that the expansion of the export-oriented maquilas (light manufacturing) sector in Honduras improved gender equality in both employment and earnings. Because the garment and textiles sector is very female intensive, women benefited differentially more from this expansion, highlighting the significance of the *composition* of the foreign demand shocks.

5. Tunisian tariff rate data are from the World Bank's WDI Database and World Integrated Trade Solutions (WITS) interactive data tool.

6. Data on Tunisian trade as a share of GDP are from United Nations (UN) Comtrade merchandise database, the Balanced Trade in Services (BaTiS) dataset of the World Trade Organization (WTO) and OECD, and WDI GDP data.

7. Data on the sectoral shares of the Tunisian labor force are from World Bank calculations using data from Tunisia's National Survey on Population and Employment, National Institute of Statistics, 2006–16.

8. Data on the sectoral shares of Tunisian exports are from World Bank calculations using UN Comtrade merchandise data and the BaTiS dataset of the WTO and OECD.

9. Female and male labor force participation data for Tunisia, the Middle East and North Africa, and other regions or country groups are calculated from Tunisia's National Survey on Population and Employment and from International Labour Organization Statistics (ILOSTAT) data.

10. Tunisian unemployment data, aggregate and by gender, are from the country's National Survey on Population and Employment, National Institute of Statistics.

11. Shares of female employment, by industry, are calculated from Tunisia's 2016 National Survey on Population and Employment, National Institute of Statistics.

12. Annex 1B of this report presents a version of a Melitz (2003) model of trade that features this particular feature: that larger (and presumably more productive) firms tend to sell to export markets, whereas smaller (and presumably less productive) firms sell only to domestic markets.

13. Correlations between the size of Tunisian firms and the likelihood they are exporters, as well as between firms' export sales and total employment, are calculated using World Bank Enterprise Survey data.

14. More precisely, because exports are potentially endogenous, sector-specific exposure to foreign demand shocks is used as an instrument for sector-specific exports. See annex 1A on shift-share methodology for details.

15. Regional exposure to exports is defined as $\tilde{X}_{r,t+b} = \sum_i \frac{L_{r,i,t}}{L_{i,t}} \cdot \tilde{X}_{i,t}$, where $\tilde{X}_{i,t}$ denotes total exports of industry i at period t; $L_{r,i,t}$ denotes total employment

in region r and industry i; and $L_{i,t} \equiv \Sigma_{r \in R} L_{r,i,t}$ is total aggregate employment in industry i.

16. Tunisia is a small open economy. Therefore, it is unlikely that changes in foreign demand are correlated with unobserved factors that drive changes in local labor markets—that is, this instrument is likely valid. Furthermore, changes in exposure to exports are strongly correlated with changes in exposure to foreign demand shocks—that is, the instrument is relevant. Satisfying the exclusion restriction and instrument relevance, we can appropriately interpret the results in this section as the causal effect of exports on local labor markets in Tunisia during this time. Because the change in exports was higher in male-intensive industries, the theoretical mechanism described above predicts that the female-to-male employment ratio should decline.

References

Ben Yahmed, Sarra, and Pamela Bombarda. 2020. "Gender, Informal Employment and Trade Liberalization in Mexico." *The World Bank Economic Review* 34 (2): 259–83. https://doi.org/10.1093/wber/lhy020.

De Hoyos, Rafael, Maurizio Bussolo, and Oscar Núñez. 2012. "Exports, Gender Wage Gaps, and Poverty in Honduras." *Oxford Development Studies* 40 (4): 533–51. https://doi.org/10.1080/13600818.2012.732562.

Gaddis, Isis, and Janneke Pieters. 2012. "Trade Liberalization and Female Labor Force Participation: Evidence from Brazil." Discussion Paper No. 6809, Institute of Labor Economics (IZA), Bonn.

Juhn, Chinhui, Gergely Ujhelyi, and Carolina Villegas-Sanchez. 2013. "Trade Liberalization and Gender Inequality." *American Economic Review* 103 (3): 269–73. https://doi.org/10.1257/aer.103.3.269.

Juhn, Chinhui, Gergely Ujhelyi, and Carolina Villegas-Sanchez. 2014. "Men, Women, and Machines: How Trade Impacts Gender Inequality." *Journal of Development Economics* 106: 179–93. https://doi.org/10.1016/j.jdeveco.2013.09.009.

Kis-Katos, Krisztina, Janneke Pieters, and Robert Sparrow. 2018. "Globalization and Social Change: Gender-Specific Effects of Trade Liberalization in Indonesia." *IMF Economic Review* 66 (4): 763–93. https://doi.org/10.1057/s41308-018-0065-5.

Melitz, Marc J. 2003. "The Impact of Trade on Intra-industry Reallocations and Aggregate Industry Productivity." *Econometrica* 71 (6): 1695–1725.

OECD (Organisation for Economic Co-operation and Development). 2012. *Closing the Gender Gap: Act Now*. Paris: OECD Publishing. https://doi.org/10.1787/9789264179370-en.

CHAPTER 5

Egypt Case Study: Exploring the Link between Trade and Labor

Claudia N. Berg and Mexico A. Vergara Bahena

Key Messages

- Liberalization of trade in the Arab Republic of Egypt, with its bigger trade flows, did not yield the expected improvements in its labor market. Moreover, any short-run impacts (positive and negative) dissipated over time.

- Our results show that higher exports in Egypt correlate with lower real wages, especially for low-skilled workers, and no meaningful improvements in informality or female labor force participation.

- Firm-level studies can explain this puzzling result: although employment rose in response to higher exports, the increase did not occur on a large enough scale to be felt at the economy-wide level.

- For Egypt to seize the benefits of trade, it must deepen reforms to incentivize large growth of the export sector, integrate more into global value chains, and favor labor-intensive industries over capital-intensive ones.

Introduction

The Arab Republic of Egypt offers an excellent opportunity to deepen our understanding of the relationship between trade liberalization and better labor markets. On the trade front, it implemented a series of new trade agreements over a short period of time: since 2004, it has signed 6 of the 10 trade agreements now in force.[1] It also launched several bold and important reforms in 2016 to improve macroeconomic stability, restore confidence, and enhance socioeconomic conditions. And it increased public investment in road infrastructure, digital connectivity, and supplies of electricity and gas (IFC 2020).

Yet these bold economic reforms have not done much for the labor market, which is rife with challenges such as lagging private-sector economic growth, rising informal employment, and increasing wage inequality. A widespread regional divide also persists between regions in terms of employment growth and job quality, according to the 2016 Labor Force Survey (LFS). In addition, whereas employment shares of labor-intensive manufacturing sectors (like garments and furniture) have steeply declined, those in capital-intensive nontraded services (like construction, storage, and communications) have expanded.

Moreover, poverty remains a big challenge. The share of extreme poverty—that is, those living on less than US$1.90 per person a day in 2011 purchasing power parity (PPP) dollars—rose from 1.5 percent in 2012 to 3.8 percent in 2017, and the share living between US$1.90 and US$3.20 per person per day (2011 PPP) rose from 19.0 percent to 28.9 percent (World Bank 2021). Although poverty rates had improved between 2012 and 2015, this trend was reversed in 2017 following double-digit inflation.

It is well accepted that expanding trade offers the potential to boost a country's economy and reduce poverty in the long term, but it is less clear how this dynamic plays out in the short term (Zaki 2016). Trade has possible effects from (a) imported goods that compete with domestic production of final goods; (b) imported inputs that complement production of exports; and (c) exports. One might expect the effects of the first to be negative but the effects of the second and third to be positive.

This chapter builds on the bilateral trade flow results of chapter 2—which demonstrated that Egypt's signing of free trade agreements increased its trade flows—and asks how this outcome affected Egypt's labor market. Specifically, it focuses on how imports and exports affect wages, informality, and female labor force participation (FLFP) at the subdistrict level. Although data limitations constrain our ability to differentiate between the two competing effects of imports, we undertake an initial examination and leave a deeper analysis for future research. The chapter then explores the relationship between export sales and labor demand at the firm level to see whether the structure of Egypt's firms could help explain why the labor market has not improved as other low- and middle-income countries' labor markets have in response to higher trade flows.

This chapter adds to the empirical literature by exploring the impacts of both exports and imports on the labor market. Most of the previous literature has focused on shocks arising from increased competition due to imports from China (Autor, Dorn, and Hanson 2013; Feler and Senses 2017); automation (Acemoglu and Restrepo 2017); exchange rates (Goldberg and Tracy 2000); or tariff reduction (Amiti and Davis 2011). Further, this chapter's analysis extends beyond labor-intensive manufacturing industries, which has been the main area of focus to date. It also estimates effects on both manufacturing and services for the overall worker population—including potential effects on different types of workers (such as urban, rural, young, high-skilled, and female workers).

Egypt's Trade Flows and Labor Markets: A Snapshot

Egypt is the second-richest country in the Middle East and North Africa (after Saudi Arabia), accounting for about 28 percent of the region's gross domestic product (GDP) and 26 percent of its population in 2020. Home to 102 million people—and the most populated country in the Middle East and North Africa—it is emerging from a period of social and economic turmoil. In 2011, Egypt's Arab Spring uprisings took place; two years later, the first civilian president was overthrown, and Abdel Fattah El-Sisi has been in office since 2014.

In 2016, Egypt launched a successful round of ambitious macroeconomic reforms aimed at restoring stability and confidence and improving socioeconomic conditions. In addition to ongoing trade liberalization, reforms included exchange rate liberalization, fiscal consolidation, upward adjustment of energy prices, introduction of a value added tax, and new laws relating to the business environment (for example, for investment and bankruptcy). These reforms had the intended effect of achieving macroeconomic stability, accelerating real GDP growth, reducing the fiscal deficit, and putting public debt on a downward trajectory (IFC 2020). They also built on macroeconomic reforms that predated the Arab Spring.

Key Trade Trends

Beginning in the early 1990s, Egypt began implementing policies to boost its trade. The first of these, the Economic Reform and Structural Adjustment Program, aimed at rectifying the macroeconomic imbalances, including chronic balance of payment deficits and high inflation (Korayem 1997). As part of this liberalization, the country reduced its maximum tariff rate from 110 percent in the 1980s to 40 percent by the end of the 1990s—followed in 2004 by a second wave of reforms, with tariff rates further reduced and simplified. Steps were also taken to improve the business environment (Zaki 2016). A few key trade trends stand out.

Trade agreements drove a reduction in tariff rates and an increase in trade flows. Egypt's weighted mean applied tariffs fell from 20.0 percent to 6.6 percent between 2002 and 2016, before rebounding to 10.4 percent in 2019 (figure 5.1).[2] Exports shot up 196 percent between 2000 and 2020, while imports soared 231 percent despite a drop-off in the wake of the 2008-09 Global Financial Crisis as worldwide trade decelerated (figure 5.2).[3] Trade (exports plus imports) as a percentage of GDP fell between 2009 and 2015, then began to rebound until the COVID-19 pandemic hit in 2020. Throughout these decades, imports were higher than exports, with the former accounting for 25.7 percent of GDP and the latter close to 17.5 percent of GDP in 2019.[4]

Exchange rate liberalization made little difference in net trade flows. Although leading to a significant depreciation of the Egyptian pound,[5] exchange rate liberalization had only modest repercussions on

FIGURE 5.1

Mean Applied Tariff on All Products, Egypt, 1995–2019

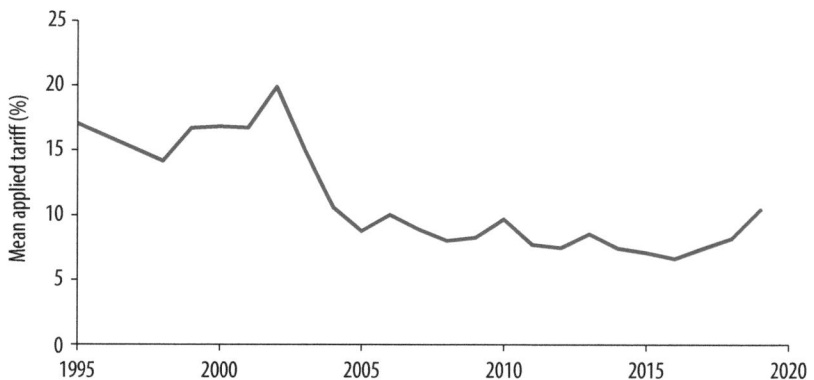

Source: World Bank based on data from Our World in Data (https://ourworldindata.org/).
Note: Weighted mean applied tariff is the average of effectively applied rates weighted by the product import shares corresponding to each partner country.

FIGURE 5.2

Exports and Imports of Goods and Services, Egypt, 1980–2020

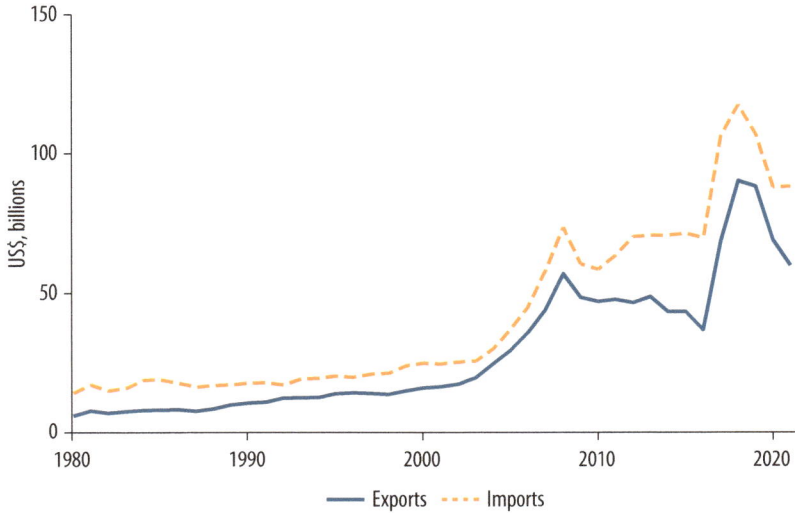

Source: World Bank based on data from the World Development Indicators Database.

trade. With Egyptian exports relatively less expensive for the country's trading partners, exports of goods increased from 5.6 percent of GDP in 2016 to 9.4 percent in 2019, while exports of services rose from 4.8 percent of GDP in 2016 to 8.1 percent in 2019.[6] Yet Egypt's overall export performance remained lower than in previous years—with the total trade-to-GDP ratio at 17.5 percent of GDP in 2019, below the 20.5 percent ratio in 2011 (IFC 2020). The increase of exports was offset by the increase in import prices, given that 75 percent of Egyptian imports are intermediate and raw materials for domestic and export production (Zaki 2016).

Participation in global value chains (GVCs) remains low. In 2015, less than 5 percent of Egypt's total output was related to GVCs, an increase of less than 1 percentage point since 1990. This is less than half of Morocco's and Tunisia's output for GVCs—11.0 percent and 15.3 percent, respectively.[7] Between 2009 and 2018, more than half of Egypt's goods exports consisted of primary and resource-based products, and a quarter consisted of medium- and high-technology exports (IFC 2020). This is a problem because the countries receive the biggest boost in incomes and employment when they transition away from exporting commodities and importing inputs and toward exporting basic manufactured products. Thus, greater participation in GVCs has the potential to boost Egyptian incomes, create more-productive and better jobs, and reduce poverty (World Bank 2020).

The export basket is capital intensive. Between 2013 and 2020, Egypt's export basket has changed little, with fuel still accounting for one-third of exports in terms of value (33.6 percent in 2013 and 32.3 percent in 2020) (figure 5.3).[8] This sector is capital intensive and characterized by distortionary policies such as subsidized energy prices (IFC 2020). Another important export is chemicals, accounting for 16.5 percent and 15.9 percent of export value in 2013 and 2020, respectively. Together, the fuels and chemicals sectors account for almost half of export value but do not contribute much to employment growth given that they are both capital intensive rather than labor intensive.

Import industries are also capital intensive. For most years between 2005 and 2019, the machinery industry has imported the most goods (14–22 percent), topped only by minerals (10–17 percent), mainly oil-related, from 2012 to 2014 (figure 5.4).[9] These imports, which are almost double the value of exports, are typically used as intermediate

FIGURE 5.3

Decomposition of Export Value, by Industry, Egypt, 2013, 2016, and 2020

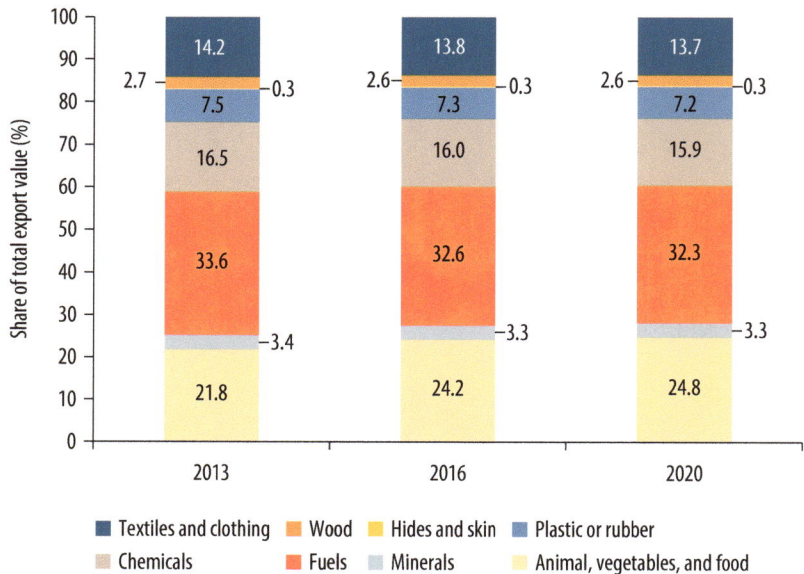

Source: World Bank based on data from the United Nations Comtrade database.
Note: Shares of exports are by value in percentage of total exports.

FIGURE 5.4

Shares of Import Value, by Industry, Egypt, 2005–19

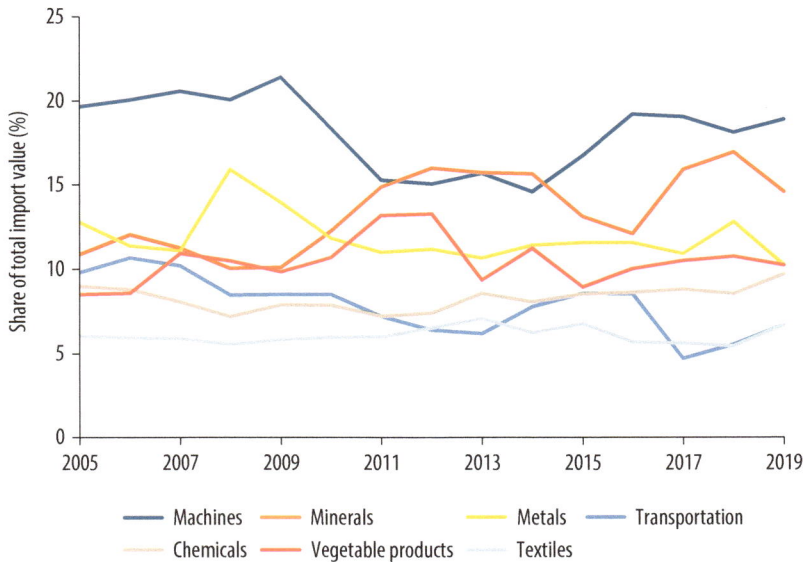

Source: World Bank based on data from the United Nations Comtrade database.
Note: Shares of exports are by value in percentage of total imports.

goods for production. Take the case of machinery imports: An essential part are final consumption products (such as broadcasting equipment, computers, and telephones). The rest are machines for industrial production (such as wires, valves, pumps, excavation machinery, and motors).[10] An increase in imports could have a potentially positive effect on the labor market because it means more inputs for production of exporting goods. But given that Egypt has few backward links in GVCs, higher imports may substitute for domestic production, which would have a negative effect on the labor market.

Exports and imports are moderately diversified among several trading partners. In 2019, Egypt's top five export markets were the United States (7.2 percent), the United Arab Emirates (6.8 percent), Türkiye (5.7 percent), Saudi Arabia (5.6 percent), and Italy (5.5 percent).[11] Together, these five countries buy 30.8 percent of Egypt's exports.

Egypt's imports are relatively more concentrated. The country buys most of its imports from China (15.3 percent), followed by the United States (6.6 percent), Saudi Arabia (6.6 percent), Germany (5.5 percent), and Türkiye (4.7 percent). Together, these five countries account for 38.7 percent of its imports.

Key Labor Trends

Rising exports have been linked to poverty reduction through the generation of new employment opportunities. They also tend to raise wages (Lopez-Acevedo and Robertson 2012), lower prices of goods and services for poor consumers (Bartley Johns et al. 2015), and generate economic growth (Bhagwati and Srinivasan 2002; Dollar and Kraay 2004; Frankel and Romer 1999; Noguer and Siscart 2005). But in Egypt, three key labor market indicators—real wages, FLFP, and informality—show no benefit from increasing trade and may have even gotten worse. Several labor trends stand out.

Nationwide Employment Trends

Employment growth has failed to keep up with population growth. Between 2006 and 2019, Egypt's working-age population (ages 15–64) grew by an average annual rate of 2.5 percent, while the number of jobs grew by an average annual rate of only 1.9 percent. This translated into a decrease in the employment rate (the share of working-age persons who are employed) from a peak of 47 percent in 2008 to 39 percent in 2019. Egypt has relatively fewer large firms relative to other economies, which is problematic since large firms tend to be engines for job creation, especially for the middle class (World Bank 2021).

Unemployment remains a problem, especially for women. Over the past 15 years, Egypt's unemployment rate has had significant swings, climbing from 8.8 percent in 2010 to above 12.0 percent between 2012 and 2015—and peaking at 13.2 percent in 2013. Stabilization efforts launched in 2016 brought the rate down to a 30-year low of 7.8 percent in 2019, but the COVID-19 pandemic in 2020 pushed it back up to 9.3 in 2021. Further, the 2019 unemployment rate for women (23.6 percent) was much higher than for men (5.8 percent), part of a long-standing pattern (figure 5.5). Although Egypt's unemployment rate, along with Morocco's, has been lower than in the Middle East and North Africa overall since 2010 (except for 2011–16), Tunisia's rate has been much higher.[12]

Youth unemployment is also a serious concern. As of 2020, the youth unemployment rate (ages 15–24 years) stood at 23.4 percent, more than twice the national rate—with the rate for females close to 57.8 percent versus 15.2 percent for males.[13] Egypt is a relatively young country: 90 percent of the unemployed are younger than 30 (ILO, n.d.); and about 76 percent of the population are younger than 40, while 27 percent are ages 15–29. Moreover, the country's universities add an estimated 800,000 graduates to the labor market every year (IFC 2020). This means that nearly 6 million additional jobs would need to be

FIGURE 5.5

Unemployment Rate, Aggregate and by Gender, Egypt, 2004–20

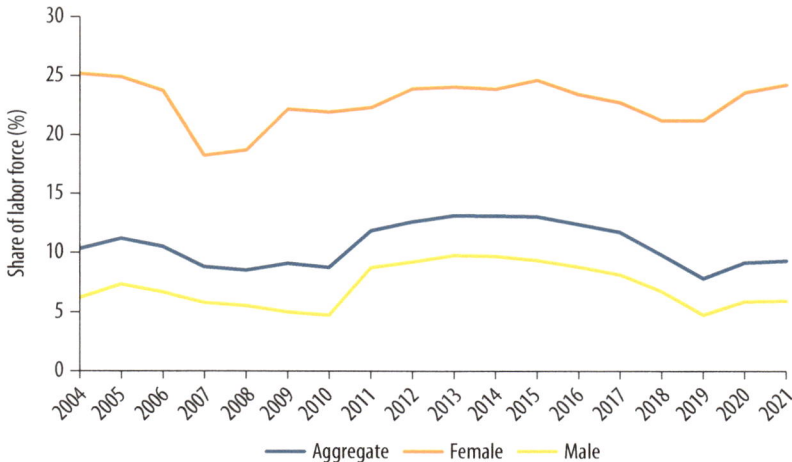

Source: World Bank based on the World Development Indicators Database.
Note: The unemployment rate is calculated by dividing the number of unemployed people by the active working-age (ages 15–64) population. The "active" population comprises those who are either (a) employed or (b) unemployed and seeking a job.

created between 2019 and 2030 just to maintain the employment rate at 2019 levels. This looks to be a major challenge, given that between 2009 and 2019, the economy added only about 3 million jobs, mostly in the informal sector (World Bank 2021).

Female labor force participation is low. Between 1990 and 2019, FLFP rates ranged from 20 percent to 26 percent, averaging 23 percent—an average similar to that of the Middle East and North Africa region, where 20 percent of women are out of the labor force.[14] Moreover, Egypt's FLFP has not surpassed 24 percent in any year since 2009 (figure 5.6). In contrast, male labor force participation is considerably higher, averaging 76 percent during the same time period, although the rate has been dropping since 2009, reaching a low of 66.9 percent in 2017. Subnationally, there is widespread variation across regions and over time (see annex 5C, table 5C.3).

The services sector accounts for the biggest share of employment. In 2017, the services sector accounted for 38 percent of employment in Egypt, up from 34 percent in 2008, as it continued to replace employment in agriculture, forestry, and fishing, which fell from 31 percent to 25 percent (figure 5.7).[15] At the same time, the other sectors accounted for about 8–13 percent.

FIGURE 5.6

Labor Force Participation Rate, Aggregate and by Gender, Egypt, 2004–19

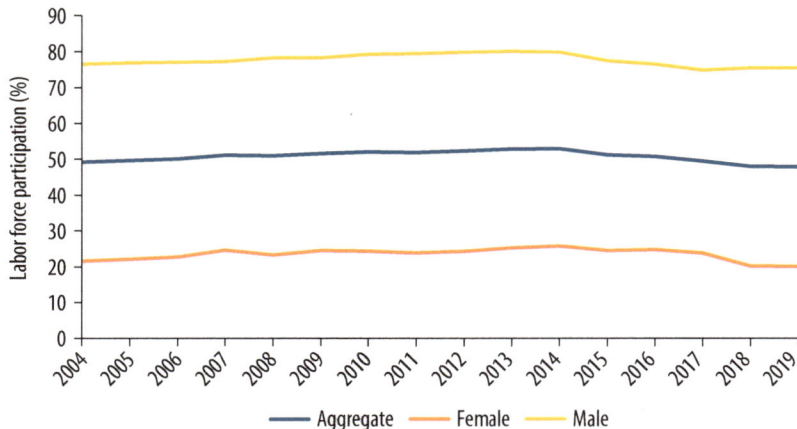

Source: World Bank based on the World Development Indicators Database.
Note: "Labor force participation" (either aggregate, female, or male) is calculated as the active population divided by the working-age (ages 15–64) population. The "active" population comprises those who are either (a) employed or (b) unemployed and seeking a job.

FIGURE 5.7

Employment Share in Selected Industries, Egypt, 2008–17

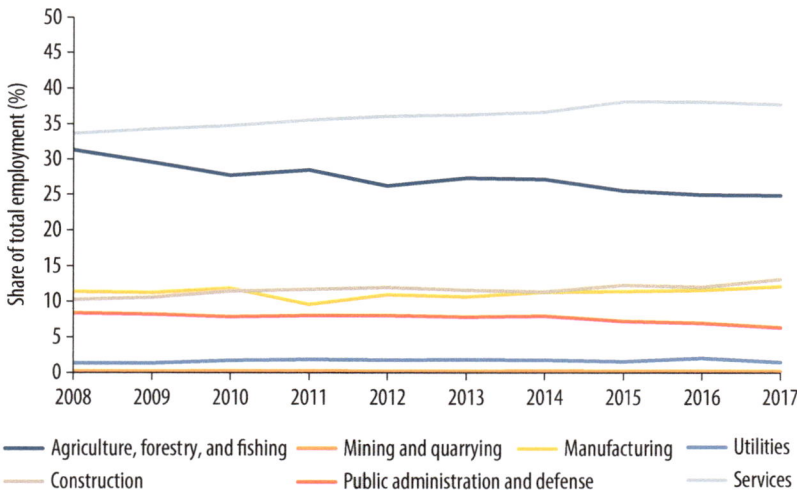

Source: World Bank based on Labor Force Survey data, Central Agency for Public Mobilization and Statistics (CAPMAS).
Note: Population weighted average for employed working-age (ages 15–64) individuals. "Services" include accommodation and food services, financial and insurance activities, real estate, and human health and social work activities.

In most industries, the share of female employment remained low (not more than 10 percent). However, female participation in 2017 was 44 percent in services and 37 percent in agriculture (figure 5.8).

Informality rates are high and growing. Between 2008 and 2017, the informality rate—the share of working-age people who are self-employed, unpaid family workers, or workers without social security coverage—rose from 58.4 percent to 66.7 percent.[16] This is comparable to the Middle East and North Africa average, which at 68 percent is one of the highest informality rates in the world (Lopez-Acevedo et al. 2023).

Within the country, informality rates vary widely by region and over time (see annex 5C, table 5C.2). Interestingly, the women's informality rate is lower than that of men—62.3 percent versus 67.9 percent in 2017 (figure 5.9), because women are more likely than men to be employed in government jobs (World Bank 2021). Overall, job creation in Egypt is concentrated in smaller-scale, less formal, and less productive economic activities (Adly 2020; Assaad et al. 2019).

The gender wage gap is rising. Between 2008 and 2016, real wages increased steadily before falling in 2017, but at different rates and levels for men and women.[17] The average monthly wage for men increased by 25.8 percent, for an annual average increase of 2.5 percent.

FIGURE 5.8

Share of Female Employment, by Industry, Egypt, 2008–17

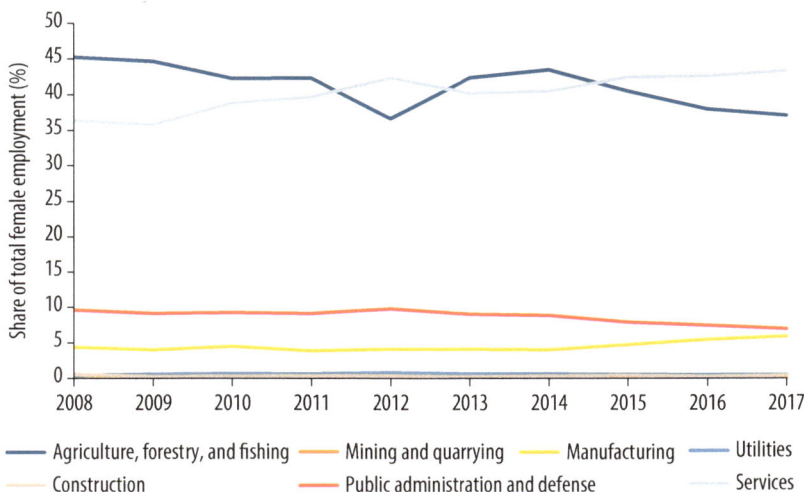

Source: World Bank based on 2008–17 Labor Force Survey data, Central Agency for Public Mobilization and Statistics (CAPMAS).
Note: "Services" include accommodation and food services, financial and insurance activities, real estate, and human health and social work activities.

FIGURE 5.9

Informality Rates, by Gender, Egypt, 2008–17

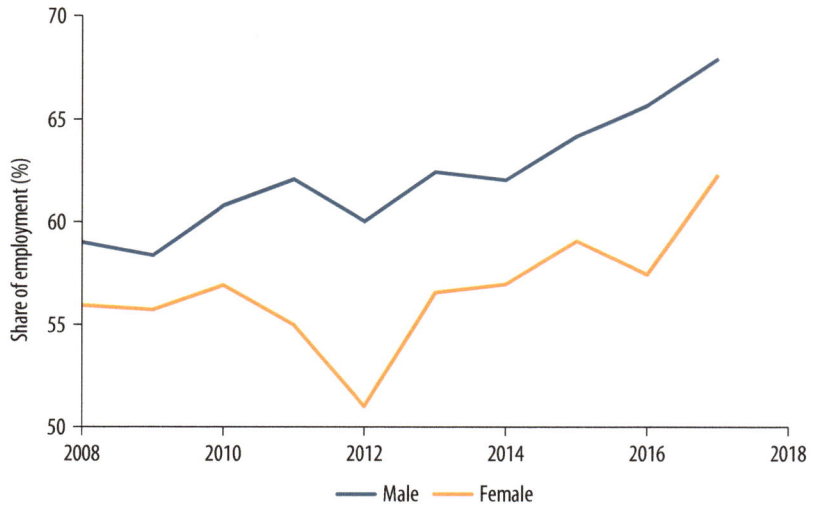

Source: World Bank based on 2009–17 Labor Force Survey data, Central Agency for Public Mobilization and Statistics (CAPMAS).
Note: The informality rate is the share of working-age individuals (ages 15–64) who are self-employed, unpaid family workers, or workers without social security coverage.

Women's wages, from a lower base, increased more slowly, by 13.9 percent, for an average annual increase of 1.4 percent.[18] As a result, the gender wage gap widened—from women earning LE 0.92 for every LE 1 earned by men in 2008 to women's LE 0.83 per men's LE 1 in 2017. Overall, the gender wage gap has not improved significantly during this time period (figure 5.10). (For details on calculation of the gender wage gap, see annex 5B.) Even so, the wage gap is modest relative to the region because Egyptian women who are employed tend to be more educated and work in government jobs.

Labor Market Segmentation across and between Governorates

Egypt's labor market is segmented along multiple dimensions, closely tracking trade patterns. Barriers to labor mobility seem to be stringent, and the structure of occupations in Egypt could be a potential explanation, since it is skewed toward manual and physical jobs in the private sector, with low regional mobility (World Bank 2021).

Using the World Bank's 2017 Enterprise Survey and Egypt's Labor Force Survey from the same year, we show that regions with a higher number of exporting firms (map 5.1, panel a) are also the regions with

FIGURE 5.10

Real Average Monthly Wages, by Gender, and the Gender Wage Gap, Egypt, 2008–17

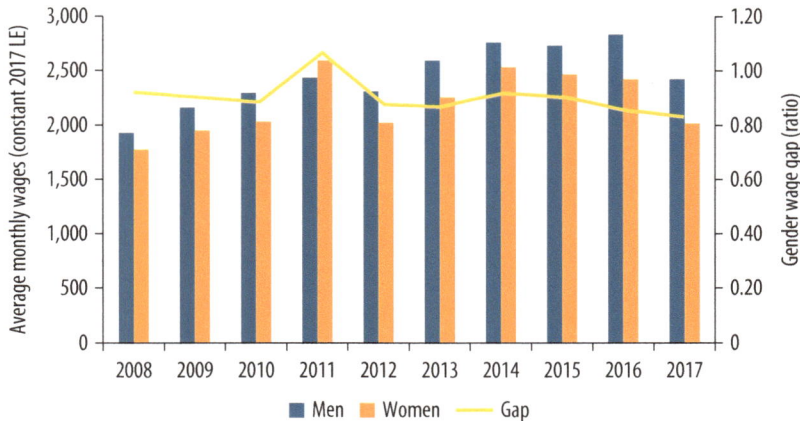

Source: World Bank based on 2008–17 Labor Force Survey data, Central Agency for Public Mobilization and Statistics (CAPMAS).
Note: Average wages (left axis) are calculated using weights. The gender wage gap (right axis) is calculated as the female wage divided by the male wage. (For more about this calculation, see annex 5B.)
LE = Egyptian pound.

MAP 5.1

Concentrations of Jobs and Exporting Firms, by Governorate, Egypt, 2017

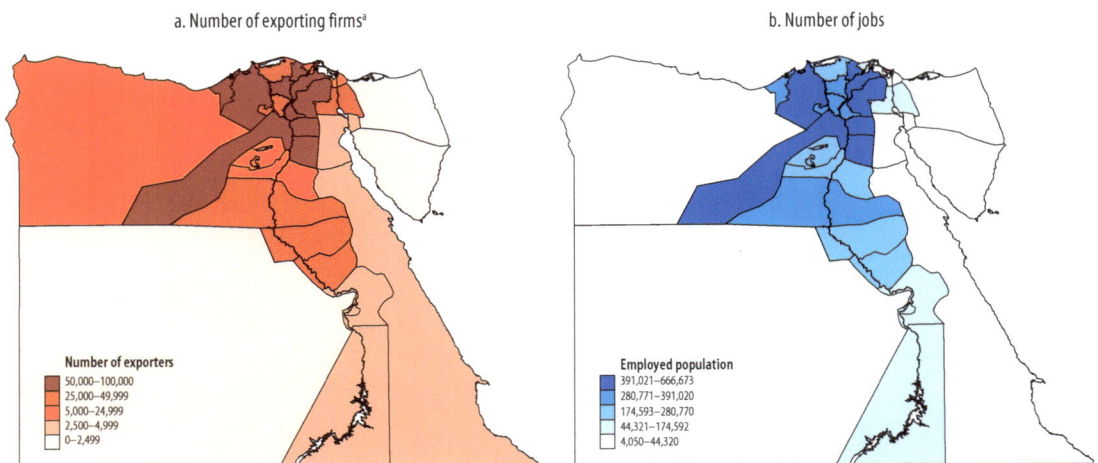

a. Number of exporting firms[a]

b. Number of jobs

Number of exporters
- 50,000–100,000
- 25,000–49,999
- 5,000–24,999
- 2,500–4,999
- 0–2,499

Employed population
- 391,021–666,673
- 280,771–391,020
- 174,593–280,770
- 44,321–174,592
- 4,050–44,320

Source: World Bank based on 2017 World Bank Enterprise Survey and Egyptian Labor Force Survey data.
Note: Darker colors indicate higher concentration of firms (panel a) and employment (panel b).
a. "Exporters" are those firms that export at least 10 percent of their sales directly.

a major employment concentration (map 5.1, panel b). Intuitively, there seems to be a link between trade and local labor markets.

Regional differences between regions are stark. For example, Cairo is the governorate with the most employees (about 10 percent of total workers), followed by Behira (about 8 percent) over the 2008–17 period. But bigger employment numbers (more labor demand) do not imply higher wages, with average monthly wages varying widely across governorates. New Valley and Suez showed the highest average weekly real wages in 2008 (at LE 670 and LE 610, respectively), although these regions do not have the highest numbers of exporting firms.[19] In 2015, North Sinai surpassed both with higher average real wages of LE 730. (For detailed average real wage data by governorate, see annex 5C, figure 5C.1.)

There is also regional specialization across industries. In some governorates (Behira, Beni-suef, Kafr-el-sheik, and Menia), more than 40 percent of all workers are in the agriculture, forestry, and fishing sector (figure 5.11). But this sector does not play a large role in employment in regions with more workers in the manufacturing sector (Cairo, Damietta, Giza, Suez) and where services are becoming more relevant.

Even though the national manufacturing employment share is close to 10 percent, some regions have an employment share of more than double the national estimate (Alexandria, Damietta, Kalyoubia, Suez). Importantly, these regions also happen to have most of the exporting firms (Cairo, Giza, Port Said), with a manufacturing employment share close to 20 percent.

Informality rates vary across Egypt's governorates. The regionally segmented labor market exhibits 2008 informality rates ranging from 6.7 percent in New Valley (El-wadi El-Gidid) to 78.9 and 79.8 percent in Beni-suef and Menia, respectively. By 2017, more people had entered the informal market, pushing the informality rate up everywhere except in four governorates (Behira, Beni-suef, North Sinai, and Red Sea). At the low end, informality in 2017 reached 24.6 percent in Red Sea, and at the high end, Menia had increased marginally to 80.4 percent. The change in New Valley was especially striking, growing to 30.1 percent.[20] (For detailed informality rates by governorate, see annex 5C, figure 5C.2.)

FLFP also varies significantly among regions. For example, it is higher in two governorates that specialize in agriculture (Behira and Beni-suef) and two regions that have the highest share of employment in the services industry (Port Said and Suez). In other words, FLFP is greater in regions where industries have the highest shares of female employment. (For detailed FLFP rates by governorate, see annex 5C, figure 5C.3.)

FIGURE 5.11

Sectoral Decomposition of Employment by Governorate, Egypt, 2017

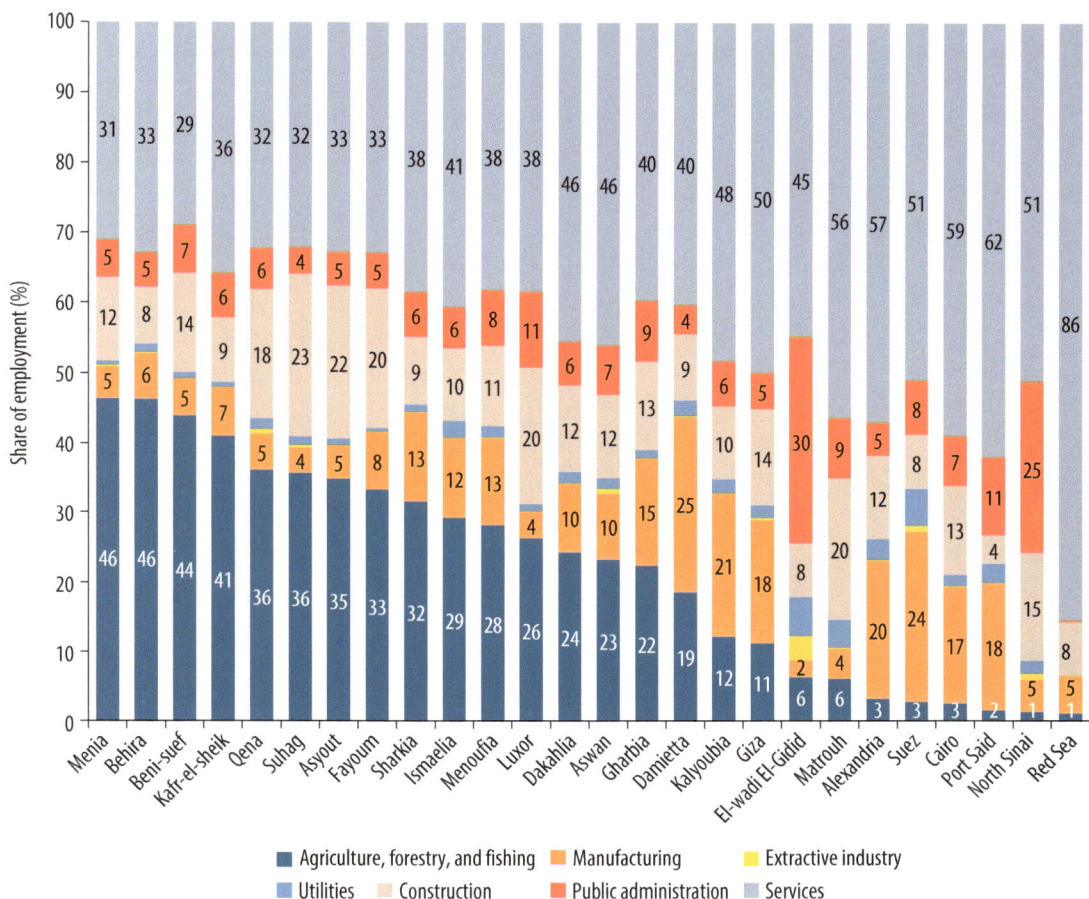

Source: World Bank based on 2017 Labor Force Survey, Central Agency for Public Mobilization and Statistics (CAPMAS).
Note: "Services" include accommodation and food services, financial and insurance activities, real estate, and human health and social work activities.

How Trade Affects Local Labor Market Outcomes

Against this trade and labor market backdrop, we can ask how trade affects local labor markets in Egypt. Following the methodology outlined in chapter 1's annex 1A, we apply a geography-based Bartik (1991) approach to estimate how imports and exports affect Egypt's labor market at the subdistrict level (kism or markaz).[21] This shift-share approach allows us to analyze the effect of exogenous changes to trade flows on local labor market outcomes. Specifically, we focus on how a trade exposure index affects wages, informality, and FLFP (box 5.1).

BOX 5.1

How a Trade Exposure Index Affects Local Labor Market Outcomes

We estimate the following equation:

$$\Delta y_{t,t+n}^{d} = \beta_0 + \beta_1 x_{t,t+n}^{d} + X^{d'}\gamma + \varepsilon_t^{d},$$

where Δy_t^{d} is the change in labor market outcome (wage, female labor force participation, or informality) of subdistrict d between time t and $t+n$. The variable of interest is the trade exposure index, $x_{t,t+n}^{d}$, which measures the concentration of non-oil trade per worker between time t and $t+n$, weighted by the labor force. Our analysis focuses on the imports and exports of final goods. Finally, X^{d} is a vector of exogenous control variables.

To analyze exports and correct for endogeneity, we construct an instrument using time series regressions of the Arab Republic of Egypt's exports to the United States (US) and European Union (EU) on the US and EU gross domestic product (GDP) by industry at the four-digit level, from 1991 to 2018 annually. Predicted values from these regressions would serve as a proxy for Egypt's exports to the US and EU explained exclusively by the latter's domestic aggregate demand.

To test the effect of imports, we also run the Bartik (1991) model.[a] For that case, the instrument uses time series regressions from Egypt's imports from the US and EU on the US and EU GDP by industry at the four-digit level from the same study period. Predicted values from these regressions would serve as a proxy for Egypt's imports from the US and EU. Both instruments, by construction, are orthogonal to every supply- or demand-side factor in the international market and every Egypt local market condition.

a. For a full description of the Bartik (1991) model, see chapter 1, annex 1A.

Our analysis explores the effects of trade in the short and long term. In the case of Egypt, we rely on the Labor Force Survey data to construct the labor market variables analyzed in the Bartik analysis. These data for Egypt are collected annually and span 2009–17. For the purposes of this analysis, we define the short run as 2009–12 and the long run as 2009–17. Our unit of analysis corresponds to the 259 subdistricts of Egypt. We present the results as the percentage change in labor market outcomes from a US$100 change in trade per worker.

Egypt is a good case for applying the Bartik approach. Recall that a fundamental condition of this approach is that labor markets be segmented. As demonstrated, Egypt's employment, FLFP, informality, and wages are all highly segmented along geographical lines—and we find that these labor market outcomes are segmented at the beginning and end of our study period (2009–17). We estimate the impact of the trade exposure index on labor market outcomes for the economy as well as various subgroups of workers: (a) working in the manufacturing or service sectors, (b) men and women, (c) low- and high-skilled, (d) young and old, and (e) rural and urban.

An important note here is that results must be statistically significant to serve as a basis for policy decisions, and the magnitude must be large enough for them to matter economically. Statistical significance helps determine whether a result is due to chance or to some factor of interest (Gallo 2016). In the following tables, statistical significance is indicated by stars—with more stars meaning a greater degree of confidence in the result. An estimate that is not statistically significant (having no stars) is unlikely to be different from zero.

Effects of Higher Exports

What happens at the local labor market—in Egypt's case, the subdistrict level—when there is an increase in exports per worker? To assess this link, we apply the Bartik approach and reach several key findings.

Higher exports correlate with lower real wages, especially for low-skilled workers. Our results show that in the short run, subdistricts that are more exposed to exports experience a decrease in average real wages, but this outcome dissipates in the long run (table 5.1). Specifically, between 2009 and 2012, a US$100 increase in exports per worker leads to a statistically significant decline in average wages of LE –207.85, which drops to almost zero by 2017. The effect is negative for both genders, although for women it is not statistically significant, and for young workers the coefficient has the same sign in the long run but remains statistically insignificant.

The effect on average wages is observed economywide, and it is more prominent for certain types of workers. In subdistricts more exposed to the trade shock, average wage decreases are substantially higher for low-skilled workers relative to high-skilled ones and slightly higher for older relative to younger, and the estimated negative effect on urban workers is almost three times that on rural workers, in absolute terms.

Higher exports correlate with little change in informality. In the short run and long run, higher exports do not appear to have any statistically significant effect (table 5.2). This means that there is little change in the informality rate. In the short run, for most types of workers, the correlation between exports and informality is negative—that is, as exports rise, informality decreases (meaning less informality). In the long term, the correlation between exports and informality is negative at the aggregate level and for younger workers.

Higher exports correlate with little change in FLFP. Here, too, our results show that in the short run and long run, higher exports do

TABLE 5.1

Estimated Effect on Average Annual Real Wages (in 2010 Egyptian Pounds) from a US$100 Increase in Exports or Imports per Worker in Egypt

Type of worker		Exports		Imports	
		Short-run effect (2009–12)	Long-run effect (2009–17)	Short-run effect (2009–12)	Long-run effect (2009–17)
All	Coefficient	−207.85**	−0.300	−16.878**	−28.603
	t-statistic	(−2.55)	(0.00)	(−2.09)	(−0.93)
	N	250	246	250	246
Manufacturing	Coefficient	−195.71	291.39	−59.313**	−82.338
	t-statistic	(−0.56)	(0.91)	(−2.16)	(−1.03)
	N	119	110	119	110
Services	Coefficient	−119.41	111.96	−10.951**	−48.816
	t-statistic	(−1.10)	(0.33)	(−2.44)	(−0.96)
	N	250	246	250	246
Males	Coefficient	−244.49***	47.95	−20.973**	−39.37
	t-statistic	(−3.32)	(0.17)	(−2.26)	(−0.63)
	N	250	246	250	246
Females	Coefficient	−67.59	−19.54	−6.757	−26.857***
	t-statistic	(−0.41)	(−0.11)	(−1.00)	(−3.41)
	N	201	205	201	205
Low skill	Coefficient	−286.06***	−60.47	−2.676	−16.527
	t-statistic	(−2.61)	(−0.17)	(−0.45)	(−0.75)
	N	247	242	247	242
High skill	Coefficient	−149.22	−246.79	−13.085	−11.56
	t-statistic	(−0.64)	(−0.91)	(−1.46)	(−1.24)
	N	236	231	236	231
Young	Coefficient	−203.63***	−420.47	−14.549	4.643
	t-statistic	(−2.81)	(−1.10)	(−1.48)	(0.29)
	N	246	244	246	244
Old	Coefficient	−242.24**	378.4	−15.797*	−49.896
	t-statistic	(−2.11)	(1.08)	(−1.91)	(−0.75)
	N	250	246	250	246
Rural	Coefficient	−133.67**	−54.67	68.709	−8.61
	t-statistic	(−2.19)	(−0.45)	(−0.09)	(−0.05)
	N	149	146	149	146
Urban	Coefficient	−380.90*	153.7	−17.139**	−23.081
	t-statistic	(−1.72)	(0.25)	(−2.20)	(−1.01)
	N	156	149	156	149

Sources: World Bank calculations using Labor Force Surveys of the Central Agency for Public Mobilization and Statistics (CAPMAS) and the United Nations Comtrade database.
Note: "Low-skill" refers to primary or less education and "high-skill" to secondary or above. "Young" refers to ages 35 or younger and "old" to ages above 35. Robust t-statistics are within parentheses.
***p < 0.01 **p < 0.05 *p < 0.1.

TABLE 5.2

Estimated Effect on the Informality Rate from a US$100 Increase in Exports or Imports per Worker in Egypt

Type of worker		Exports		Imports	
		Short-run effect (2009–12)	Long-run effect (2009–17)	Short-run effect (2009–12)	Long-run effect (2009–17)
All	Coefficient	−0.00026	−0.01514	0.000***	0.000
	t-statistic	(−0.09)	(−1.09)	(2.74)	(−0.60)
	N	250	246	250	246
Manufacturing	Coefficient	−0.00827	−0.01831	0.001	−0.006
	t-statistic	(−0.73)	(−1.23)	(1.41)	(−0.26)
	N	150	139	150	138
Services	Coefficient	−0.00081	−0.00065	0.000	0.000
	t-statistic	(−1.50)	(−0.88)	(0.53)	(−0.54)
	N	250	246	250	246
Males	Coefficient	−0.00194	−0.01775	0.000	−0.001
	t-statistic	(−0.62)	(−1.19)	(0.27)	(−0.55)
	N	250	246	250	246
Females	Coefficient	−0.00067	0.00216	0.000	0.000
	t-statistic	(−0.65)	(0.97)	(1.39)	(0.11)
	N	226	224	226	224
Low skill	Coefficient	−0.00127	−0.02031	0.000	0.000
	t-statistic	(−0.45)	(−0.88)	(0.44)	(−0.36)
	N	247	242	247	242
High skill	Coefficient	−0.00012	−0.00116	0.000	0.000
	t-statistic	(−0.06)	(−0.31)	(−0.53)	(−1.34)
	N	241	238	241	238
Young	Coefficient	0.00028	−0.01981	0.001**	0.000
	t-statistic	(0.08)	(−1.12)	(2.02)	(−0.20)
	N	250	246	250	246
Old	Coefficient	−0.00125	−0.01342	0.000	−0.001
	t-statistic	(−0.44)	(−1.11)	(0.87)	(−0.59)
	N	250	246	250	246
Rural	Coefficient	−0.00017	−0.00319	−0.012	0.004
	t-statistic	(−0.12)	(−1.13)	(−0.62)	(1.59)
	N	149	146	149	146
Urban	Coefficient	−0.00086	−0.02437	0.000	−0.001
	t-statistic	(−0.14)	(−0.91)	(1.12)	(−0.64)
	N	156	149	156	149

Sources: World Bank calculations using Labor Force Surveys of the Central Agency for Public Mobilization and Statistics (CAPMAS) and the United Nations Comtrade database.

Note: "Low-skill" refers to primary or less education and "high-skill" to secondary or above. "Young" refers to ages 35 or younger and "old" to ages above 35. Robust t-statistics are within parentheses.

***$p < 0.01$ **$p < 0.05$ *$p < 0.1$.

not appear to have any statistically significant effect. Thus, there is little change in FLFP—which is less than half of the world's average, is historically stubborn, and has been 24 percent or less since 2005. In the short run, the estimated effect of exposure to exports is negative (that is, lower female participation) except among high-skilled female workers, who seem to marginally benefit, although this benefit disappears in the long run.

In sum, Egypt's higher exports do not translate into better local labor markets in the same way that has occurred in other low- and middle-income countries (such as Bangladesh, China, India, and Vietnam) (Erten and Leight 2021; McCaig 2011; Topalova 2010). Our findings suggest that this outcome is in spite of Egypt's success in undertaking bold economic reforms and signing several free trade agreements—and that rising exports, if anything, seem to have suppressed wages in the short term.

Effects of Higher Imports

It is possible that Egyptian imports—which are double the value of its exports—are weakening the link between exports and labor market variables. Although around 75 percent of imports are intermediate goods necessary for both production and exports (Zaki et al. 2019), Egypt's higher trade flows could mainly be affecting wages, informality, and FLFP through higher imports rather than exports. To assess this hypothesis, we also run the Bartik model using an instrumental variable for imports—reaching the key findings described below.

Higher imports correlate with lower wages. In the short term, an increase in imports is associated with a negative effect on wages, although the effect is only 1–10 percent of the effect from an increase in exports. Between 2009 and 2012, a US$100 increase in imports per worker led to a statistically significant decline in average wages of LE 16.88. This decrease is especially pronounced for male, older, and urban workers. In contrast, women and low-skilled, high-skilled, young, and rural workers do not experience a statistically significant effect on wages.

The group that experiences the biggest wage decrease is workers in the manufacturing sector, with the impact being more than five times greater than for workers in the service sector (LE 59.31 versus LE 10.95, respectively), and it is statistically significant. This effect is in line with the literature finding that most of the negative effects of increasing imports are in labor-intensive industries (Autor, Dorn, and Hanson 2013; Feliciano 2001).

However, in the long run, the negative impact on wages is short-lived for most. Whereas the point estimate increases in absolute value, its statistical significance decreases. In other words, the true long-run estimate is unlikely to be different from zero. Between 2009 and 2017, the estimated effect of imports on wages is LE 28.60 on average, but the result is not statistically significant.

Higher imports correlate with little change in informality. In the short run, an increase in imports is associated with a positive, albeit very small, effect on the informality rate (that is, informality gets worse), unlike with higher exports, where there is a slight improvement. This outcome resembles findings in the low- and middle-income world where imports increase informality in Argentina (Cruces, Porto, and Viollaz 2018); Brazil (Ulyssea and Ponczek 2018); and Vietnam (McCaig and Pavcnik 2018).

In Egypt, this effect appears to be driven by the impact on young workers (ages 15–35), the only subgroup to experience such a setback. Specifically, a US$100 increase in imports between 2009 and 2012 is related to an increase of 0.001 percentage points in the informality rate for workers (table 5.2). In the long run, none of the results is statistically significant, and most are zero, except for old and urban workers who have a slight negative.

Higher imports correlate with little change in FLFP. The FLFP rate reacts much more strongly to imports than to exports, but the effects are still negligible. In the short run, a US$100 increase in imports is associated with an FLFP rate decrease of less than 0.001 percentage points (table 5.3). The latter is true for all types of workers except rural, but the effect is statistically significant only for the aggregate worker population, older workers, and urban workers. In the long run, all effects dissipate, and none is statistically different from zero.

In sum, Egypt's higher imports after liberalization do not seem to have helped local labor markets. Although most effects are negligible and short-lived for wages and informality, they are negative (that is, wages would go down and informality would improve) and statistically significant, as found in the literature.

Here it is important to note that the gravity model estimates suggest that the average increase in trade for Egypt from signing new trade agreements is 5.8 percent, which is much less than the literature has found (see chapter 2). In other words, new regional trade agreements are not flooding the Egyptian market with new imports to compete with domestic production.

TABLE 5.3

Estimated Effect on Female Labor Force Participation from a US$100 Increase in Exports or Imports per Worker in Egypt

		Exports		Imports	
Type of worker		Short-run effect (2009–12)	Long-run effect (2009–17)	Short-run effect (2009–12)	Long-run effect (2009–17)
All	Coefficient	−0.00117	0.00107	−0.00039**	−0.0003
	t-statistic	(−0.74)	(0.39)	(−2.06)	(−0.43)
	N	250	246	250	246
Low skill	Coefficient	−0.0016	−0.00389	−0.00012	−0.00014
	t-statistic	(−1.44)	(−1.10)	(−1.35)	(−0.37)
	N	248	244	248	244
High skill	Coefficient	0.00078	−0.00507	−0.0001	−0.00001
	t-statistic	(0.27)	(−1.09)	(−0.51)	(−0.04)
	N	245	242	245	242
Young	Coefficient	−0.00189	0.00082	−0.00012	0.00028
	t-statistic	(−0.79)	−0.24	(−0.51)	−0.94
	N	250	246	250	246
Old	Coefficient	−0.00001	0.00019	−0.00059***	−0.00096
	t-statistic	(−0.01)	−0.06	(−6.13)	(−0.63)
	N	248	245	248	245
Rural	Coefficient	−0.00051	−0.00079	0.00598	0.00036
	t-statistic	(−0.25)	(−0.25)	(0.22)	(0.11)
	N	149	146	149	146
Urban	Coefficient	−0.00072	0.00026	−0.00028**	−0.00021
	t-statistic	(−0.35)	−0.06	(−2.37)	(−0.44)
	N	156	149	156	149

Sources: World Bank calculations using Labor Force Surveys of the Central Agency for Public Mobilization and Statistics (CAPMAS) and the United Nations Comtrade database.
Note: "Low-skill" refers to primary or less education and "high-skill" to secondary or above. "Young" refers to ages 35 or younger and "old" to ages above 35. Robust t-statistics are within parentheses.
***$p < 0.01$ **$p < 0.05$ *$p < 0.1$.

Role of Firms in the Broken Link

How do we explain what appears to be a broken link between trade and local labor markets? The structure of Egyptian firms could represent one explanation. To determine whether this is the case, we dive into a firm analysis. After all, even though exports do not connect to labor markets at the macro level, as we would expect, there may be micro-level effects. Certainly, rising exports have the potential to increase employment through increased labor demand. So if that does not happen, why not? There are four possible reasons.

First, exporting firms may be too small of a segment in the local labor market to significantly affect aggregate employment. In the case of Egypt, this reason may be valid, given that Egypt's export market is characterized by a few large firms. According to the World Bank's 2017 Enterprise Survey in Egypt, which contains the universe of enterprises, only 1 percent of firms are exporters (defined as exporting at least 10 percent of their sales directly). The average sizes of exporting and nonexporting firms are 18.9 and 3.2 employees, respectively.[22]

This explanation is further corroborated by the 2020 Enterprise Survey, covering a subset of formal firms with at least five employees (figure 5.12, panel a). In this sample, the 2020 average employment size for exporters is 363 versus 95 for nonexporters. And consistent with the kernel density, there is a strong positive correlation between employment and export sales in 2020 (figure 5.12, panel b). Thus, even if labor demand increased in these firms, they are too small a segment of the market to have much impact at the macro level.

Second, exporting firms are often in capital-intensive sectors (such as extractive industries and high technology exports), which can expand production without significantly increasing their workforce. This reason may also be valid. In Egypt, as elsewhere, exporting firms tend to be relatively more capital intensive

FIGURE 5.12

Correlation of Firm Size and Export Activity, Egypt, 2020

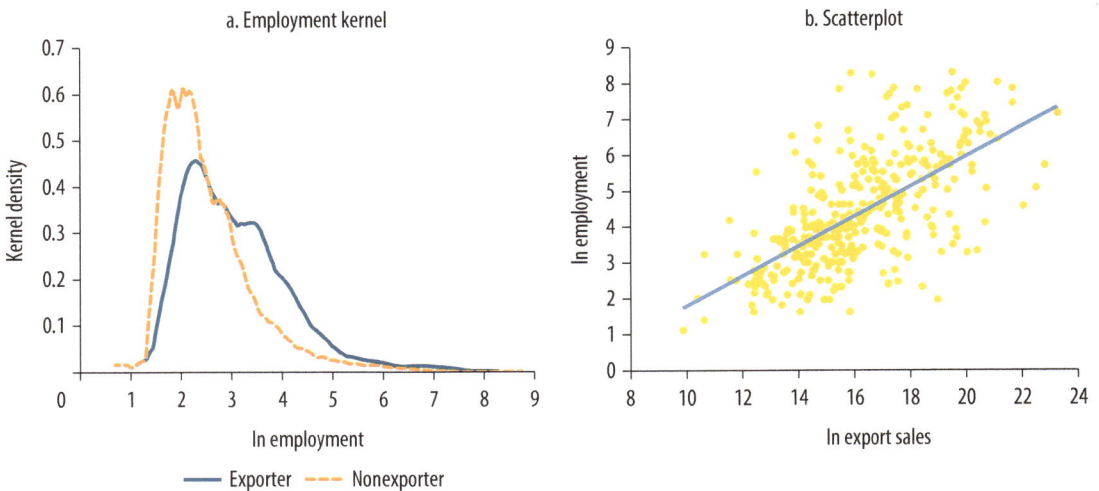

Source: World Bank based on 2020 World Bank Enterprise Survey for Egypt.
Note: "Exporters" are those firms that export at least 10 percent of their sales directly. All other firms are classified as "nonexporters." The numbers on the x-axis (panel a) and y-axis (panel b) show the natural logarithm (ln) of employment. The numbers on the x-axis of panel b show the ln of export sales and the slanted solid line, the linear relationship between both variables.

than their nonexporting counterparts. Using the ratio of the firm's value of machinery (as a proxy for capital) to its labor cost, we find the capital–labor ratio is 31 for exporting firms and 26 for nonexporting firms.

Third, exporting firms may have excess capacity of workers (possibly owing to labor market distortions) and use the relatively idle workers to provide the additional production for exports. This reason does not appear to be valid. If firms increased exports by mobilizing idle workers without expanding their workforce, then we would not expect to find a positive export–employment elasticity. However, our results show that in Egypt there is a statistically significant positive effect—that is, a 100 percent increase in export sales would boost employment by about 20 percent (box 5.2 and table 5.4).

Fourth, firm-level production may simply shift from the domestic to the international market, without expanding production or employment. This reason also appears not to be valid. In Egypt, some firms shift production from the domestic to the foreign market without increasing their employment, but this represents a minor effect related to the disconnect between exports and the labor market. To test this

---

BOX 5.2

How to Determine the Employment–Export Elasticity

We estimate the elasticity of employment relative to an increase in export sales at the firm level. Using 2017 and 2020 World Bank Enterprise Survey data for Egypt, we estimate the following model of derived labor demand of the firm:

$$\ln N_{it} = \alpha + \beta \ln E_{it} + X'_{it}\gamma + \mu_i + \varepsilon_{it},$$

where N_{it} is the number of employees at firm i at time t; E_{it} is export sales of firm i at time t; and X_{it} are a set of time-varying controls.

Estimating the above equation is challenging because of endogeneity driven by the fact that the export decision is not

made at random. The decision to export, and how many employees to hire conditional on export, is driven by unobserved factors (μ_i and ε_{it}). Guided by the empirical literature, we address these endogeneity issues by fixed effect estimation with a Heckman correction (Heckman 1979).

In table 5.4, the probit estimate in column 1 suggests that the main predictors of exporting appear to be use of foreign technology and imported inputs. The ordinary least squares estimate in column 2 and the fixed effect with Heckman correction estimate in column 3 point to a positive relationship between exports and employment at the firm level.

TABLE 5.4

Estimates of Extensive and Intensive Margin

	(1)	(2)	(3)
Dependent variable	Exporter (yes = 1)	ln(employment)	
Estimator	Probit	OLS	FE-Heckit
ln(export sales)		0.075***	0.207**
		(5.99)	(2.18)
ln(value of machinery)	0.003*	0.048***	0.006
	(1.94)	(6.03)	(0.36)
ln(cost per worker)	0.026*	−0.181***	−0.478***
	(1.82)	(−2.95)	(−3.68)
ln(age of firm)	0.006	0.477***	0.181
	(0.38)	(6.80)	(0.30)
Indirect exporter (yes=1)		−0.481	0.213
		(−1.44)	(0.72)
Innovation (yes=1)	0.137**	−0.215	
	(2.43)	(−1.12)	
Foreign owners (yes=1)	0.133**	0.229	
	(2.19)	(0.97)	
Female owners (yes=1)	0.013	0.216	
	(0.25)	(1.02)	
Registered (yes=1)	0.018	0.370**	
	(0.44)	(2.14)	
Training (yes=1)	0.015	0.777***	
	(0.37)	(4.57)	
Foreign tech (yes=1)	0.328***	0.378*	
	(4.10)	(1.76)	
Imported inputs (yes=1)	0.135***	0.590***	
	(4.40)	(4.70)	
Lambda			−0.545*
			(−1.70)
Constant		2.854***	6.288**
		(4.68)	(2.52)
Year dummies	Yes	Yes	Yes
Observations	594	594	594
R-squared	0.209	0.363	0.579

Source: World Bank calculations using the 2017 and 2020 World Bank Enterprise Surveys.

Note: Probit marginal effects reported in column 1. The dependent variable in column 1 is a dummy equal to one if the firm is an exporter and zero otherwise. The dependent variable in columns 2 and 3 is log employment. Column 2 is estimated by ordinary least squares (OLS), and column 3 by fixed effect with a Heckman correction (FE-Heckit). The exclusion restrictions are innovation, foreign owners, female owners, registered, training, and foreign tech. Unweighted. Robust t-statistics in parentheses. ln = natural logarithm.
***p < 0.01 **p < 0.05 *p < 0.10.

hypothesis, we analyzed changes in employment with changes in the share of sales sold internationally between 2016 and 2020 among the exporting firms in our sample. Our results show that more export sales correlate with more employment and vice versa.

How to Fix a Broken Link

It would be incorrect to conclude from the lack of labor market response that "trade doesn't work." Instead, the story is much more nuanced. The lackluster response of Egypt's labor market following its trade liberalization is largely because its export market remains a very small share of its economy. Microanalysis at the firm level demonstrates a positive employment response to export expansion but also shows that this is not occurring at a large enough scale to be felt at the macro level.

For Egypt to seize the benefits of trade, it requires deeper reforms that create incentives to substantially grow the export sector, especially in favor of labor-intensive industries, and to integrate more into GVCs. It will be important, therefore, to improve the business environment. Barriers to investment (especially foreign direct investment) must be lowered. The private sector should become more attractive relative to the public sector in terms of wages and job security. Also, the formalization costs that firms face must be lowered.

Increasing imports and competing firms should not be a concern for liberalization efforts. Our results show that increased imports have negligible negative and short-lived effects. This is occurring for two reasons.

First, all major imported goods in Egypt are capital intensive. Most papers studying the relationship between labor market outcomes and imports find adverse effects of increasing imports because they focus on labor-intensive and manufacturing industries (Autor, Dorn, and Hanson 2013; Feliciano 2001). But even if imports were substituting for domestic production, since imported goods are not labor intensive, the impact on local labor markets would be low. Further, capital-intensive imported goods could be increasing the productivity of labor for Egyptian firms. For example, some of the main imported goods—computers, telephones, medicaments, and pesticides—could boost labor's marginal productivity.

Second, Egypt's most important trade partners are high-income countries. Trade theory predicts that competing imports are most disruptive when countries trade with low-wage countries (Krugman 2000). Egypt's trade partners are mainly high-income countries with higher salaries, whose imports come mostly from high-wage Organisation for Economic Co-operation and Development (OECD) countries. In 2009, Egyptian imports from the OECD accounted for 58.26 percent of total imports, and the United States and European Union alone accounted for 40.13 percent.[23] Other important trade partners—such as Brazil, Japan, the Republic of Korea, the Russian Federation, and Saudi Arabia—accounted for 17.36 percent of total imports, and all have higher real wages.

This is important not only because it reduces potential harmful local job effects from increasing imports but also because most high-technology goods come from wealthier countries, which would push firms to upgrade. Egypt has a low diversified export basket of goods with eroding demand, meaning it could rethink its export basket and its participation in GVCs.

Annex 5A. Free Trade Agreements

TABLE 5A.1

Egypt's Free Trade Agreements in Force

Agreement name	Entry into force	Current partners
Agadir Agreement[a]	2007	Egypt, Arab Rep.; Jordan; Morocco; and Tunisia
Common Market for Eastern and Southern Africa (COMESA)–Accession of Egypt	1999	Angola; Burundi; Comoros; Congo, Dem. Rep.; Eritrea; Eswatini; Ethiopia; Kenya; Lesotho; Malawi; Mauritius; Rwanda; Sudan; Tanzania; Uganda; Zambia; and Zimbabwe
Egypt–Türkiye	2007	Türkiye
European Free Trade Association (EFTA)–Egypt	2007	Iceland, Liechtenstein, Norway, and Switzerland
European Union–Egypt	2004	Austria, Belgium, Bulgaria, Croatia, Cyprus, Czech Republic, Denmark, Estonia, Finland, France, Germany, Greece, Hungary, Ireland, Italy, Latvia, Lithuania, Luxembourg, Malta, Netherlands, Poland, Portugal, Romania, Slovak Republic, Slovenia, Spain, and Sweden
Global System of Trade Preferences among Developing Countries (GSTP)	1989	Algeria; Argentina; Bangladesh; Benin; Bolivia; Brazil; Cameroon; Chile; Colombia; Cuba; Ecuador; Egypt, Arab Rep.; Ghana; Guinea; Guyana; India; Indonesia; Iran, Islamic Rep.; Iraq; Korea, Dem. People's Rep.; Korea, Rep.; Libya; Malaysia; Mexico; Morocco; Mozambique; Myanmar; Nicaragua; Nigeria; Pakistan; Peru; Philippines; Singapore; Sri Lanka; Sudan; Tanzania; Thailand; Trinidad and Tobago; Tunisia; Venezuela, RB; Vietnam; and Zimbabwe
Pan-Arab Free Trade Area (PAFTA)[b]	1998	Bahrain; Egypt, Arab Rep.; Iraq; Jordan; Kuwait; Lebanon; Libya; Morocco; Oman; Qatar; Saudi Arabia; Sudan; Syrian Arab Republic; Tunisia; United Arab Emirates; and Yemen, Rep.
Protocol on Trade Negotiations (PTN)	1973	Bangladesh; Brazil; Chile; Egypt, Arab Rep.; Israel; Korea, Rep.; Mexico; Pakistan; Paraguay; Peru; Philippines; Serbia; Tunisia; Türkiye; and Uruguay
Southern Common Market (MERCOSUR)–Egypt	2017	Argentina, Brazil, Paraguay, and Uruguay
United Kingdom–Egypt	2021	United Kingdom

Source: World Trade Organization's Regional Trade Agreements Database.
a. The Agadir Agreement is also known, more formally, as the Agreement on the Establishment of the Free Trade Area between the Arab Mediterranean States.
b. The Pan-Arab Free Trade Area (PAFTA) is also known as the Greater Arab Free Trade Area (GAFTA).

Annex 5B. Mincerian Wage Regression

To better understand the wage dynamics at play in Egypt, we estimate a Mincerian wage equation (Mincer 1958) as follows:

$$\ln wage_i = \beta_0 + \beta_1 female_i + \beta_2 textiles_i + \beta_3 \left(female_i \times textiles_i \right) + X_i'\gamma + \varepsilon_i,$$

where $\ln wage_i$ is log real wages of individual i; $female_i$ is a dummy taking the value of one if individual i is female; $textiles_i$ is a dummy taking the value of one if individual i works in the textile and garment industry; and X_i is a vector of exogenous control variables including age, age squared, a dummy indicating high skill (defined as those with a college degree or higher), number of hours worked, and dummies for the other 31 sectors.

Table 5B.1 reports the estimated results of the Mincer regression. There is no noticeable improvement in the gender wage gap, even after controlling for confounding factors. We find that the wage differential between men and women peaked in 2015, when women earned an estimated 29 percentage points less than men, double the gap in 2009. Thereafter, the wage gap followed a downward trend, reaching 22 percentage points in 2017.

We also note that the returns to higher education have decreased over time. In 2009, highly skilled individuals earned, on average, 25 percentage points more than the low-skilled individuals, but by 2017, this education premium had fallen to 17 percentage points. In Egypt, and

TABLE 5B.1

Mincer Wage Equation

Worker type	2009	2010	2011	2012	2013	2014	2015	2016	2017
Female	−0.096***	−0.192***	−0.088***	−0.234***	−0.166***	−0.137***	−0.127***	−0.079***	−0.077***
	(−15.68)	(−25.19)	(−12.54)	(−17.36)	(−21.74)	(−17.40)	(−16.44)	(−11.86)	(−11.96)
Textile	−0.063***	−0.148***	0.004	−0.720***	−0.114***	−0.050***	−0.031**	−0.098***	−0.118***
	(−4.13)	(−10.78)	(0.27)	(−17.14)	(−7.99)	(−3.38)	(−2.12)	(−6.07)	(−7.32)
Female x textile	−0.046	−0.127***	−0.090***	0.098	−0.033	−0.139***	−0.165***	−0.195***	−0.142***
	(−1.31)	(−4.59)	(−2.59)	(1.16)	(−1.08)	(−4.17)	(−4.78)	(−6.35)	(−3.18)
High skill	−0.096***	−0.192***	−0.088***	−0.234***	−0.166***	−0.137***	−0.127***	−0.079***	−0.077***
	(−15.68)	(−25.19)	(−12.54)	(−17.36)	(−21.74)	(−17.40)	(−16.44)	(−11.86)	(−11.96)
N	57,238	60,853	65,136	62,654	57,242	56,877	57,732	63,028	56,832
R-squared	0.148	0.186	0.133	0.180	0.185	0.156	0.143	0.130	0.159

Source: World Bank based on 2009–17 Labor Force Surveys, Central Agency for Public Mobilization and Statistics (CAPMAS).
Note: Sample restricted to working-age population (ages 15–64). "High skill" means secondary education and above. Regression controls for age, age squared, hours worked, and other sectors (32 in total, plus one omitted as reference). Other coefficients for all other sectors are omitted for brevity. Robust t-statistics in parentheses.
*p < 0.01 **p < 0.05 ***p < 0.10.

in most Middle East and North Africa economies (chapter 2), the public sector employs a significant share of workers with higher education. Given the generous conditions that public employment provides (such as job security and nonmonetary benefits), more than half of young job seekers prefer to work in the public sector (World Bank 2012).

Annex 5C. Subnational Labor Market Trends

FIGURE 5C.1

Average Real Monthly Wages, by Governorate, Egypt, 2008–17

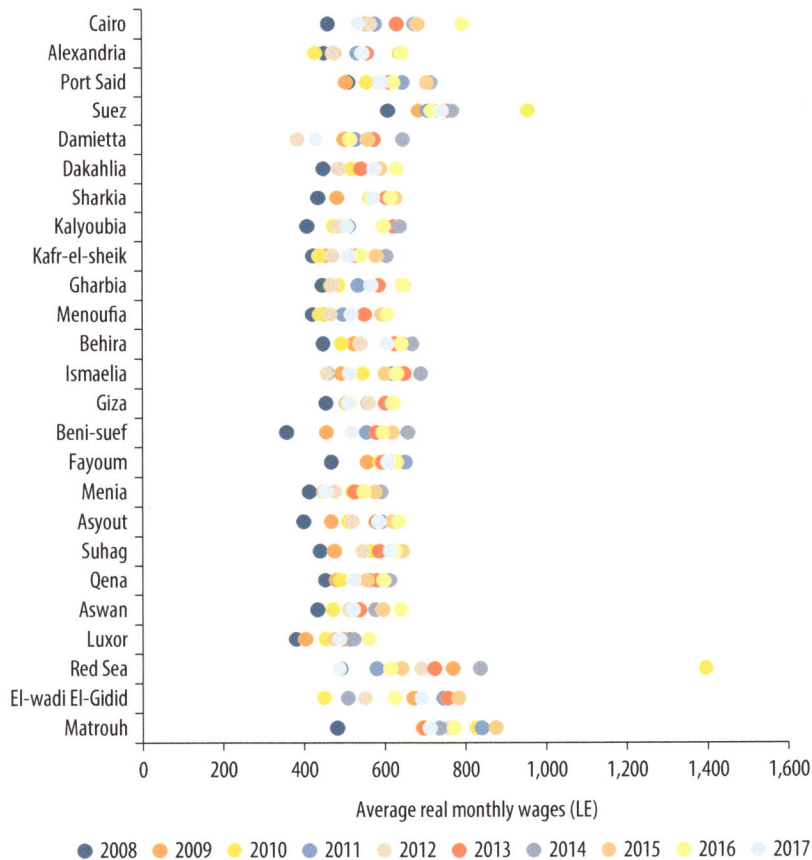

Source: World Bank based on 2008 Labor Force Survey data, Central Agency for Public Mobilization and Statistics (CAPMAS).
Note: Sample restricted to working-age population (ages 15–64). Wages are in constant 2010 Egyptian pounds (LE).

FIGURE 5C.2

Informality Rate, by Governorate, Egypt, 2008–17

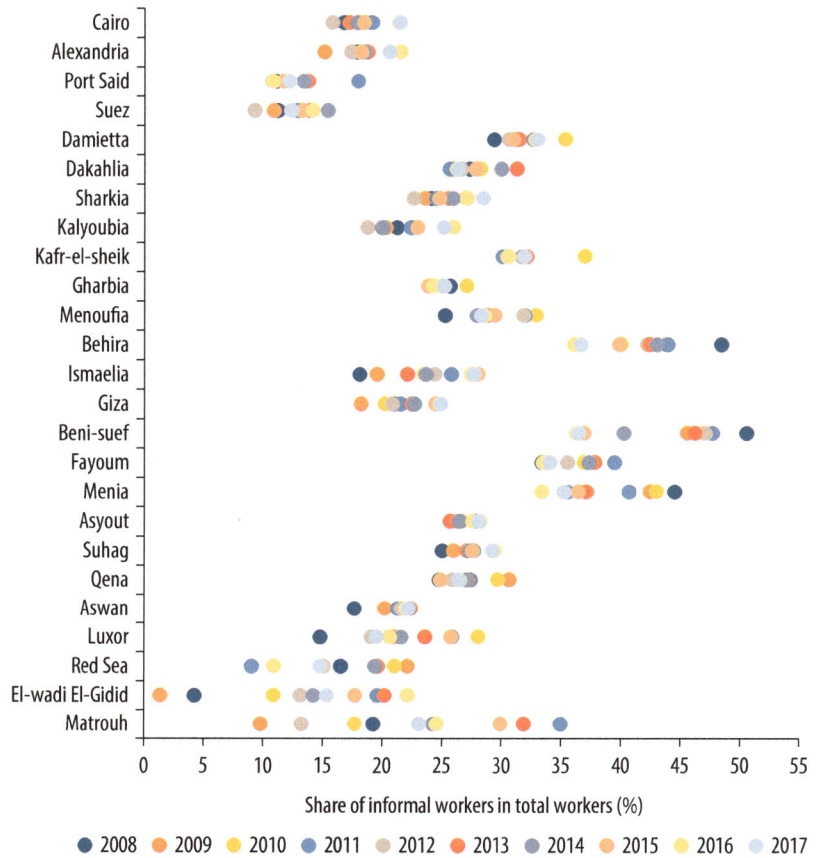

Source: World Bank based on 2008–17 Labor Force Survey data, Central Agency for Public Mobilization and Statistics (CAPMAS).
Note: The informality rate is the share of working-age population (ages 15–64) who are self-employed, unpaid family workers, or workers without social security coverage.

FIGURE 5C.3

Female Labor Force Participation, by Governorate, Egypt, 2008–17

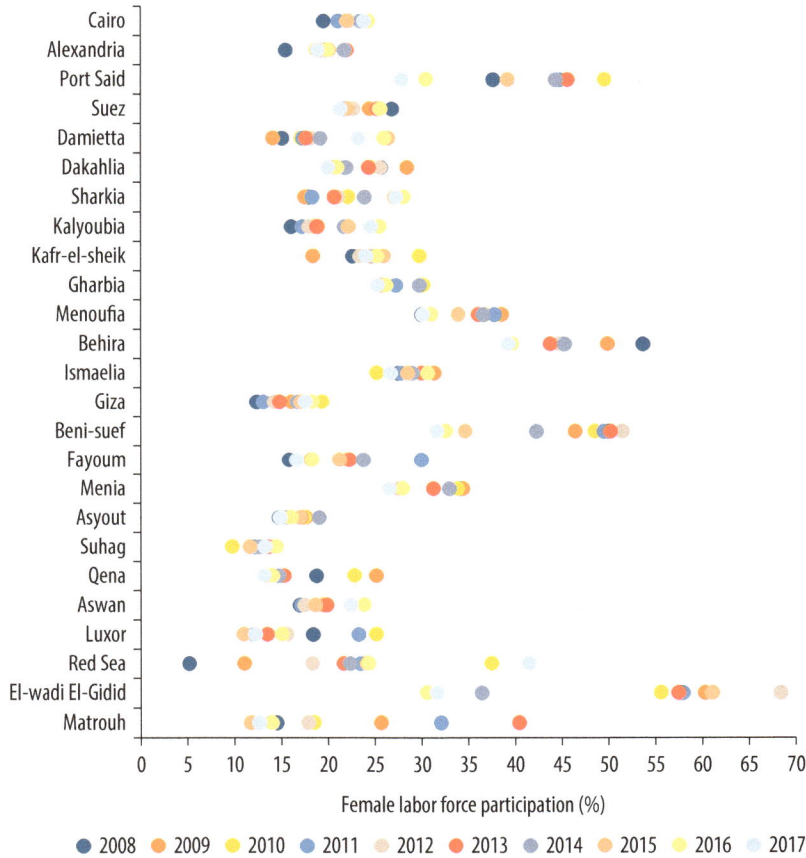

Female labor force participation (%)

● 2008 ● 2009 ● 2010 ● 2011 ● 2012 ● 2013 ● 2014 ● 2015 ● 2016 ● 2017

Source: World Bank based on 2008–17 Labor Force Survey data, Central Agency for Public Mobilization and Statistics (CAPMAS).
Note: "Female labor force participation" is calculated as the active female population divided by the working-age (ages 15–64) population. The "active" population comprises those who are either (a) employed or (b) unemployed and seeking a job.

Notes

1. Trade agreement data are from the World Trade Organization (WTO) Regional Trade Agreements Database (updated April 22, 2022), http://rtais .wto.org/UI/PublicMaintainRTAHome.aspx. Also see the table in annex 5A.

2. Egyptian applied tariff rate data are from Our World in Data (https:// ourworldindata.org/).

3. Egyptian import and export data are from the World Bank's World Development Indicators (WDI) Database.

4. Data on Egyptian imports and exports, as a share of GDP, are from the WDI Database.

5. In November 2016, the Central Bank of Egypt announced the flotation of the Egyptian pound, which depreciated by 45 percent against the US dollar, reaching LE 13 by the time of decision and LE 18 soon after (Zaki, Abdallah, and Sami 2019).

6. Data on changes in Egyptian exports of goods and services, 2016–19, are from "Egypt, Arab Rep. Trade Statistics," WITS Database, World Bank: https://wits.worldbank.org/countryprofile/en/egy.

7. Data from "GVC Output Table," World Integrated Trade Solution (WITS) database, World Bank: https://wits.worldbank.org/gvc/gvc-output-table .html.

8. Shares of Egyptian exports, by industry, are calculated from United Nations Comtrade data.

9. Shares of Egyptian imports, by industry, are calculated from United Nations Comtrade data.

10. Data about machinery imports are from Egypt trade data, WITS database, World Bank: https://wits.worldbank.org/.

11. Data about Egypt's top export and import markets are from "Egypt, Arab Rep. Trade Statistics," WITS Database, World Bank: https://wits.worldbank .org/countryprofile/en/egy.

12. For the unemployment rate trends in Morocco and Tunisia, see chapters 3 and 4, respectively.

13. Egyptian unemployment rate data, by age group and gender, are from the WDI Database.

14. Egyptian labor force participation data are from the WDI Database.

15. Egyptian employment data, by sector, are from 2008–17 Labor Force Surveys, Central Agency for Public Mobilization and Statistics (CAPMAS).

16. Egyptian informality rate data are from 2009–17 Labor Force Surveys, CAPMAS.

17. For subnational real wages across time (averaged for men and women), see annex 5C, figure 5C.1.

18. Data for average real wages of men and women, 2008–17, are from Egyptian Labor Force Surveys 2009–17 conducted by CAPMAS. Sample restricted to the working-age population (ages 15–64). Wages are in constant 2010 Egyptian pounds.

19. Average real wage data from 2008–17 Labor Force Surveys, CAPMAS.

20. All informality and female labor participation data are from 2008–17 Labor Force Surveys, CAPMAS.

21. Urban areas are divided into kism and rural areas into markaz.

22. The World Bank's Enterprise Surveys, which target larger firms (those with five or more employees), similarly find that exporters are on average considerably larger than nonexporters (313 versus 65, respectively, in 2020).

23. Egyptian import data are from the WITS database, World Bank: https://wits.worldbank.org/.

References

Acemoglu, Daron, and Pascual Restrepo. 2017. "Robots and Jobs: Evidence from US Labor Markets." Working Paper No. 23285, National Bureau of Economic Research, Cambridge, MA.

Adly, Amr. 2020. *Cleft Capitalism: The Social Origins of Failed Market Making in Egypt.* Stanford, CA: Stanford University Press.

Amiti, Mary, and Donald R. Davis. 2011. "Trade, Firms, and Wages: Theory and Evidence." *Review of Economic Studies* 79 (1): 1–36.

Assaad, Ragui, Caroline Krafft, Khandker Wahedur Rahman, and Irene Selwaness. 2019. "Job Creation in Egypt: A Sectoral and Geographical Analysis Focusing on Private Establishments 1996–2017." Policy Paper, Economic Research Forum, Cairo.

Autor, David H., David Dorn, and Gordon H. Hanson. 2013. "The China Syndrome: Local Labor Market Effects of Import Competition in the United States." *American Economic Review* 103 (6): 2121–68. https://doi.org/10.1257/aer.103.6.2121.

Bartik, Timothy J. 1991. *Who Benefits from State and Local Economic Development Policies?* Kalamazoo, MI: W. E. Upjohn Institute for Employment Research.

Bartley Johns, Marcus, Paul Brenton, Massimiliano Cali, Mombert Hoppe, and Roberta Piermartini. 2015. *The Role of Trade in Ending Poverty.* Washington, DC: World Bank; Geneva: World Trade Organization.

Bhagwati, Jagdish, and T. N. Srinivasan. 2002. "Trade and Poverty in the Poor Countries." *American Economic Review* 92 (2): 180–83. https://doi.org/10.1257/000282802320189212.

Cruces, Guillermo, Guido Porto, and Mariana Viollaz. 2018. "Trade Liberalization and Informality in Argentina: Exploring the Adjustment Mechanisms." *Latin American Economic Review* 27 (1): 1–29. https://doi.org/10.1186/s40503-018-0061-1.

Dollar, David, and Aart Kraay. 2004. "Trade, Growth, and Poverty." *The Economic Journal* 114 (493): F22–F49.

Erten, Bilge, and Jessica Leight. 2021. "Exporting Out of Agriculture: The Impact of WTO Accession on Structural Transformation in China." *Review of Economics and Statistics* 103 (2): 362–80.

Feler, Leo, and Mine Senses. 2017. "Trade Shocks and the Provision of Local Public Goods." *American Economic Journal: Economic Policy* 9 (4): 101–43.

Feliciano, Zadia M. 2001. "Workers and Trade Liberalization: The Impact of Trade Reforms in Mexico on Wages and Employment." *Industrial and Labor Relations Review* 55 (1): 95–115. https://doi.org/10.2307/2696188.

Frankel, Jeffrey A., and David Romer. 1999. "Does Trade Cause Growth?" *American Economic Review* 89 (3): 379–99.

Gallo, Amy. 2016. "A Refresher on Statistical Significance: It's Too Often Misused and Misunderstood." Analytics and Data Science digital article, *Harvard Business Review*, February 16. https://hbr.org/2016/02/a-refresher-on-statistical-significance.

Goldberg, Linda, and Joseph Tracy. 2000. "Exchange Rates and Local Labor Markets." In *The Impact of International Trade on Wages*, edited by Robert C. Feenstra, 269–307. Chicago: University of Chicago Press.

Heckman, James J. 1979. "Sample Selection Bias as a Specification Error." *Econometrica* 47 (1): 153–61.

IFC (International Finance Corporation). 2020. "Creating Markets in Egypt: Realizing the Full Potential of a Productive Private Sector." Country Private Sector Diagnostic, IFC, Washington, DC.

ILO (International Labour Organization). n.d. "Employment for Youth in Egypt (EYE): Working Together in Qalyoubia and Menoufia." Description of Project EGY/16/02/NOR, ILO, Geneva. https://www.ilo.org/africa/technical-cooperation/WCMS_571875/lang--en/index.htm.

Korayem, Karima. 1997. "Egypt's Economic Reform and Structural Adjustment (ERSAP)." Working Paper No. 19, Egyptian Center for Economic Studies, Cairo.

Krugman, Paul R. 2000. "Technology, Trade and Factor Prices." *Journal of International Economics* 50 (1): 51–71.

Lopez-Acevedo, Gladys, Marco Ranzani, Nistha Sinha, and Adam Elsheikhi. 2023. *Informality and Inclusive Growth in the Middle East and North Africa.* Middle East and North Africa Development Report. Washington, DC: World Bank.

Lopez-Acevedo, Gladys, and Raymond Robertson. 2012. "The Promise and Peril of Post-MFA Apparel Production." *Economic Premise* No. 84, World Bank, Washington, DC.

McCaig, Brian. 2011. "Exporting Out of Poverty: Provincial Poverty in Vietnam and US Market Access." *Journal of International Economics* 85 (1): 102–13.

McCaig, Brian, and Nina Pavcnik. 2018. "Export Markets and Labor Allocation in a Low-Income Country." *American Economic Review* 108 (7): 1899–1941.

Mincer, Jacob. 1958. "Investment in Human Capital and Personal Income Distribution." *Journal of Political Economy* 66 (4): 281–302.

Noguer, Marta, and Marc Siscart. 2005. "Trade Raises Income: A Precise and Robust Result." *Journal of International Economics* 65 (2): 447–60.

Topalova, Petia. 2010. "Factor Immobility and Regional Impacts of Trade Liberalization: Evidence on Poverty from India." *American Economic Journal of Applied Economics* 2 (4): 1–41.

Ulyssea, Gabriel, and Vladimir P. Ponczek. 2018. "Enforcement of Labor Regulation and the Labor Market Effects of Trade: Evidence from Brazil." Discussion Paper No. 11783, Institute of Labor Economics (IZA), Bonn, Germany.

World Bank. 2012. "Reclaiming Their Voice: New Perspectives from Young Women and Men in Upper Egypt." Report No. 71674, World Bank, Washington, DC.

World Bank. 2020. *World Development Report 2020: Trading for Development in the Age of Global Value Chains*. Washington, DC: World Bank.

World Bank. 2021. "Unlocking Egypt's Potential for Poverty Reduction and Inclusive Growth." Egypt Systematic Country Diagnostic Update, Report No. 164656, World Bank, Washington, DC.

Zaki, Chahir. 2016. "Employment, Gender and International Trade: A Micro-Macro Evidence for Egypt." *Review of Economics and Political Science* 1 (1): 29–60.

Zaki, Chahir, Alia Abdallah, and May Sami. 2019. "How Do Trade Margins Respond to Exchange Rate? The Case of Egypt." *Journal of African Trade* 6 (1–2): 60–80. https://doi.org/10.2991/jat.k.190528.001.

www.ingramcontent.com/pod-product-compliance
Lightning Source LLC
Chambersburg PA
CBHW041442210326

41599CB00004B/102